DEAR Gail ~

ENJOY LONG BEACH ARCHITECTURE !

BEST

2019

LONG BEACH ARCHITECTURE
The Unexpected Metropolis

Cara Mullio & Jennifer M. Volland

Forewords by D. J. Waldie & Thom Mayne

HENNESSEY + INGALLS
SANTA MONICA 2004

First published 2004 by

Hennessey + Ingalls
214 Wilshire Boulevard
Santa Monica CA 90401

www.hennesseyingalls.com

© 2004 by Hennessey + Ingalls, Inc.

ISBN 0-940512-39-4 (cloth)

California Architecture and Architects, No. 25

Printed in China
Designed by Michael Worthington
Edited by Gabrielle Gayagoy

Library of Congress Cataloguing-in-Publication Data

Mullio, Cara, 1970-
    Long Beach architecture : the unexpected metropolis / Cara Mullio
and Jennifer M. Volland ; forewords by Thom Mayne, D.J. Waldie.
        p. cm. – (California architecture and architects ; no. 25)
    Includes index.
    ISBN 0-940512-39-4 (cloth)
    1. Architecture—California—Long Beach. 2. Architects—California—
Long Beach. I.
Volland, Jennifer M., 1970- II. Title. III. Series.

NA735.L54M85 2004
720'.9794'94—dc22   2004052370

Front cover image: Long Beach skyline, c. 1968
Back cover image: Belmont Shore and Alamitos Bay, 1941

CONTENTS

PROJECTS

FOREWORD

by D. J. Waldie

I don't live in Long Beach, but in a city on its fringe. L.A. is so large, so heterogeneous, that its distant edges have their own edges. But even though I'm not its citizen, Long Beach is the big city with which I have some intimacy.

"Big city" and "Long Beach" do not make an oxymoron. Long Beach is one of California's major cities and the second largest in Los Angeles and Orange counties. The city's history, of which its 19th- and 20th-century buildings are mute survivors, is largely about running second.

Early on, Long Beach sought a sense of place through denial: a churchly city of Sabbatarian purists, a temperance city with no saloons, a city racially segregated even more rigorously than Los Angeles, a city that resisted its Mexican past and which looked, as its builders wanted it to, like the capital of an improved Iowa.

"Iowa-by-the-Sea" its detractors called it and "the city of the newly wed and the nearly dead" for its twin distinctions of being a Midwest honeymoon destination and the retirement home of so many small-town shopkeepers and prosperous farmers from what everyone here called "back East."

Not even the earthquake of 1933, which took down the poorly built remnants of the city's first boom years, unsettled Long Beach's complacency. The earthquake was good for Long Beach, as was the Depression. Okie and Arkie construction workers got jobs, federal dollars built energetically Art Deco public buildings and port facilities, and the city's moderately well-to-do put up houses in all the fashionable styles, from Tudor to Spanish Revival to Domestic Moderne.

World War II transformed that Long Beach into an arsenal of the Cold War. It was a city drunk on city-owned oil leases, free-spending sailors from the Pacific Fleet, and the prosperity of suburban subdivisions. That's all gone now.

Ease defined Long Beach's sense of itself for so much of its history, even as the city tried to edit so much out of its story. The area is one of the nation's most racially and ethnically diverse. It has a large gay and lesbian community (and one of the oldest on the West Coast). It's a city known for its poor neighborhoods and its rich ones, with an aging public infrastructure and too little money, and it's filled with conflicted aspirations. It struggles to deal with the collapse of its oil, aerospace,

military, and suburban development economies while holding on to its dream of an untroubled past of exceptional sweetness.

Old buildings can be mistaken for monuments to desires we are now ashamed to have. They can be mistaken as completely innocent, too, as if the buildings had only an aesthetic past. Long Beach's sense of itself, declared in its complex architectural heritage, is as unsettled and open to reinterpretation as any in Southern California.

The authors of this loving survey of Long Beach's built past understand the ambiguity in what they see. The city they present is dense with stories and filled with meaning.

left/ City Hall, c. 1923

FOREWORD

by Thom Mayne

What makes L.A. unusual, if not unique, is that it is a primary example of what architectural historian Charles Jencks has termed a *heteropolis* —a new form of urban agglomeration that flourishes on difference. Unlike the European model of a city with a clear, locatable center, Los Angeles sprawls with heterogeneity, plurality, and difference made manifest in buildings and urban organization strategies that epitomize the variety of the city as a whole.

By plan Los Angeles is a fragmented city. It is a city of dispersal in its very earliest stages whose growth pattern involves the emergences and intensifications of its parts. Pasadena, Riverside, Downtown, San Bernardino, Long Beach: these are all distinctive areas of intensification within the larger organism of Southern California that will be seen by some as uniquely their own. It is perhaps more apt to understand them as an inextricable part of the great whole of this region. They are parts that at this early stage of emergence may appear distant but that, due to their genetic and historical connections, may someday occupy the center.

The authors of *Long Beach Architecture: The Unexpected Metropolis* offer a definitive study of one such city on the rise that deepens the understanding of the region as a whole. As with a sample of DNA, Long Beach holds within it the genetic code that informs the larger metropolis of Los Angeles. Within the city, one can find a great deal of architectural synchronicity with Los Angeles. There are obvious similarities between the cities such as Naples to Venice Beach, oceanfront to suburb, and ubiquity of freeways. Architecturally, Long Beach is a microcosm of Los Angeles. Here one can find a sampling of classic modern architects including Neutra, Lautner, Soriano, Killingsworth, and Kappe. Beaux Arts from the early part of the century and classic neo-Spanish coexist with Art Deco and kitsch in an arcane and idiosyncratic manner that has come to define Los Angeles. Beyond the stylistic, however, there is evidence of a serious, if yet unbuilt, interest in architecture through the works of Eisenman, Pei, and others.

To look carefully at the city is to come to a more complete understanding of not only Long Beach itself, but of Los Angeles. It is a piece of the same flesh, a marker or a mirror that exists on a scale that allows one, when properly guided, to achieve a greater comprehension of the Southern California landscape that emanates from and beyond the city of Los Angeles.

The authors have provided a careful study of the development of Long Beach, especially with respect to its architectural lineage. We are fortunate to have a thoughtful tome that adds to an increasingly multivalent understanding of our metropolis.

left/ City Hall, c. 2000

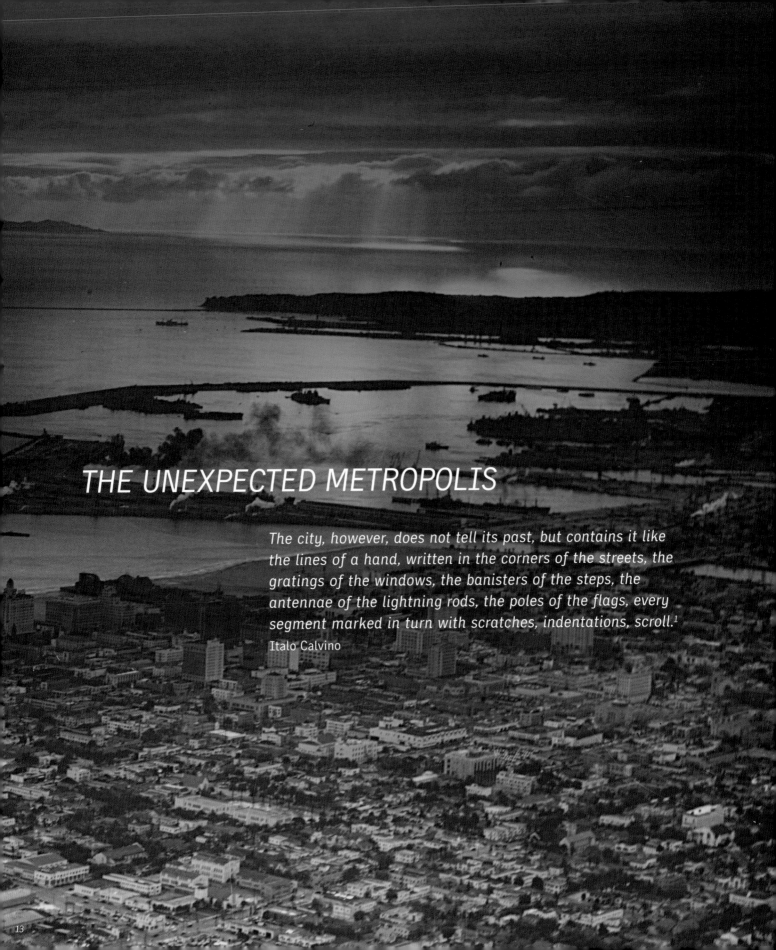

THE UNEXPECTED METROPOLIS

The city, however, does not tell its past, but contains it like the lines of a hand, written in the corners of the streets, the gratings of the windows, the banisters of the steps, the antennae of the lightning rods, the poles of the flags, every segment marked in turn with scratches, indentations, scroll.[1]
Italo Calvino

PREFACE

"Unexpected" is indeed an apt description for Long Beach. The city embodies a complex interplay of the historic and the new, conservative values and progressive movements, conflict and peaceful coexistence. With a size of 50 square miles and a population of more than 470,000, Long Beach lies in a congested region of California between Los Angeles and Orange County, amidst the concrete convergence of major highways and urban sprawl. Strategically oriented to the sea, Long Beach appeals to the transfer of goods, services, and people. It is this tactical position that dictated the original development of this city and continues to act as the nucleus of activity and sustenance.

The industrial roots that spawned Long Beach's rapid growth also characterize its intriguing polarity. Unable to shake its reputation as a rough port town, the city suffers from stale, enduring images: the ugly stepsister of Los Angeles, the home of a seedy amusement zone, and the blue-collar, labor-strong city based on a quintessentially American foundation of trade, military, oil, aerospace, and defense. Yet this multifaceted amalgamation of identities managed to site itself on a prime piece of California property flanked by a generous port to the west and wide swaths of beaches to the south.

As with the evolution of any metropolis, however, new layers have deposited—strong immigrant and ethnic populations, a burgeoning gay community, an emerging arts district, and neighborhoods and residents intensely passionate about preservation and community awareness. Despite this rich, multifarious environment, the city still exists on the periphery of people's awareness. Has anyone really taken a close, hard look at Long Beach lately? While other regions in Southern California such as Santa Barbara, Santa Monica, and Pasadena become increasingly homogenized in terms of people, cost of living, and public offerings, Long Beach stubbornly maintains a unique presence, identity, and diversity.

Much of this individuality is captured in Long Beach's remarkable architecture. That is the narrative we present in *Long Beach Architecture: The Unexpected Metropolis*, a tale based on the eyes that see and a re-examination of the area's current, past, razed, and unrealized cityscape. We pose one viewpoint of the city's historical continuum and although it opens the discussion, it is in no way the definitive, end-all discourse. Our perspective evolved through a lengthy analysis and exploration of Long Beach, encompassing many hours of driving the streets and investigating neighborhoods, following up on numerous leads from architecture experts local and afar, studying published and unpublished materials, interviewing residents and architects, and relying on the expertise of historians, city officials, designers, and developers. The revealing portrait depicts a city that embraces all of its stereotypes, one that continues to leave its footprint in the built and unbuilt realm.

This book records the development of the vicinity from its rancho days in the mid-1800s to the sprawling conurbation of the 21st century. The visual nature of our approach—featuring a historical overview and 100 significant projects—allows the reader to experience Long Beach on many levels, whether examining works and their authors in isolation or constructing a project's particular relevance in the city's timeline. An exploration of districts, arteries, and patterns of expansion weaves into the account, as do the anecdotal and cultural episodes that contribute to the definition of any community. In order to demarcate an already massive area, the book strictly focuses on Long Beach and what lies in the city confines, and does not venture to examine the architectural merits of adjacent cities such as San Pedro, Signal Hill, Lakewood, and Seal Beach.

Publications and annals that highlight regional architecture and the built realm, and how both relate to the formation of a city, are indispensable resources for uncovering the past. However, there is currently a huge gap in architectural historiography regarding Long Beach. Coverage mainly consists of pamphlets with limited, narrow-scoped information focusing on a particular architect or a specific period. Or Long Beach tends to be lumped in with larger chronicles on the Los Angeles region, which de-emphasize the significant contributions of this city. David Gebhard and Robert Winter's *Los Angeles: An Architectural Guide* is certainly a seminal work, but the sheer massiveness of its subject matter does not permit in-depth coverage of specific areas. Still other publications, such as Walter Case's *Long Beach and Vicinity* or Bill Hillburg's more recent *Long Beach: The City and Its People,* strictly highlight the history of Long Beach. Writers Dana Cuff, Mike Davis, Dolores Hayden, and Kevin Starr adopt more critical approaches to urbanism and extol broad and compelling perspectives of American cities. While these chronologists and theorists often acknowledge Long Beach, they mix it into larger discussions about Los Angeles. *Long Beach Architecture: The Unexpected Metropolis* attempts to fill the void, touching on critical moments in history but more importantly how they relate to architecture and development. The book allows readers to formulate and comprehend a distinct progression of events, assimilating the region on a micro- and macroscopic scale.

We first conceived this project when we collaborated on a 2002 essay for *Arcade,* the Northwest journal for architecture and design. In this text, we compared Tacoma, Washington, and Long Beach, California. Both share a strategic orientation to the sea that spurred a rich port-based economy, the railroad, and parallel periods of prosperity and decay. We delved into the idea that every major metropolis has a smaller "second city" that lives in the shadow of its more popular sibling. Struggling to establish an identity, this type of city often carries the stigma of the ugly and ignored step-sister. The examples are numerous—Seattle/Tacoma, Los Angeles/Long Beach, San Francisco/Oakland, and Manhattan/Brooklyn, to name a few. Many such cities have been relegated to a scorned existence, lying on the margins and unable to emerge as their own entities. Long Beach often is overlooked despite its claim as the fifth-largest city in California and its various contributions to the local economy, not to mention its political and social effects on the national and international markets. But with time, the second city typically breaks the mold, forging its own identity.

In 2004, Long Beach sits at precarious crossroads, as the very success that defines and sustains it also threatens to damage its livability. This second city exists as a new frontier for inhabitants of Los Angeles because of the abundance of relatively affordable housing and an unbeatable quality of life. However, a rich diversity, one of Long Beach's most appealing characteristics, could be destroyed, as gentrification and homogeneity instigate a vicious and irrepressible cycle that allows access to some while alienating others. Questionable and short-sighted actions in recent development have been counterintuitive to protracted prosperity and survival of the city, contributing to an uncertain future. The continuation of Long Beach's progress demands integrated urban planning focused on economic, environmental, and social sustainability. Many groups, such as the Cultural Heritage Commission and Long Beach Heritage, fight hard to preserve the architectural legacy of the city, and progressive local urban planners, architects, and designers ensure that quality design is interwoven into the future landscape. Yet further awareness on both a govern-mental and public level is still a critical factor in the ongoing process.

Overall, Long Beach appears to be on course, emit-ting a contagious energy as it evolves. As the port continues to expand and create jobs, emerging tech-nological sectors further diversify and invigorate already varied economies. At the same time, Long Beach needs to increasingly rely and draw upon its intrinsic assets. The city's rich architectural inheri-tance should be preserved and highlighted, and future choices regarding development must also incorporate rigorous design standards and intelli-gent, long-term planning. The recent proliferation of projects in Long Beach attests to the important role of architecture and design in modern-day life, providing a sense of continuity between the past and the present. It is a reminder that current decisions will set the stage for the future viability and appeal of this unique environment.

Cara Mullio & Jennifer M. Volland

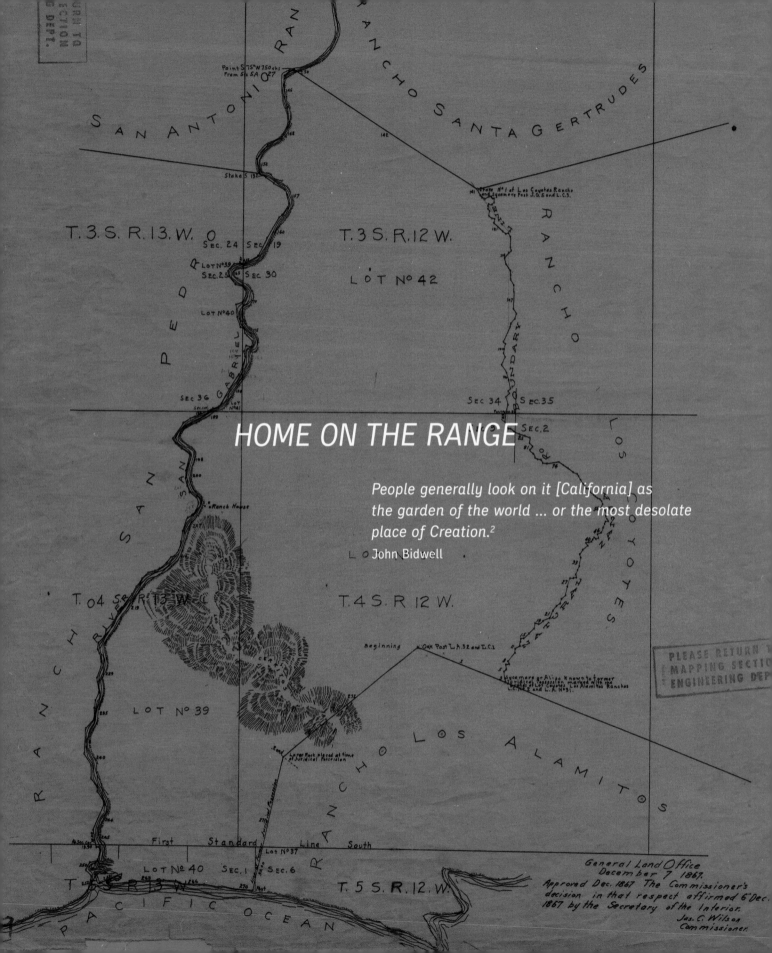

HOME ON THE RANGE

People generally look on it [California] as the garden of the world ... or the most desolate place of Creation.[2]

John Bidwell

EARLY INHABITANTS

It is difficult to imagine that Long Beach was first incorporated in 1888, a mere infant in the history of the world. Architecture, of course, played a critical role in the development of the area long before the establishment of a formal city, first as a matter of necessity, and later to mark progress and wealth.

Tongva Indians lived and thrived in the area that today comprises Long Beach for at least a millennium before encountering European explorers. Archaeologists have identified two Tongvan village sites that now are listed on the National Register of Historic Places. A settlement called Tibahang-na (also known as Tevaaxa'anga) lay on the current site of Rancho Los Cerritos. A larger community and sacred Indian settlement, Puvunga, occupied what is now Rancho Los Alamitos. Like those who later inhabited the area, the Tongva appreciated the mild climate and fertile land. They could exist with little clothing and simple, flexible shelter. The Tongvan settlements followed regular patterns: An unroofed sacred enclosure, known as the yovaar, marked the center of the community; outside the brushwork wall of the yovaar lay the dome-shaped reed houses of the chief and elite members of society, and beyond them, the houses of other community members. Large, cleared areas for games existed adjacent to the settlement and semi-subterranean sweathouses with earthen roofs were located near streams or pools of water.[3]

The Spanish navigator Juan Rodriguez Cabrillo first encountered these early inhabitants on October 8, 1542. He sought out the excellent harbor and natural protection afforded by the lofty peninsula on the north side of the crescent-shaped bay. At the time of Cabrillo's arrival, Indian villages were sparsely scattered along the inner shore of the bay and the cliffs around Point Fermin, with others a little farther inland.

Although California's natives remained relatively undisturbed for more than 150 years, their fate was already sealed. In 1769, Spain launched colonization efforts in Alta California. Around the same time, Father Junipero Serra began to spread his Christian beliefs and established missions up and down the coast. The Tongva later became known as the Gabrielinos for their affiliation with the San Gabriel Mission. Legally speaking, the missions held all of the land surrounding their compounds in trust for the natives, who would be given back their holdings once they had become "properly civilized." As history revealed, this never happened. It is estimated that 300,000 Native Americans inhabited what is now the Golden State prior to the Spanish conquest. Following Spanish settlement, many Gabrielinos perished from imported diseases or were stripped of their identity and absorbed into the new culture. The Indian population in California continued to decline under Mexican and later U.S. rule, dropping to 50,000 in 1855 and 16,350 in 1910.

Fifteen years after colonization efforts began, Governor Pedro Fages bestowed huge land grants on three veterans of the expedition for their devoted service to the Spanish crown. Manuel Perez Nieto received the largest grant, a 300,000-acre parcel (which was later reduced to approxi-

1./ Panoramic view of Rancho Los Cerritos adobe, west wall, and gate, 1872
left/ General Land Office map of ranchos, December 7, 1867

mately 167,000 acres) that extended from the hills above the San Gabriel Mission to the Pacific Ocean, bordered the Los Angeles River on the west, and ran for miles down the coast. Today, the city of Long Beach and a dozen surrounding communities occupy this area. These rancheros became the first landholders in California.

After Nieto died in 1804, his land was divided among his heirs into six separate ranchos: Los Cerritos, Los Alamitos, Los Bolsas, Los Coyotes, Santa Gertrudes, and Palo Alto. Manuela Nieto de Cota received Rancho Los Cerritos officially in 1834. Rancho Los Cerritos and Rancho Los Alamitos served as the centers of social life for the burgeoning community in the Mexican era, hosting rodeos, bullfights, fandangos, barbecues, and other divertissements. Under subsequent ownership, the ranchos held family gatherings and biannual shearing parties. For many years, the rest of the area was vast ranching land, and the only dwelling between the ranchos and the ocean was a small wood hut called the Shepherd's Hut (located where Pine Avenue and 1st Street intersect today) that provided cover for shepherds. Built in the 1870s, it was soon to be joined by other dwellings and an emerging town. The ranchos remain an important example of pre-1900 American architecture and agricultural land usage from a time when the West was still a vast frontier, and their subsequent alterations demonstrate the changing trends.

2./ Garden and veranda of Rancho Los Cerritos soon
after the garden was replanted, 1931

It was constructed of three-foot-thick adobe walls on the first floor
narrowing down to two feet thick on the second floor. The north and south
one-story wings accommodated workrooms, storage, a blacksmith shop, and
living quarters for the ranch foreman. With two-foot-thick adobe walls, they
projected out from the two-story central block to form a courtyard. Sarah
Bixby Smith, whose family played a predominant role in the early development of Long Beach and inhabited the rancho after Temple, recalled its
appearance in her book *Adobe Days*:

> The approach to the house was through the large gate in the
> wall that closed the patio. I think the court never was planted
> to any extent, the garden being on the farther side of the house.
> It afforded only a few locust trees, one large pink oleander
> and several hitching posts. There was always much going and
> coming here, for the ranch business involved the use of saddle
> horses and carriages.[4]

While packed earth floors were standard in the wings, Temple was able to
obtain enough handhewn redwood from Northern California and ship it to
San Pedro to use for beams, floors, and other interior woodwork in the two-
story building. Similarly, windows in the wings originally only included bars
and shutters, but Temple installed double-hung windows with glass panes
imported from the East in the main portion of the house.

The adobe bricks, made by local Indian laborers, were manufactured near
the San Gabriel River flowing just east of the present house; 30 years later
the pit was still used for making bricks for repairs. Abundant in supply, the
material kept the heat out in the summer and retained it in the winter. Any
exposed exterior woodwork was painted in a bright turquoise and the walls
were mud-plastered and whitewashed with a lime mixture at least once a
year to protect the surface from moisture. The original roofs were flat and
made of redwood planks covered with sand or gravel and likely sealed with
hot *brea*, possibly from the tar pits in Los Angeles.

Temple lavished his care and attention on the elaborate formal garden east
of the adobe, coordinating an overall scheme that placed equal importance
on the landscape and the architecture. One of the finest in Southern California, it displayed a range of flora from rose beds to fruit orchards. Lined
with brick imported from the East Coast, the garden followed a grid pattern,
an arrangement familiar to Temple from his New England origins. When
Temple sold the rancho for $20,000 in 1866, he was said to have spent more
than that amount on the garden, an inordinate sum of money for outdoor
design at that time.

THE FIRST FAMILIES

Although the difficult conditions involved in the settlement of the West deterred many Easterners, others
recognized the opportunities inherent in the forgiving
climate and fertile land and began to acquire property.
Massachusetts-born Jonathan Temple was one such
character. He converted to Catholicism to appeal to
the colonial authorities and became a Mexican citizen.
In 1843, Temple purchased the 27,000-acre Rancho
Los Cerritos from Cota's widow and children during
the Mexican Period when Alta California was a state
of Mexico.

One of the wealthiest individuals in the county, Temple
retained a primary residence on Main Street near
the plaza in Los Angeles, where he ran a mercantile
business. The rancho, meanwhile, served as Temple's
headquarters for his large-scale cattle operation.
Temple built an adobe on the property in 1844 and occupied the main two-story Monterey Colonial-style portion
while in residence during the summer months. This
section featured a symmetrical facade, central hall,
stairs, and double wooden verandas on three sides.

Flint, Bixby & Co. purchased the ranch from Temple in 1866 after successive
years of severe drought and flooding decimated the local cattle industry.
The Bixby family, whose roots were established in Maine, is inextricably
linked to Long Beach. From 1866 to 1881, Jotham Bixby and his family
resided in the adobe. During this time, Bixby installed a gabled, wood-
shingled roof on the two-story portion of the structure and later to both

wings, reminiscent of an East Coast aesthetic. Bixby began to sell or lease parts of the property as early as 1878. In 1887, rising land values usurped the importance of his sheep operation, and Bixby leased and sold thousands of acres to developers and farmers for what would later become Long Beach. The communities of Lakewood, Bellflower, Paramount, half of Signal Hill, and small portions of South Gate and Downey also developed on the original Rancho Los Cerritos property.

A succession of ranch workers and families lived in the building after Bixby's family but it slowly began to deteriorate and, during the years 1927 to 1930, it sat completely vacant. Bixby's nephew, Llewellyn Bixby Sr., purchased the rustic adobe in 1930 and extensively renovated it as his family's main residence. Kenneth S. Wing, a prolific local architect, drew up the plans for the project. He preserved the basic layout of the wings and courtyard and saved much of the adobe walls underneath new white plastered walls. The remodel embodied the Mission Revival style popular during the 1920s and 1930s with features such as the red-clay roof tiles. Ralph R. Cornell, famed for his landscape designs for the University of California, Los Angeles, campus from 1937 to 1972, updated the formal garden, planted an orchard to the south of the adobe, and beautified the inner courtyard. Rancho Los Cerritos remained under Bixby family ownership until 1955 when the City of Long Beach acquired the residence and 4.7 acres. The city has operated it as a museum and research library since 1956.

Eastward on a hilltop, the Nieto family built an adobe on Rancho Los Alamitos sometime between 1800 and 1834. The family did not occupy the structure; instead the rancho vaqueros and horses lived there. Governor José Figueroa acquired ownership in 1834 and formed a partnership to run cattle on the land. This venture was short-lived and cattleman Abel Stearns purchased the land in 1842. Stearns fixed up the old adobe for use as a summerhouse and in 1850 he added the north wing for the vaqueros. When gold was discovered, the growing population of the north required sustenance, and the period of 1849 to 1855 brought great prosperity to cattle ranchos. But lack of rain from 1862 to 1864 brought an end to the windfall, and Stearns lost Rancho Los Alamitos to foreclosure. Michael Reese acquired the rancho at a sheriff's sale in 1866, and while he did not live there, he leased the land for stock grazing.

Banker and local investor Isaias W. Hellman purchased Rancho Los Alamitos along with J. Bixby & Co. (co-owned by Jotham Bixby and Flint, Bixby & Co.) for $125,000 in 1881. John Bixby, another member of the prolific clan, came to California in 1871 to work for Jotham at the rancho. John married Susan Patterson Hathaway in 1873 and began leasing Rancho Los Alamitos in 1878. He planted a garden and began transforming the old adobe into a home. Between 1878 and 1887, he built new barns and upgraded livestock by introducing purebred sheep, horses, and registered Holstein dairy cattle. He started the south wing on the house, adding two small rooms. Additionally, John enlarged windows and added fireplaces. Just before he died, John set aside 5,000 acres for the townsite of Alamitos Beach.

3./ Barn and tree at Rancho Los Alamitos, 1980
4./ Aerial view of Rancho Los Alamitos, Anaheim Road, 1936

In 1891 the ranch was partitioned: The southern third went to the Hellman family (the 6,800 acres today encompasses Los Alamitos and the retirement community of Leisure World in Seal Beach); John Bixby's family retained the middle acreage with the ranch house; and the northern land was given to the J. Bixby & Co. partners.

In 1906, Fred Bixby and his wife, Florence, inherited the portion of the Alamitos ranch that included the headquarters building. Fred extended the south wing, adding several bedrooms, and put a second story on the house in 1925. Florence expanded the gardens between 1920 and 1936 with the involvement of such notable landscape designers as the Olmsted Brothers, Florence Yoch, and Paul Howard. Fred died in 1952, and Florence lived at the ranch house until her death in 1961. Seven years later, their descendants gave the furnished house, gardens, and six barns to the City of Long Beach to maintain and develop as a regional historic and educational facility.

LAYING TRACKS

The completion of the Transcontinental Railroad in 1869 provided coast-to-coast mobility. Venturesome souls populated new areas and infused lifeblood into emerging cities.

Phineas Banning, a leading proponent of transportation and seaport trade in Southern California, recognized the promises of rail at an early stage. During an 1853 conversation with Abel Stearns regarding the practicability of rail routes to Southern California, Banning said:

> Los Angeles is the natural trading point for all the land in that triangle. San Pedro is the only possible port for our pueblo. It isn't a matter of opinion, but of geography, of mountain ranges, of grades, of passes, and shoreline, of the way the country's made. I don't know when the railroad will be built, but some day it will be. We'll have to work to bring it about, but nature will be fighting on our side.[5]

Officials of the Southern Pacific Railroad wanted Los Angeles to surrender control of an existing 22-mile rail line to Wilmington that was built by Banning in 1869. Called the Los Angeles and San Pedro Railway, it offered seven trains daily with stops at Long Beach, stimulating growth between city and sea. The Southern Pacific basically gave the communities on its prospective routes an ultimatum, which many thought amounted to extortion: They could either pay Southern Pacific a large sum of money, for which the railroad would grant rights-of-way and provide a large piece of land for the depot, or the railroad would reroute the line through another community. Because fast-growing cities desperately needed this amenity, they usually succumbed. But Banning stood strong. By 1885, the Santa Fe railroad reached Los Angeles, giving the city another eastern rail connection, thereby breaking the monopoly of the Southern Pacific. The competition sparked a rate war with Southern Pacific, encouraging

5./ Train arrives in front of Ocean View Hotel, c. 1892
6./ Bird's-eye perspective of Long Beach, 1887

unprecedented transcontinental travel that resulted in a flood of western immigration.

In 1891 Long Beach's city council granted the Los Angeles Terminal Railroad Company the right to connect Long Beach by rail with Los Angeles. The industrialization of western Long Beach was set in motion. Several years later, in 1896, Congress approved a $1.9 million breakwater project for San Pedro Bay. The move effectively scuttled rival proposals for ports in Santa Monica Bay, Newport Bay, Anaheim Bay, and Alamitos Bay. The San Pedro Bay location prevailed, and when the first breakwater boulders were dumped into the Pacific in 1899, the rival ports of Long Beach and Los Angeles began to take shape.

7

7./ Long Beach Hotel, c. 1885

AMERICAN COLONY

William E. Willmore first envisioned the future of Long Beach during a visit to the area in 1870. Emigrating from London, Willmore began to look for ventures. He secured a job promoting Southern California real estate with Jotham Bixby and served as the southern manager for the California Immigrant Union, which encouraged settlement and facilitated the real-estate transactions between the owners of large tracts of rural property and possible customers.

In 1881 Willmore persuaded Bixby to subdivide a section of Rancho Los Cerritos shoreline property and offer it for sale. Willmore agreed to give Bixby $100,000 for 4,000 acres, to be payable in three installments plus eight percent interest. The two businessmen then announced initial plans for American Colony, their first development. Also referred to as Willmore City, the proposal included a central business district and a seaside devoted to parks and resort hotels. Magnolia Avenue and Alamitos Avenue served as the west and east limits of the townsite, while 10th Street provided the northern boundary. Farm lots in five, 10 and 20-acre parcels lay beyond the tract, the smallest being those nearest the town. A main thoroughfare, Ocean Park Avenue, followed the contour of the bluff. Except for one or two hotel sites, no buildings were permitted on the oceanfront side of the street and the beach was to remain a natural playground for citizens and visitors. American Avenue (now Long Beach Boulevard) marked the main north-south street, with a row of eucalyptus trees down the center.[6]

Willmore marketed this new city in newspapers nationwide, enticing Easterners and Midwesterners with train excursions and courting local customers with wagon rides to and from Los Angeles. An 1883 advertisement from the *Los Angeles Times* touted the new community:

> *Good Soil! Abundance of Water! Beautiful Location! Delightful Climate! Magnificent Beach! The land is sold in tracts of from 5 to 40 acres, with perpetual water rights, at from $50 to $75 per acre ... Reached by cars to Willmore Station, on Wilmington and Los Angeles railroad; thence by horse car three miles.*[7]

Only a handful of individuals purchased land in Willmore City because during the same period the federal government gave away millions of acres to anyone willing to homestead for several years. Because of the dropping prices of land, in 1884 Willmore defaulted on his installment payment to Bixby. Bixby reassumed control of American Colony and renamed the community Long Beach in 1885 at the suggestion of Belle Lowe, the wife of the town storekeeper and postmaster. Shortly after Willmore's departure, the town began to thrive and Southern California embarked on the first of many real-estate booms. In 1886, John Bixby carved out a development just east of Willmore City called Alamitos Beach Townsite on some of his prime oceanfront property.

Early in the city's history, droves of tourists and beach-goers flocked to Long Beach. The 130-room Long Beach Hotel, the first *grande dame* resort on the local shoreline, rose on the bluff at Ocean Boulevard and Cedar Avenue in 1885. Similar to the Hotel Del Coronado near San Diego, the wood-framed Long Beach Hotel soared five stories, three stories higher than the bluff. The dining hall's southern walls, comprised entirely of glass, overlooked the ocean.

In 1888, only eight years after Willmore's first conversation with Bixby, residents voted to incorporate Long Beach.

LONG BEACH MAKES ITS MARK

To dream a dream and to live to see it
realized is not given to every man. I am
one of the fortunate ones.[8]
Colonel Charles Rivers Drake

VISIONS OF GRANDEUR

At the turn of the century, Long Beach was still a small town with just over 2,200 souls. The millionaire land-speculator Colonel Charles Rivers Drake, who had recently retired to Long Beach from Arizona, recognized the area's potential as a seaside resort. Drake invested in waterfront real estate and petitioned the city council to expand the Pacific Electric streetcar service from Los Angeles to Long Beach. On July 4, 1902, the first run of the Red Cars—as the streetcars were called—coincided with the opening of the $100,000 bathhouse Drake built at the end of the line. An estimated 60,000 people crowded the area and many resorted to sleeping on the beach when local accommodations reached capacity. The establishment of Red Car service and the building of the bathhouse led to the formation of a seaside amusement area called "The Walk of a Thousand Lights," more popularly referred to as the Pike.

The eagerly anticipated bathhouse, which later became known as the Plunge, was the most expensive facility of its type at the time of its erection in 1902 and accommodated the biggest indoor pool in the West. Classical Revival in style, the monumental structure featured a curved facade with two-story Corinthian columns topped by a dentil cornice. Accommodating 4,000 visitors, the grand bathhouse held a spectators' gallery with rows of seats, more than 500 dressing rooms, and pools for women and children. Residents as well as tourists enjoyed the warm saltwater pool and beach-front location. Since it was a main attraction for Pike visitors over the years, the Plunge required modernization in 1923 to a tune of $400,000. The owners created an even larger pool facility with 1 million white vitreous tiles that lined the sides and bottom of the basin and a central fountain that continuously swirled pure, clean saltwater.

Within a few years of the Plunge's opening, Drake's company built a board-walk along the beach and lined it with game booths, a roller rink, a Ferris wheel, a carousel, and a vaudeville theater. At first only 12 feet wide, the boardwalk later expanded to 15 feet and in 1906 eventually grew to a 35-foot cement walk. Sunburst-motif lampposts along with the strings of overhead lights reinforced the name of The Walk of a Thousand Lights.

More attractions and concessions appeared in the years to follow, drawing thousands of annual visitors, and transforming the Pike into the Coney Island of the West. To the delight of children, the Looff carousel material-ized on the boardwalk in 1911. Charles I. D. Looff, originator of the Coney Island style of carousel carving and designer of the Santa Monica Amusement Pier, built the Hippodrome for his handcarved wooden horses and ornate imported organ. Looff moved his carousel factory to Long Beach and lived above his fanciful jeweled creations on the Pike. One of the last remaining relics of the boardwalk, the carousel dome will top the new home of the Historical Society of Long Beach at The Pike at Rainbow Harbor.

The blossoming of the real-estate market coincided with the influx of commercial ventures, and Drake invested in other parts of the city. His Knoll Park development (later renamed Drake Park) offered sites that enticed the

1./ View of Pike and Plunge signage, Ocean Center Building in background, c. 1930
left/ First Congregational Church and The Willmore looking down Cedar Avenue, c. 1928

city's leading citizens, who built large Victorian houses that fronted curving streets and once commanded views of the harbor area. Drake also appealed to the high-end tourist market with the luxurious million-dollar Hotel Virginia, which he developed in partnership with other city leaders in 1908. He then leased land in what is now Recreation Park and established the Virginia Country Club for the exclusive use of wealthy citizens and the hotel's guests. The country club moved to a site adjacent to Rancho Los Cerritos in 1921.

On the residential front, communities such as Alamitos Beach Townsite, Carroll Park, and Belmont Heights were annexed into Long Beach in 1905, 1908, and 1911, respec-tively. One of the most interesting early developments was that of Naples on Alamitos Bay Peninsula. The idea began in 1904 when father-and-son team Arthur M. Parsons and Arthur C. Parsons announced plans for a "Venetian-style" community that featured a series of canals and pedestrian walkways. To accomplish this, they enclosed, dredged, filled in, and stabilized a marshland with concrete bulkheads to create the seaside neighbor-hood. These quaint passages recalled the real romance of Venice, Italy. The first six houses, built as speculative homes, defined the visual appearance, and the area then became dubbed the "City of Red Tile Roofs."

Described in a July 21, 1905 advertisement in the *Daily Telegram* as "the coming resort of the world," Naples competed with Venice, a similar concept on the Santa Monica Bay, developed by Abbot Kinney.[9] Waterfront lots in Naples ranged from $900 to $4,000, which was costly

2./ Aerial view of Naples, c. 1920

a community, and Long Beach development was a striking demonstration that those things which appeal to the lower inclinations are not necessary in the foundation of a permanent, substantial city. Long Beach was known as a saloon-less town for more than 20 years before the Volstead law was enacted.[11]

Aside from the rare occasions of hotels serving wine, prohibitionist tendencies prevailed in Long Beach. The conservative tenets overshadowed the desire for liquor, at least in early days.

Religious life played an important role in the foundation of Long Beach. Church activities date from 1884, when the Methodist Resort Association decided to make Long Beach the site of its annual camp meeting. Several years later, the Methodists built a wooden tabernacle on a site between Locust and American avenues and 3rd and 4th streets. This building was the home of an important devotional institution and drew large crowds until it was torn down in 1915 to make room for a business block.

Long Beach attracted all denominations to build new and larger edifices. Religious institutions of particular architectural note include the Classical Revival First Christian Church of 1914 and the Second Church of Christ Scientist of 1924, with its Roman facade and large dome, both by Elmer Grey; the 1926 Spanish Renaissance Forest Lawn-Long Beach (until recently Sunnyside Mausoleum) in the outer reaches of the city; and St. Anthony's Church of 1933 with its Gothic Revival towers by Emmet Martin and Lawrence Waller.

for the time. In 1907, the Parsons partnered with oil-and-rail baron Henry Huntington to incorporate a stop at Naples on the Pacific Electric Railroad's Newport Line. Naples provided a welcome diversion from "dry" Long Beach. Chocolate heiress Almira Parker Hershey bought 300 parcels and built a lavish retreat called the Hotel Napoli in 1909. The hotel's architecture reflected that of the Hollywood Hotel, another one of Hershey's fancies. Despite the investment in roof tile imported from Italy and carved woodwork, the hotel never opened its doors. It sat empty until 1927 when Hershey sold the property to C. F. Higgins, who transformed and updated the interiors, adding sophistication to the neighborhood.[10] It had subsequent owners and usages, and in 1959 a developer razed the hotel for condominium apartments.

PORT POWER

The port presented another huge draw in terms of commercial opportunity and jobs. In 1906, the Los Angeles Dock and Terminal Company initiated development of the Long Beach harbor by purchasing 800 acres of sloughs and salt marshes. The formal opening of a new municipal dock marked the official founding of the Port of Long Beach on June 24, 1911. Also in 1911, the State of California granted the tidelands areas to the City of Long Beach —in trust for the people of the state—for port operations. This trust not only restricted the use of the tidelands, but also directed oil income and revenue generated from businesses and activities to municipal projects that benefited the general public. In 1916, the Los Angeles Dock and Terminal Company declared bankruptcy and turned over the harbor's dredging projects to the City of Long Beach, which completed the digging of channels.

The shipping industry developed at the port. In 1907, John F. Craig moved his family-owned business, Craig Shipbuilding Company, from Toledo, Ohio, to 43 acres in Long Beach's inner harbor. Other cities offered contracts to lure Craig, but he recognized the city's potential and anticipated it would grow as the company evolved. The *Daily Telegram* remarked in 1910 that this was the city's first big industry and it promised great things for the future of the port, saying "today it is employing 250 men and has business enough in sight to

CONSERVATIVISM

Upon Long Beach's incorporation in 1888, the new municipal government adopted an ordinance prohibiting saloons and gambling within the city limits. An April 1922 issue of the *Daily Telegram* described the history:

Long Beach early determined to exclude from within its boundaries those things which until recently were considered necessary in many communities to attract outsiders and develop

double that number if skilled workmen are procurable here."[12] The Craig Shipbuilding Company continued to prosper in the war years.

BOOMING INDUSTRIES

As money from port operations flowed into Long Beach, cultural diversions penetrated the town. Most people credit Hollywood with the birth of the film industry, but some of the founding fathers and studios set up shop in Long Beach. California Motion Picture Manufacturing Company entered the scene in 1911 followed by Edison Studios in 1913 (which only lasted a few months); a third, founded by J. Searle Dawley on the same site as the other two studios, opened as Balboa Amusements Producing Company. Dawley sold the studio to H. M. Horkheimer, who cranked out silent movies at a fast rate. The expansion garnered the attention of a *Daily Telegram* reporter who wrote in 1915:

> *The start was made in one modest building, on the southeast corner of Sixth and Alamitos streets. As the business grew, the remaining corners were built up, one after another, until now the company is utilizing all four corners of the intersecting streets where it originally located and, in addition, has eleven acres of land on Signal Hill. This is indeed a record unique in the history of the film business, which today stands second only to Standard Oil, in the matter of commercial importance.[13]*

The studio grew to encompass 20 buildings. By 1917, Balboa Films was one of the largest movie studios in the business and a local economic powerhouse. The studio worked with stars such as Charlie Chaplin, Buster Keaton, and Roscoe "Fatty" Arbuckle, many of whom resided in the area. But the good fortune of Balboa Films suddenly ended in 1918 when the firm produced too many movies for distributors to handle and went bankrupt. Other companies continued to use the studio until its demolition in 1925.

With the growth of the community and new industries, banks emerged to cater to the need for capital and financial security. The Bank of Long Beach opened in 1896, followed in 1900 by First National Bank. By 1907, three new banks had been founded: City National, Exchange National, and Farmers & Merchants. Farmers & Merchants exemplifies the pioneering spirit of the town's new residents and remains an enduring local institution.

Farmers & Merchants founder C. J. Walker left the East Coast to journey West by wagon train as a teenager and arrived in Long Beach in 1885. He became a prominent, respected, and well-established businessman in Long Beach when he assumed the role of president for the mismanaged First National Bank. Using his strong business sense, Walker prevented the bank from going under and redirected it toward financial stability. However, he resigned from his position after six weeks when the Los Angeles owners of the bank began issuing directives that Walker felt no longer served the community's best interests. Inextricably linked to the development of Long

3./ Balboa Films, c. 1918
4./ Long Beach Realty Co., 1923

Beach, Walker felt the city should have its own locally owned bank. He turned his attention to establishing an institution to serve the financial needs of the people. On November 23, 1907, Walker and his wife, Carrie, established Farmers & Merchants Bank using $25,000 of their own money as capital.[14]

The Farmers & Merchants bank and tower buildings rose in 1923 and 1925, respectively. In those years Pine Avenue was an unmanicured dirt road with no curbs or sidewalks. Walker hired the architecture firm Curlett & Beelman with W. Horace Austin to create a sound and stable structure—one that continues to operate as the bank's main branch and corporate headquarters.

A MATURING METROPOLIS

Here you have, on one side, the ocean; on the other, the mountains, now snow-capped; and below the lovely town. Here you have glorious sunsets, not only tinting the snow peaks, but transforming the ocean into molten gold, and painting Catalina and the San Pedro hills in pastel colors.[15]

Charles Mulford Robinson

The City Beautiful Movement flourished in the United States in the first decades of the 20th century, focusing on classical principles of realigning streets into wide, tree-lined avenues that culminated in civic structures. Daniel Burnham, the plan's major proponent, first espoused his views at the World's Columbian Exposition in 1893. He later published his ideas for Chicago in 1909, the first city-scale master plan. This proposal spoke to the growing needs of cities but it proved to serve more as a guideline. In his book *The Modern Urban Landscape*, Edward Relph described the inherent limitations of comprehensive planning in the attempt of cities to define their physical layout: "After the first flush of enthusiasm city governments had neither the inclination nor the funds to carry out pretty master plans, especially while there were pressing needs for social reform, for the improvement of basic living conditions, for paving roads and for the installation of sewerage systems."[16]

Still trying to forge its way, Long Beach was no exception. The population of Long Beach leaped from 2,252 in 1900 to 17,809 in 1910. To accommodate the swell, the community focused on the simple yet vital requirements of shelter, jobs, and transportation. However, city leaders were cognizant of basic planning principles and protecting the intrinsic beauty of the coast. In a 1909 letter to the mayor and council of Long Beach, Charles Mulford Robinson, an East Coast-based city planner and journalist, offered suggestions for municipal improvement, arguing for the city to acquire the property between the high-tide line and the bluff from Locust Avenue eastward. Robinson felt leaving the land in private ownership was "to part with the birthright of Long Beach ..." adding that the prospect was "absolutely suicidal as far as the city's future is concerned."[17] Thus, at an early stage, the recreational aspects of the beach and waterfront struggled against pervading commercial interests.

As people became less consumed with the hardships of a pioneer lifestyle, they shifted their attention to cultural divertissements. Attention to workmanship and quality design factored into the equation of residential and commercial building, which no longer was driven by purely utilitarian concerns. A 1917 *Daily Telegram* noted:

> The word "architecture" has taken hold, and the necessity and the commercial value to the individual owner and to the city as a whole of well-designed buildings is better understood. The days of every-man-his-own-architect are passing and there is a growing demand for the services of the men who are specially trained for this work. The desirable new and prospective residents judge our city by the appearance of our buildings both civic and of private ownership.[18]

This new found interest in the aesthetics of building was reflected in noteworthy projects by the San Francisco firm of Coxhead & Coxhead, the Pasadena office of Greene & Greene, and Los Angeles-based architect Irving J. Gill. The appearance of work by these practitioners in Long Beach attested to the city's growing importance as a destination of recognition and

1

1./ Adelaide A. Tichenor House, c. 1920s
left/ Aerial view of Long Beach coastline, c. late 1930s

significance. But it wasn't only landmark residences that lent to Long Beach's distinctive architecture. An overall approach to design, as evidenced in more modest neighborhoods, reinforced the emerging aesthetic as well. In 1922, the *Long Beach Press* featured an article entitled "Setting Nation's Style in Homes," and attributed the city as a leader in styles of Swiss Chalet, Bungalow, Aeroplane, and Spanish.[19] Comprehensive decisions regarding local architecture were implemented by the Long Beach Architectural Club in the 1920s, an organized group of architects that included Hugh R. Davies and Schilling and Schilling.

MILITARY MIGHT

Long Beach was proclaimed the nation's fastest-growing city in the years just prior to World War I. In 1920, Long Beach had 55,600 residents. By 1923, it topped out at 120,000 and by decade's end it reached more than 145,000.

Many factors contributed to the population boom. The Navy designated Long Beach as the headquarters for its new Pacific Fleet in 1919, bringing more than 3,000 officers and enlisted men to the area by the end of the 1920s. By 1932, the city was home port to more than 50

2./ Sailors strolling on Pine Avenue Pier, c. 1925

3./ Oil derricks, c. 1922

4./ Pacific Southwest Exposition, 1928

Navy ships and 8,500 officers and enlisted men, thus creating a welcome and enduring demand for housing. The top brass took up residence and established offices in the fancy hotels and apartment buildings.

Across town the beginning of another industry, air transportation, sprouted. Aviation pioneer Earl S. Daugherty established his own airfield, Chateau Thierry, in 1919 near today's intersection of Long Beach Boulevard and Bixby Road. By 1924 the land became so valuable that Daugherty decided to move the airfield to its present location off Lakewood Boulevard. Daugherty lobbied the city to turn it into a municipal airport and the related industry blossomed into one of Long Beach's most lucrative endeavors.

OIL: THE CITY'S GOLD

With the momentous discovery of oil on Signal Hill in 1921 came great individual and collective prosperity. By the decade's end, it was one of the most lucrative oil fields in the world, with 3,000 wells pumping profits. The city, teeming with people, required temporary and permanent housing, as well as hotels and apartments. Real-estate prices soared and bungalows popped up throughout the city.

In his novel *Oil!*, Upton Sinclair, who kept a beach house in Long Beach, detailed the development of the oil industry in Southern California and the almost overnight transformation of the landscape:

> But suddenly there was no possibility of secrecy; literally all the world knew—for telegraph and cable carried the news to the farthest corners of civilization ... The inside of the earth seemed to burst out through that hole; a roaring and rushing, as Niagara, and a black column shot up into the air, two hundred feet, two hundred and fifty—no one could say for sure—and came thundering down to earth as a mass of thick, black, slimy, slippery fluid.[20]

As with the discovery of gold in the foothills of Northern California in 1849, the promise of fortune altered the landscape. Long Beach rapidly transformed into a major metropolitan center. The influx of money and individuals sparked a "million dollar a month" building campaign that resulted in many of the skyline's landmarks. The 1926 Pacific Coast Club and the 1929 Villa Riviera reflected indulgences in wealth and discriminating taste. During this time of consumerist visions, the first residential high-rises with the "own-your-own" concept appeared on the scene including the Artaban, Omar Hubbard, Cooper Arms, and Sovereign apartments. By 1925, a total of nine movie theaters operated, including the Fox West Coast Theater designed by Meyer and Holler of Grauman's Chinese Theater fame.

Simultaneously, automobiles became a fixture in Southern California. The exceptional climate and thousands of miles of paved roads encouraged travel. "They know that in California the pleasure car rates a higher percentage of use than in any other section of the United States, and they appreciate the fact that one who is auto-less here will have cause practically every day in the year to regret it," stated a 1922 *Daily Telegram* article, eerily foreshadowing dependence on cars.[21] Tourists praised Long Beach as a favorite destination, and the city itself contained approximately 15,000 motor vehicles. Anaheim Street featured a majority of the car dealerships in the 1920s, which employed stylish and ornate architecture to lure buyers into their showrooms.

In 1928, riding on the wave of international attention, Long Beach staged the Pacific Southwest Exposition, an event modeled on a world's fair celebrating the cultures of all the countries bordering the Pacific. The 60-acre waterfront exposition boasted a conglomeration of faux Moorish buildings spread across a desolate sand pit in the harbor area. Designed by local architect Hugh R. Davies, the buildings consisted of stretched canvas buttressed by a coating of stucco that simulated the ancient walls of Northern Africa. Included were 50 structures touting the latest technological wonders and Long Beach's many assets. The event attracted hundreds of thousands of visitors to the harbor area and opened the way for the growth of global commerce.

5

5./ Bird's-eye perspective of Lincoln Park and Magnolia Avenue Pier, 1890

GREENING SO CAL

Attempts to guide Southern California into a cohesive existence persisted, as the negative effects of population and transportation became more pronounced. Developers subdivided land at an alarming rate for housing, commercial uses, and industrial sites with seemingly indiscriminate site selection and lack of consideration for environmental ramifications.

In 1930, the landscape architects and urban park planners Olmsted Brothers and Bartholomew and Associates submitted the report *Parks, Playgrounds and Beaches for the Los Angeles Region* to the Los Angeles Chamber of Commerce. The Olmsted Brothers were not new to Long Beach and its landscape. In 1923, the firm designed Santa Cruz Park, which incorporated eucalyptus saplings, Moreton Bay fig trees, and a rolling lawn. An 1889 deed for the land noted that the site was to be dedicated to the city in perpetuity. Santa Cruz Park was subsequently reduced in size to less than two acres and is now dwarfed by its high-rise neighbors.

The ambitious Olmsted/Bartholomew plan envisioned a regional parks system that stretched from the Antelope Valley in the north to the Long Beach harbor in the south, from the Malibu coast east to Riverside County. The plan had remarkable foresight and vision into the possible plight of the zone:

> [T]he scenic resources are dwindling. The beaches are being fenced off and withdrawn from general use with alarming rapidity. The opportunities now existing for the enjoyment of views out over the sea from the highways along the shore and from privately owned open spaces are being rapidly lost. A practically continuous row of buildings, walls and planting between motorists and the

> seacoast of Los Angles County is in prospect. There are now only six miles of highway along the entire coast of Los Angeles County where views of the sea cannot be so cut off at the will of private landowners. There are no large parks or permanent public open spaces along the coast, such as the waterfront parts of Chicago, Belle Isle of Detroit, or Stanley Park, Vancouver. The few small squares, shore parks, and narrow beaches now existing are wholly out of scale with the present population and are deplorably inadequate for the future.[22]

The plan attempted to address this inevitable misfortune by initiating and promoting sustainable urban communities through the preservation of swaths of green. The report emphasized open space as the essence of a city's underpinning and warned that its prevailing slow erosion impoverished a future of public space.

Although the proposal suggested a remedy, it was essentially doomed from the beginning because it lacked the necessary financing in the midst of the Great Depression and the cooperation required to enact such a comprehensive undertaking. A plan of this magnitude needed city and county support, and no formal authority came forth to spearhead this effort. If realized, this plan would have offered more green space than imaginable, buffering communities and enhancing seaside zones like Long Beach.

The country needs and, unless I mistake its temper, the country demands bold, persistent experimentation. It is common sense to take a method and try it. If it fails, admit it frankly and try another. But above all, try something.[23]
Franklin Delano Roosevelt

ASSEMBLING DEMOCRACY

The catastrophic stock market crash of 1929 was a difficult pill to swallow following decades of prosperity. Despite the pleasurable offerings still existent in Long Beach, the tourist industry took a severe hit. With lack of disposable income, building growth slowed and extraneous amusements dropped off the personal expenditure radar. Tourism was negatively affected resulting in the closure of the Hotel Virginia in 1932. Landmark structures emptied and the city went quiet. But thanks to Long Beach's diversified economy of trade and oil, it fared slightly better than countless other towns across the country.

In the midst of the Great Depression, Long Beach experienced a violent earthquake on March 10, 1933, that registered 6.3 on the Richter scale and claimed close to 100 lives, half of those in Long Beach. Despite the fact that the city already had some of the toughest building codes in California (precipitated by the 1913 Empire Day Disaster, when the Pine Avenue Pier collapsed killing nearly 50 people), many structures, particularly the downtown masonry buildings and public schools, were severely damaged or destroyed. While natural disasters have the tendency to devastate communities for interminable periods, the earthquake lifted Long Beach out of its economic slump. Governmental aid flowed into the city in the form of reconstruction grants and loans. City permits for new construction, which drastically dropped following the 1920s boom, increased dramatically, infusing new life into the city in the form of jobs, optimism, and stability. A rebuilding program ensued in the Streamline Moderne style, most apparent in the city's public schools. As a result of the earthquake, Long Beach Assemblyman Harry B. Riley pushed the Riley Act through the state legislature, which set down even stricter engineering and building requirements in an effort to ensure that schools were built to withstand future quakes.

In 1935, President Franklin Delano Roosevelt established the Works Progress Administration (later known as the Work Projects Administration) to help curb unemployment and increase the purchasing power of persons on relief by employing them on useful projects. The WPA building program included the construction of literally tens of thousands of buildings, bridges, and miles of road. Long Beach appealed to the federal government for help in rebuilding post-earthquake, and the WPA in turn supported the development of civic, recreational, and educational facilities. Projects included the construction of Silverado Park Clubhouse, Harbor Department transit shed, Recreation Park bowling green, Bluff Park comfort stations, and several branch libraries and fire stations. The Federal Art Project, part of the WPA initiative, subsidized art, literature, music, and drama, and engaged artists to create work for state and municipal institutions. Long Beach possesses an enduring legacy of public art produced by the New Deal projects, which can be viewed at the Long Beach Airport, the Promenade, and various public schools throughout the city.[24]

World War II soon overshadowed the devastating events of the 1930s, and once again Long Beach reaped economically while other communities languished. In 1937 the Navy opened its first permanent base in Long Beach, Reeves Field, on the western end of Terminal Island, and designated it the headquarters for the Pacific Fleet's growing air arm.

1

1./ Ships in dry dock
left/ Workers polishing nose cones, c. 1940

Douglas Aircraft Company built a new plant on the edge of Long Beach Airport in 1940 to produce Army bombers and transport planes. Employees turned out 9,440 warplanes throughout the years, and the plant was decorated with a banner announcing Long Beach as "The Arsenal of Democracy." The plant was the world's largest enclosed and air-conditioned production facility, eventually producing jobs for more than 43,000. Douglas continued to be a major economic force in Long Beach, employing 13,000 during the Korean War from 1950 to 1953. In the same decade, the company began work on its first-generation jet airliner and the main runway was lengthened at the airport. This expansion created thousands of new jobs, although it caused an uproar from the residents in the adjoining neighborhoods of Los Altos and California Heights.

On December 7, 1941, the Japanese attacked Pearl Harbor. This event resonated deeply in Long Beach: Many of the crew and officers of the battleship *Arizona* had homes and families in Long Beach. The city altered its coastline into a fortresslike compound. The government funded the Roosevelt Naval Base, the Naval Shipyard, and the Naval Hospital. Allied Engineers Inc., Architects and Engineers, which included the architect Paul R. Williams, articulated a program for the base into a cohesive whole. The smooth, unornamented concrete International Style buildings of the project exuded utility and solidarity. In 1941, work also began on the 8.9-mile federal breakwater, the largest such structure in the world, which would create 30 square miles of protected anchorage for the Navy and commercial ships. This barrier permanently altered the coastline and diminished the essence of surf and sand in Long Beach.

PARADIGMS OF DOMESTIC LIVING

The suburb ... has served as an experimental field for the urban development of a new type of open plan and a new distribution of urban functions ... Some of the lessons that modern planners first mastered in the suburb must be incorporated into the new concept of the city.[25]

Lewis Mumford

From early on, planned communities existed in Long Beach, not the superficial and hastily planned areas that dot today's landscape and define suburbia, but more distinctive districts that added to a rich community fabric. Housing-expansion patterns radiated from the downtown core as well as along rail and transit lines. While wealthy Easterners and landowners like Adelaide A. Tichenor and Jotham Bixby snatched up prime oceanfront plots and built stately residences in Bluff Park, most people settled in the city's more modest developments or outlying farms.

The Sunrise Boulevard District stands out as one of the first smaller, planned neighborhoods. Located in north-central Long Beach, it is fashioned in a similar manner to core housing areas like Carroll Park and Drake Park with curving streets and a clearly defined border. The Pacific Electric Railway line served as the impetus for this 1906 subdivision. Offering small, medium, and large parcels, the area appealed to a wide variety of potential buyers, including a milk sanitarium called the S. S. Porter Milk Diet. This health resort occupied a rambling Victorian structure on a large parcel from 1907 to 1923, attracting Easterners with California's restorative climate. When the sanitarium was demolished, El Cortez, an early motor court, assumed its place on the site, offering small, one-room accommodations.

1./ Atlantic Village scale model, c. late 1930s
left/ Frank House, Case Study House #25, 1963

Following periods of expansion in the first two decades of the 20th century, urban design required a revised, sensitive approach. Charles Henry Cheney, a consultant hired by the city, spearheaded the new movement in California, encouraging cities to create planning commissions and prepare master plans. In Long Beach, Cheney laid out Cerritos Park, a 1,200-acre residential section that extended along Atlantic Avenue, north of Bixby Road to 52nd Street. An integral part of the scheme was Atlantic Village. It was touted in a 1937 *Press-Telegram* advertisement as

> *The West's first modern home district in which parks and play-grounds take the place of old fashioned "horse and buggy" streets—the first neighborhood which offers welcome refuge from the noise, dirt and smoke of the city and from the ever increasing menace of motor traffic. Its residents will find here a clean, quiet, pleasant manner of living obtainable in no other community of comparable price class!*[26]

Clearly acknowledging the negative effects of the motor age, the plan incorporated elements of urban visionary Ebenezer Howard's Garden City model, particularly from his 1898 book entitled *Tomorrow: A Peaceful Path to Real Reform.* A utopian idealist in dealing with overcrowding and sprawl, Howard favored "clean streets with free countryside all around; a belt of fine gardens and orchards so that from every point in the city one can reach the pure air, the grass and the distant horizon."[27] Atlantic Village also can be analyzed within the principles of the Radburn Plan, initiated by planners Clarence Stein and Henry Wright in New Jersey in 1928. This plan espoused "superblocks" consisting of park areas, houses with pathways leading to large-scale green spaces, clearly delineated pedestrian and vehicular traffic routes, and centrally located commerce and community functions. The

development of Atlantic Village incorporates these ideologies into a residential subdivision: detached, one- and two-family houses cluster around cul-de-sacs; business is centralized; profusely landscaped parkways lead to communal areas, the green space accounting for one-fourth of the total development.

As planned communities dotted outlying areas, the high-rise phenomenon took hold downtown in the 1920s, offering own-your-own units in luxurious, seaside settings. These self-contained residences offered easy, carefree living for tourists and part-time residents and generated great activity in the urban downtown district, with direct access to the beach, amusements, shopping, and business. To address the issues of cross-town traffic elicited by disengaged domestic zones, the Los Angeles County Regional Planning Commission selected a site in Long Beach to test a new idea. The Traffic Circle, a large roundabout designed in the early 1930s to connect major arteries such as Pacific Coast Highway, Bellflower Boulevard, and Lakewood Boulevard, proved a good means to eliminate congestion and expedite the passage of vehicles.

The focus of building shifted in the years leading up to and during the war. The tremendous volume of defense work contributed to a severe housing shortage in the city.

2./ Aerial view of Carmelitos, 1939

In addition to the tens of thousands of military personnel, the employees of Douglas, the shipyards, and other defense-related industries required accommodations. A series of pre-World War II housing development units were built on the fringes of Long Beach where land was cheap and plentiful. Large and characterless, these developments evinced uniformity and drabness.

Carmelitos was a Los Angeles County Housing Authority project located between Atlantic and Orange avenues north of the Union Pacific Railroad tracks. Built in 1939, Carmelitos offered housing for 607 low-income families, especially sailors whose income was less than $100 a month. Designed by local architects Cecil Schilling and Kenneth S. Wing, the homes were constructed of reinforced concrete and designed to endure for at least 60 years, which was the term of the federal government loan financing the work.[28] But because World War II efforts required large quantities of concrete and steel, the architects turned to wood and stucco to complete the job.

The erection of another housing authority project, Savannah Family Housing, commenced in 1940. Bound by the Los Angeles River and Santa Fe Avenue at 14th Street, the 40-acre tract accommodated 400 families in 200 duplex units. Soon after, the Cabrillo Housing Project was developed adjacent to Savannah on 100

acres of land extending south toward the Pacific Coast Highway. Began as a temporary housing complex, Cabrillo was demolished in 1965 to make way for the residential units that currently occupy the site. Another massive wartime-housing project was the 1,000-unit Truman Boyd Manor, built in 1941 as temporary housing for defense workers and armed services personnel. In 1953, the American Gold Star Mothers foundation purchased the 93-acre property and transformed it into a residence for the mothers of service personnel killed on active duty.

Over the years, the city witnessed a distinct change in function of government-sponsored housing. New uses materialized, some successful, others examples of neglect. Many of the developments discussed above became associated with low-income conditions and blight. At Carmelitos, the late 1950s inflation contributed to cutbacks in the maintenance program and rents were raised. The subsequent deterioration resulted in a 1969 strike, where tenants protested the living conditions, obsolete appliances, and lack of decision-making power. The City of Long Beach, in agreement with the Los Angeles County Housing Authority, sought to rebuild the entire project and devote half of the 64 acres to privately developed middle-income housing. But a Department of Housing and Urban Development environmental-impact statement declared that the concrete buildings undergo restoration for families and the 130 wood-frame buildings be razed and rebuilt for the elderly. The prospective residents voted on the models they liked the best, resulting in a scheme that appears more like a moderately priced condominium complex.[29] By that time, Carmelitos was the only intact conventional housing project in the city.

FROM FIELDS TO FRAMES

In 1944, President Franklin D. Roosevelt signed the Serviceman's Readjustment Act, a law that would spark unprecedented growth in Long Beach. Better known as the GI Bill, it compensated millions of men and women who had sacrificed their youth to the cause of freedom. Not entirely altruistic, the act also jump-started a peacetime economy by guaranteeing that any veteran with an honorable discharge could buy a home with a government-backed loan. The terms were hard to refuse: no money down and a four percent interest rate. The bill immediately made home ownership, once reserved for the middle and upper classes, within reach of millions of Americans.

Local developer Lloyd Whaley recognized the potential windfall of the GI Bill. Whaley began building individual homes in Long Beach in the late 1930s. In 1939 he formed the Home Investment Company and built wartime tract housing in west Long Beach and the vicinity of the Virginia Country Club, where buyers got finished homes and a slab for a garage, which would be built by Whaley once wartime materials rationing ended. In 1947, after the slow war years, he teamed with the Fred Bixby family to develop tracts on the former land of Rancho Los Alamitos. Named Los Altos, this area would become one of the nation's largest planned communities. The first of

25 tracts offered single-family homes, built assembly-line style and sold for $8,000 to $10,000. Designed with curving streets and T-shaped intersections to control traffic, most homes backed up on major thoroughfares rather than faced busy streets. Land was reserved for schools, parks, churches, business centers, and access to the planned San Diego Freeway. These were all-inclusive environments, relying little on the established urban cores of the past decades.

In one of Whaley's marketing brochures, the opening page appealed to the buyer stating, "every new residential development becomes a self-contained community with the building of a business center."[30] And, because of its proximity to the new Long Beach State College, he called it a potential Westwood. By the time Los Altos was built out in 1956, Whaley had added more than 10,000 houses to Long Beach.

Among the most exclusive tracts Whaley developed in Long Beach was Park Estates. This area offered large flat plots of land, and architects such as John Lautner, Richard Neutra, and Edward A. Killingsworth received commissions to design projects. Clients were given a thick pamphlet titled *Protective Restrictions of the Members of Los Altos Association*, which contained architecture, landscaping, and visual guidelines, among others. Most disturbing, although not uncommon for the time, were the racial exclusions it outlined:

> *A. No part of said property shall be sold, conveyed, rented, or leased in whole or in part to any person of African or Asiatic descent or to any person not of the white or Caucasian race. B. No part of said property shall be used or occupied or permitted to be used or occupied in whole or in part by any person who is either wholly or partially of African or Asiatic descent or by any person not of the white or Caucasian race, except that domestic servants, chauffeurs, or gardeners of other than the white or Caucasian race may live in or occupy the premises where their employer resides.*[31]

Although many developers promoted diversity in housing, the sales pitches for various exclusive, middle-class, and starter homes didn't always promise racial equality. This practice continued until the 1960s despite a 1948 ruling by the U.S. Supreme Court that banned such restrictions. Deed restrictions citywide prevented African-Americans from living in, owning, or renting homes and apartments outside a designated area near Long Beach Polytechnic High School. The African-American population in Long Beach reached 15,000 by the end of World War II, and many of these residents lived in Cabrillo II, part of the Savannah and Cabrillo war emergency housing complex in west Long Beach. When the federal government declared a housing surplus and decided to raze part of Cabrillo II and redevelop the site, much of this African-American community was evicted. With few housing options, many resettled in "nonrestrictive" tracts in Watts and Compton. Those who stayed found opportunities in west Long Beach in new neighborhoods built on former government-housing sites and small farms.

3./ Aerial view of Traffic Circle, c. 1960
4./ Aerial view of Los Altos area, 1951
5./ "Mansions in the Sky," Moore Realty marketing brochure, Marina Tower, 1958

Long Beach's heterogeneity contributes greatly to its appeal and can be traced back to the city's earliest days. A Japanese community populated Signal Hill and Fish Harbor in the first decade of the 20th century and at the time constituted the second-largest ethnic population in Long Beach. The West served as a refuge to African-Americans fleeing racism and violence in the South at the turn of the century. African-Americans first settled at Anaheim and California (now Martin Luther King Jr. Avenue) in 1906. They were long restricted to this area, which was the largest African-American community in the city. The largest Latino settlement occurred in an area known as Zaferia, now the eastern section of Long Beach. Mexican refugees escaping their homeland's 10-year civil war from 1910 to 1920 enlarged the Latino community present since the rancho era. The federal Bracero program, which allowed thousands of Mexican citizens to legally work and live in the United States, also bolstered the Latino community with a large wartime influx. Three decades later, large populations of Cambodian refugees settled in Long Beach after fleeing the Khmer Rouge in the mid 1970s, giving Long Beach the largest community of Cambodians outside of their homeland.

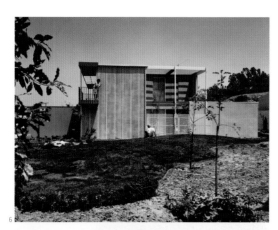

Subdivisions steadily encroached upon farmland to accommodate growth spurts in the years following World War II. Although they rapidly devoured land and wantonly destroyed existing farming operations, these sprawling developments marked progress. A 1957 newspaper article reported on the fate of Griset Brothers bean fields in the land lying between Spring and Stearns streets east of Studebaker Road: "Hemmed against the banks of the San Gabriel River, the shrinking farmlands are doomed by the subdivisions which encircle them on the north, south and west."[32]

Because of the rapid pace of development, little concern was given to the quality of the structures. In his book *Holy Land: A Suburban Memoir*, D. J. Waldie described the conditions of construction in suburbia:

6./ Cerritos Circle residence, 1964
7./ Paul Edward Tay Office and Apartments, 1964

> *The houses in my neighborhood touch the ground lightly. There is no basement. Foundations are hardly more than a foot deep. It took a bucket excavator only fifteen minutes to dig each one. Carpenters followed and nailed up three-foot foundation forms as quickly as possible. Workmen poured the concrete quickly, too. The crews poured 2,113 foundations in a hundred days. For every ten houses, they watered enough concrete for the foundation of an eleventh. Typically, the architecture was uninspired and void of personality, offering a few plans with slight variations. The style was often reflective of the budget, which was based on the dictum of getting the most for the least.*[33]

Rural landscapes were gobbled up as repeated annexations of incorporated and unincorporated communities in Los Angeles County continued. The neighboring community of Lakewood, which Waldie describes above, arose from the same tenets of urban sprawl and bedroom communities.

UNCONVENTIONAL OUTTAKES

That is not to say that all such communities evolved without a greater concern for design. A postwar tract, called Lakewood Rancho Estates, the brainchild of designer Cliff May and architect Chris Choate, is indicative of a planned environment that offered straightforward ranch-style architecture and tree-lined streets surrounded by large traffic arteries on all sides. Ross W. Cortese, the developer of this tract, which upon completion in 1954 consisted of approximately 600 houses near the Lakewood border, had been impressed with May's earlier work in Cupertino. Cortese later went on to build the Leisure World retirement community in Seal Beach. The Lakewood Rancho Estates houses, priced around $11,000, catered to middle-class families and incorporated a contemporary modernism with open floor plans, tongue-and-groove low pitched ceilings, and post-and-beam construction. Capitalizing on the Southern California climate, May substituted sheets of glass for walls and doors to facilitate indoor-outdoor living.

In 1964, Cerritos Circle, a garden apartment complex with 42 buildings, opened on the site of a former racehorse training track that was once part of the Jones family acreage. Located in the Virginia Country Club area and limited to adult tenants only, it was marketed as "a new urban living concept tailored to an area of executive homes."[34] Architect Clifton S. Jones Jr., inspired by his studies at the University of Southern California and the clean, flat-roof style of local architect Edward A. Killingsworth, incorporated open floor plans in the one- and two-story designs. Even with Jones's emphasis on modern living, the desire of most home buyers veered toward "common forms" and conservative layouts, and the complexes quickly turned to rental accommodations.[35]

Not only did a new architectural language permeate tract developments, it also evidenced itself in individual residences. Experimental ideas in architecture were a constant theme in the city's history and can be charted from the beginning of the 1900s. Examples that speak to Long Beach as a testing ground for new forms of domesticity include the Greene & Greene plan for the 1904 Reeve Residence, where one sees the architects' exploration of abstracted nature in the decorative arts and stained-glass elements. Other progressive housing prototypes include the 10 electric houses built by developer Harold E. Ketchum in 1923, Raphael Soriano's International Style Kimpson/Nixon House in 1940, Edward A. Killingsworth's Frank House, Case Study House #25, in 1963, and Ray Kappe's geometrically imposed Penn/Crowell House in 1973. The decline in original housing examples in the 1980s can be traced to several factors; it partially reflected the absence of available land and the increased enforcement of restrictive codes and prohibitive building standards. Furthermore, many creative endeavors focused on remodel projects, often hidden from passersby, or tended to spotlight adaptive reuse in urban centers as space became sacred.

Despite mass development patterns, individuality in architecture always managed to surface. This sentiment also crossed over into interior design and furnishings. Frank Bros., located on Long Beach Boulevard, was in the

8./ Kimpson/Nixon House, 1940
9./ *New Forms* exhibition, Frank Bros., February 1963

vanguard of modernist furniture and decorative objects sales in the United States during the middle of the 20th century, bringing the traditions of European and Scandinavian designers to the city. When Edward Frank joined his father Louis and brother Maurice's furniture business in 1938, he suggested that it eliminate traditional lines and instead become a specialty store focusing on the work of contemporary designers. For many years, it carried the cachet of being the primary U.S. retailer of the most recognizable names in mid-century design including Alvar Aalto, Charles and Ray Eames, Van Keppel Green, Bruno Matthsson, Paul McCobb, and Knoll, among others. The Frank Bros. educated the public through exhibitions and aggressive marketing campaigns with smartly designed ephemera, and their legacy is still evident in the enduring pieces that continue to furnish the residences of Long Beach.

Moving from an existence of scarcity to an existence of super abundance, as we know it, throughout history, means that by having gained so much, we slowly seem to be losing very much in other directions.[36]
Paolo Soleri

SINK OR SWIM

The landscape of Long Beach changed rapidly during the mid-20th century. To accommodate more people and commerce, transportation corridors expanded and new routes transpired. Long Beach erected a new academic institution, and tourism and development continued to flourish, solving some economic problems but creating others.

SPRAWL

The onset of urban sprawl spurred a complex system of freeways connecting various Southland communities. In his book *Endangered Dreams: The Great Depression in California*, State Librarian Kevin Starr reflected, "motorists of 1941 could experience the Southern California of the future: the continuous sub/urban metropolis."[37] These networks, while initially perceived as a welcome convenience, greatly reinforced the horizontality of the land. The City of Long Beach and port officials used their own funds to launch the Long Beach Freeway (Interstate 710) in 1951, providing a connection between the harbor area and Long Beach and the remainder of the Los Angeles basin. This freeway and others fostered a symbiotic relationship with the growth of suburbs. A mention of long-range plans in a 1959 *Independent* article enumerated the anticipated extent of the tentacles' reaches: "The state plans to build 1,032 miles of freeways in Los Angeles County during the 20 year period at an estimated cost of $3,152,000,000."[38] By the end of the 1960s, major freeways crossed the entire city. The San Gabriel Freeway (Interstate 605) was finished in 1966, and the San Diego Freeway (Interstate 405) connected Long Beach to Orange County and Santa Monica in 1969. Finally, in 1972, residents began to see the danger and halted the extension of the Garden Grove Freeway (State Highway 22), which had opened in 1964. Dubbed the Crosstown Freeway, the extension was slated to run through eastern Long Beach at 7th Street, which would have sliced through many of the city's residential districts, razing thousands of homes and businesses.

As freeways and suburban centers facilitated ease in business transactions, the downtown core and surrounding neighborhoods fell into blight. Even though the 710 skirted the west side, it primarily served as a spine for large transport trucks that funneled directly into the port. Hence it was little help in regenerating the downtown core, an area that experienced economic anemia in the 1960s and 1970s.

The Vincent Thomas and Gerald Desmond bridges, erected in 1963 and 1968, linked the ports to downtown Long Beach. Both were remarkable feats of engineering. At the time it was built, the Vincent Thomas Bridge was the third-largest suspension bridge in California, with a length of 6,060 feet and a main suspended span 1,500 feet long. Designed by the Bridge Department of the California Division of Highways, it was built in response to the growth of the inland basins, allowing a deep waterway passage for ocean-going ships while maintaining the flow of vehicular traffic. The Gerald Desmond Bridge spanned the back channel of the Port of Long Beach connecting Ocean Boulevard with Terminal Island. It replaced the old Pontoon Bridge, first built in 1919.

1./ Aerial of Long Beach Freeway (I-710) interchange, 1960
left/ Gerald Desmond Bridge, 1967

HIGHER EDUCATION

The GI Bill had dramatic effects on the housing market, but the bill's other middle-class entry program focused on extending education, another privilege once restricted to the wealthy or highly gifted. Intellectual and professional pursuits opened to a whole new segment of society when the government offered a free college education and small stipend for living expenses to every qualified veteran, presenting an enticing alternative to the depressed labor market.

In 1945, the University of California, Los Angeles (UCLA), was the only four-year public-college option in the Southland. The demand for postsecondary educational institutions led to the 1949 founding of Long Beach State College, which eventually would become California State University, Long Beach (CSULB). It started with 169 students, 12 faculty members, and two rented apartment buildings on Anaheim Street. In 1950, Long Beach voters approved Proposition B, which authorized the use of up to $1 million in city oil revenues to purchase a campus site and donate it to the state. By 1951, enrollment rose to 1,000 and classes and administration moved into 23 temporary buildings on Bellflower Boulevard. In 1952, architect Hugh Gibbs unveiled his master plan for a $20 million permanent

2./ Subsidence marker, c. 1958

3./ Quarry site on Catalina Island, 1942

4./ Hopper barge unloading quarried rock, preparing
breakwater, 1942

campus, and the first buildings were dedicated in 1955. The campus grew at
an exponential rate, with 10,000 students by 1960 and 23,500 by 1967. By
the late 1980s, enrollment hit 35,000. The firm of Killingsworth, Brady &
Smith assumed the role of master planner in 1962, tuning in to the needs of
a fast-growing entity.

The campus, with its large student body, effectively shaped another city
within the city. Its influence extended beyond the official perimeters of
campus. In a 1972 *Independent Press-Telegram* article, it was reported that
"one out of every 10 residents in the greater Long Beach area have been
members of the faculty, staff or student body at the university."[39] Although
long considered a commuter school, the presence of CSULB nonetheless
affected the local economy and contributed greatly to the social fabric of
the community.

A SLIPPERY SLOPE

Prosperity and growth did not always reap positive results. Although the
City of Long Beach benefited greatly from the discovery of oil, it also experienced a geological drawback—subsidence, the gradual lowering or sinking of
the earth's surface. The development of the Wilmington Oil Field in the
harbor area began in 1936 and these operations exacerbated the problem.
While the city detected subsidence in the harbor area at various times
before 1940, the effects were relatively insignificant. During the 1940s,
however, surveys showed a settling of 15 inches at the east end of Terminal
Island, with sinkage diminishing toward downtown. Damage soon became
apparent in harbor buildings, streets, railroad tracks, and underground
systems. At its worst, an area of more than 20 square miles subsided from
two up to 29 feet at the epicenter, including developed portions of the Long
Beach harbor and the southwest section of the city. The affected region,
although gradually diminishing in severity, circled Signal Hill. Experts in
engineering, geology, soil, and math mulled over the situation and reached
the consensus that a massive injection of water into the subsurface area
would result in the best chance of restoring underground pressure and
stabilizing the earth. A limited water-injection program began in 1953 and
when that proved successful, large-scale water injection commenced in
1958. In a 1959 issue of *Harbor Highlights Magazine*, Samuel M. Roberts,
the acting subsidence control administrator, described the operation as "an
engineering program of probably the greatest magnitude in the history of
the petroleum industry."[40]

The problem was rectified at a tremendous cost to Long Beach. By 1957,
expenses for damage and repair of facilities reached $90 million. The
Tidelands Fund, which dominated a long financial history in the chronicles
of the city, subsidized much of the cost. Beginning with an action of the
State Legislature in 1911, the State of California granted Long Beach the
state's right, title, and interest in the Long Beach tidelands, oil revenues
included. These lands were to be held in trust by the city for developing
harbor facilities and for development of public parks, parkways, highways,

playgrounds, and facilities for Navy personnel and merchant seamen. In 1924 and 1925 statutes were adopted to permit the use of landfill areas for public parks, highways and playgrounds. In 1938 the Supreme Court ruled Long Beach could drill for oil on these landfills but, under the aegis of the Tidelands Fund, any monies gained would have to be used for shoreline improvement. This was reiterated in 1948. The city had relied upon oil income to build and maintain its port and public coastal recreation areas. The state, in turn, received 50 percent of the profits.

By 1951, however, there was surplus money from the drilling of oil, money that wasn't needed to improve the land surrounding the tidelands. Long Beach petitioned the state to use this money for inland projects. The governor, State Assembly, and Senate agreed and signed a measure that would allow Long Beach to construct hospitals, parks, and streets with tidelands money. With these rules in mind, the city developed strategies to use the oil money to benefit the entire region and, as a result, the city gained El Dorado Park, several library branches, and many other public facilities. But when the Tidelands Fund was distributed to other programs in the 1950s such as a new marina complex on Alamitos Bay, the California Supreme Court ruled that they had no right to apply revenue from state-owned tidelands on projects other than those that would benefit all Californians. The court challenged their 50 percent share and in 1965, the state took 85 percent of all revenues, leaving Long Beach with the much-reduced but still sizable remainder. Controversy persists today regarding the use of these monies, dividing the community on the direction and future of the harbor area.

BREAKING THE MOLD

In the 1940s, the fate of the entire Long Beach waterfront faced what proved to be an irreversible alteration when the federal government allo-cated funds for a third breakwater extension. The construction eastward of the final 13,000 feet of rock wall began in 1946 and was completed in March 1949. Built to provide protection for the Navy's Pacific Fleet after the World War II attack on Pearl Harbor and almost imperceptible from the shoreline, it comprised part of the largest man-made breakwater in the world.

In its heyday, the seaside amusement area called the Pike regularly drew 50,000 visitors on the weekend. Despite the changing coastline, it continued to attract large crowds into the 1950s. But when theme parks, such as Knott's Berry Farm and later Disneyland and Magic Mountain, could simu-late the ultimate fantasy experience along with hotel accommodations and hyped-up marketing promotions as a full package for families, attention and visits diverted from the Pike and its old-fashioned attractions. The continual downsizing of the Navy was also a blow, as its personnel composed much of the patron base. A 1968 article in the *Press-Telegram Southland Magazine* reported, "Long Beach is a city in transition. With the addition of man-made Pier J, and the Queen Mary, and a continuing port improvement program, many of the prized landmarks of yesterday are falling to the ground—and

being swallowed by the progress of the times."[41] Operators dismantled the biggest Pike attraction, the Cyclone Racer, in 1972, and a few years later the rest of the rides closed.

When growth stalled during the 1960s, the city embarked on a plan to draw tourism. The Cunard Steamship Company put the Queen Mary—the most luxurious passenger liner of the 1930s—up for sale, and Long Beach won the bid. Officials anticipated it as the star attraction of the city's renaissance. Almost three-and-a-half football fields in length, its size proved overwhelming and the conversion and renovation sucked up millions in tidelands oil money. It took three years to prepare for paying customers, and then it opened to disappointing results. The appeal was more nostalgic than entertaining. And with area theme parks adding attractions all the time, the Queen Mary was certainly not on a par to compete. While it managed to draw more than 6.4 million visitors in the four years after opening, it operated at a loss and the city consid-ered ceasing operations.

The disappearance of the beach was possibly the greatest casualty of redevelopment, particularly the area from the mouth of the Los Angeles River to the foot of Alamitos Avenue. With the absence of an unspoiled coastline, recreational activities diminished. The United States Navy, during World War II, claimed the portion of the beach west of the Los Angeles River for the Naval Base and Shipyard. West Beach was the second to go. Another landfill produced ground for the Long Beach Convention Center and Arena and Shoreline Village. Redevelopment also affected green space and historic buildings. In the mid-1970s the city approved a project encompassing 421 acres of downtown. In the first phase, historic Lincoln Park (formerly Pacific Park) was virtually erased by the completion of the 1977 Civic Center. It also replaced Art Deco city offices and the historic Carnegie Public Library. Public outcry against such actions remained minimal, as the worldwide economic recession consumed the collective mind.

RECONCILING REASON WITH RAZING

It is significant that the cities doing best by their downtowns are the ones doing best at historic preservation and reuse. Fine old buildings are worthwhile in their own right, but there is a greater benefit involved. They provide discipline. Architects and planners like a blank slate. They usually do their best work, however, when they don't have one.[42]

William H. Whyte

The issue of preservation in Long Beach parallels the difficulties many cities confront but the solutions present a singular vision based on individual criteria. The preservation movement manifested in Long Beach in 1961 when a small group of neighbors banded together to fight a proposed high-rise tower at Ocean Boulevard and Paloma Avenue in Bluff Park. A developer successfully battled for the rezoning of a seven-block strip—the north side of Ocean from Kennebec Avenue on the west to Redondo Avenue on the east—from R2 to R5, a custom-made zone that permitted construction of only multiunit dwellings more than five stories in height. It was the only such zone in the city. Residents felt that the introduction of high-rise towers in an otherwise single-family home neighborhood destroyed its character and appeal. Developers saw it as a means for providing more balanced housing types and cited tall buildings as a solution for the inevitability of growth. One architect of a slated high-rise was quoted in a 1973 *Independent Press-Telegram* as saying:

> *I do not believe that neighborhoods won't form in tall buildings. People meet one another in recreation rooms, get to know each other. Those who say high-rises aren't communities are only playing on words. What IS ridiculous is to believe there still are amenities left for single-family dwellings on Ocean Boulevard. When that drive was conceived there was hardly any traffic.*[43]

Actually, the rezone attempt was a shortsighted effort to quickly boost the economy. The proposed tower was never realized, but the erection of the Galaxy Tower did succeed several years later.

Despite this setback, the residents' group remained an active force. In 1972 they incorporated as the Beach Area Concerned Citizens and embarked on a campaign to rezone Ocean Boulevard. The effort took five years of correspondence, petitions, testimony, and political lobbying, but their grass-roots advocacy ultimately paid off.

The Galaxy Tower controversy marked a pivotal point in the future of Long Beach as it brought to light issues of permissive zoning and development without regard to the surrounding environs. Long Beach could have easily followed the fate of Miami Beach or even Santa Monica, sacrificing unobstructed views in the name of profitability and pleasure for a select few. But the issue mobilized action and accomplished the identification and protection of historic resources.

Local activist Luanne Pryor proved an instrumental force in the cultural heritage movement in Long Beach. She created awareness in historically significant neighborhoods and conducted slide presentations to civic and community groups and city officials. As a result of Pryor's efforts, the city established the Cultural Heritage Committee in 1978 and authorized it to identify and protect historic resources through granting Historic District status, a designation that regulates exterior changes to all properties in the defined area. Those structures that have historic value are required to follow the Secretary of Interior's standards, whereupon owners can make

1./ Razing Pacific Coast Club, 1988
left/ Aerial view of Galaxy Tower, c. 1980

additions and changes only under certain guidelines. Subsequently, many neighborhood groups became interested in acquiring this status, particularly those in danger of losing their individual character by the thoughtless erection of 1980s "cracker box" housing and multifamily apartments.

The threatened fate of the 1906 Bembridge House also fueled the preservation movement. In the late 1960s, the city announced plans to acquire and raze preservationist and local arts aficionado Dorothy Bembridge's historic residence as part of a park extension plan. However, Bembridge, the Historical Society of Long Beach, and citizens protested and rallied together to save this treasure. Ultimately, city officials decided that the house was too valuable to destroy, and planned the park expansion around the structure. In 1976, neighborhood members coined the name Willmore City and formed the Willmore City Heritage Association, one of the city's most active preservation groups. Another early preservation group, the Long Beach Foundation for Architectural and Cultural Heritage, active since 1980, made many strides in community awareness and protection of historic resources. The name was changed to The Long Beach Heritage Coalition (today known as Long Beach Heritage) as the result of a 1990 merger with The Coalition to Preserve Historic Long Beach.

The city embarked on a wrecking spree in the 1970s and 1980s. Many monuments of not only nostalgic but also architecturally significant value faced demolition. One of the casualties was the Pacific Coast Club. A developer bought the property and proposed preserving the building for a hotel conversion. The project had funding but the city council did not approve it, citing safety and code compliance issues. The last straw came when a trespasser fell to his death between open floorboards. Regarded unsafe, the project was no longer politically feasible, proving that even historically designated buildings could face annihilation.

While in the interest of the public, the Seismic Safety Code proved daunting to the preservation process. All unreinforced masonry buildings built prior to 1933 faced certain requirements for seismic safety. This proactive approach nonetheless imposed a huge burden on property owners. Some structures, such as the Villa Riviera and Lafayette Complex, were saved only by the efforts of resident-owners, who assessed themselves millions of dollars to upgrade their dwellings to earthquake-safety standards.

Perhaps many more buildings were spared from destruction because of the economic blight of the 1970s. The lack of need and/or funding acted as a preservation buffer, when buildings stood vacant instead of being cleared for new development, particularly downtown.

The Cultural Heritage Committee became a city commission in 1988. That same year marked the first time the mayor of Long Beach would be determined by means of a citywide election. Pryor decided to run for the position based largely on the preservation platform and forced the leading candidate, Ernie Kell, into a run-off. Clear the preservation votes would affect the election, Kell wisely went to the historic-minded advocates and asked what he could do to receive their support. They insisted on the establishment of a preservation position and office, a survey of all historically significant buildings, and an ordinance that stated that the demolition of historic structures could not occur without replacement projects in place. Kell promised to fulfill their demands and won the election. This proved to be a watershed moment in Long Beach history.

In 1989 Ruthann Lehrer became the first Historic Preservation Officer for the City of Long Beach. When she began, there were three historic districts. By the time Lehrer retired in December 2003, she had expanded the perimeters of these districts and added 13 more neighborhoods to the list. Approximately 40 buildings had been designated as historic landmarks prior to her arrival; in 2004, there were more than 120, with new ones under consideration. Lehrer also completed the survey for all city structures affected by the Seismic Safety Code and established the Mills Act procedures and program

2./ City of Long Beach, Historic Landmarks and Districts, 2004
3./ View of Municipal Auditorium and downtown, c. 1935

for the city for individual properties and multiple-living units. Finally, she was able to obtain an addendum to the Seismic Safety regulation that allowed for designated landmarks to be vacated, closed to public access, and not required to undergo seismic upgrading until owners performed the rehabilitation. As a result, many otherwise doomed buildings were saved.

DECONSTRUCTING HISTORY

In the 1990s, Long Beach Heritage waged a campaign to save a collection of buildings at the Roosevelt Naval Base designed by Allied Engineers, the collaborative architecture team that included Paul R. Williams. When the 1991 Defense Base Closure and Realignment Commission closed their hometown military base in Long Beach, the land, once federally owned, was turned over to the city. This marked the end of a nearly century-long relationship with the Navy, which at one time served as the area's largest employer. In deciding the fate of the land, the city set up a process through the Economic Development Commission. The federal law requires an assessment of cultural resources, so the Navy commissioned a consultant to identify significant buildings by Williams. The study was never made public. The Economic Development Commission held hearings, and the Port of Long Beach immediately became a major player.

The port wanted to expand. When the news spread, the Historic Preservation Commission and Long Beach Heritage assumed leading roles in the controversy. After cultural resources surfaced as an issue, the State Office of Historic Preservation became involved as well as the Advisory Commission for Historic Preservation, a federal group. They organized a consultation process to bring "interested parties" into the fold. Jerry Miller, then manager of the Business Development Center for the City of Long Beach, led this process, which consisted of meetings to discuss alternatives. Concurrently the California Environmental Quality Act (CEQA) required that an environmental review be completed before granting land. Findings concluded that the city had not adequately followed CEQA compliance, and Long Beach Heritage had a case. It was a big step for the organization, which was able to uphold the process in court. The city and port were required to perform an Environmental Impact Report, fundamentally an information document that allowed for public exposure.

But preservationists were fighting a losing battle as the question arose of how to determine value. Financial compensation granted in lieu of historic preservation prevailed as the only probable alternative. The Port of Long Beach razed Roosevelt Naval Base in 1999 to make way for a new shipping terminal. Long Beach Heritage and other groups in turn received a model of the buildings, a financial-mitigation package, photographic documentation, and salvaged artifacts. The Long Beach Navy Memorial Heritage Association currently administers the grant money for preservation efforts in Long Beach. This fund—mitigation for environmental damage to a structure—is unique to the City of Long Beach. Since its inception, projects have included the restoration of Christian Outreach Appeal's original stained-glass

4./ Roosevelt Naval Base, Building 233, north side of pool area, 1996
5./ Rubble from demolished Omar Hubbard Building, 1976

windows, a naval exhibition at the Historical Society of Long Beach, and the restoration of the Carriage House at the Long Beach Museum of Art.44

The Los Angeles Conservancy recognized Long Beach's strides in the arena of historic preservation in 2003. In the conservancy's first "Los Angeles County Preservation Report Card," Long Beach received one of only six A's awarded out of the 89 cities and jurisdictions reviewed in the county. The conservancy based its grades on the strength of a municipality's preservation ordinances, if they existed; its use of state historic-tax credits and its historic districts, if any; its surveys of architectural resources; and the existence of a historic-preservation officer or commission.

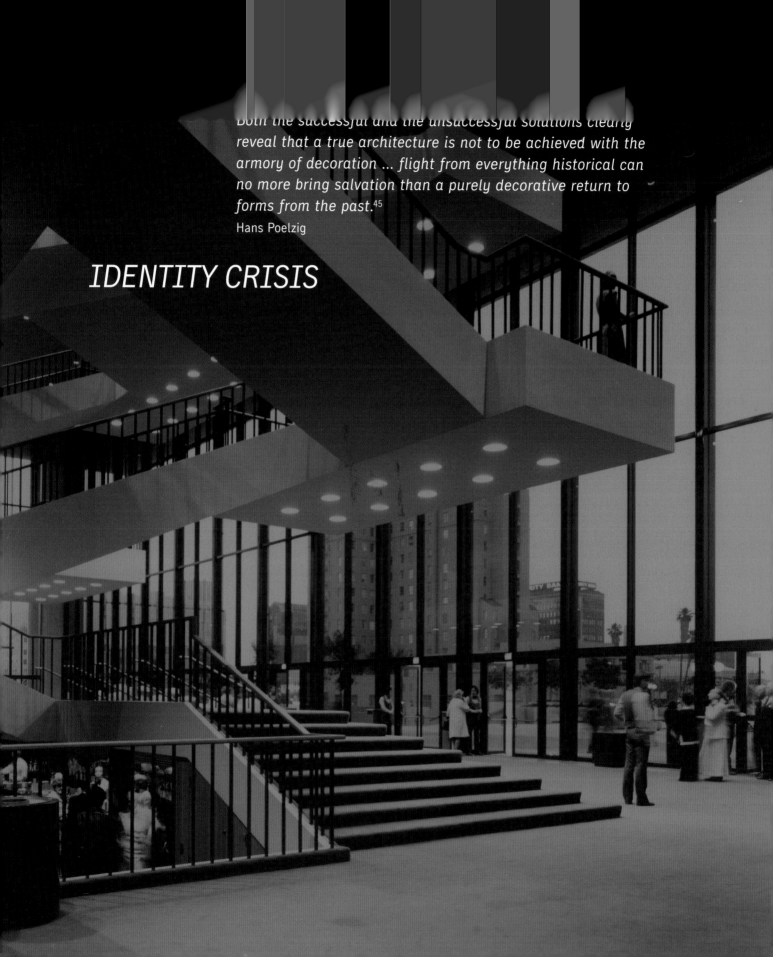

Both the successful and the unsuccessful solutions clearly reveal that a true architecture is not to be achieved with the armory of decoration ... flight from everything historical can no more bring salvation than a purely decorative return to forms from the past.[45]
Hans Poelzig

IDENTITY CRISIS

Unlike the stark and brutalist approach employed in the erection of 1970s buildings such as the concrete-formed Civic Center and Performing Arts Center, Long Beach's public projects of the following decades produced showier corporate architecture, with slick edges and reflective surfaces. Yet good or bad, the architecture from the 1960s through 1980s proffered an individuality that would be lacking in projects to come.

A 1978 federal study found Long Beach to be among the most socially, economically, and financially distressed cities in the country. Long Beach's then-Mayor Eunice Sato speculated on why the corrosion of the city had escalated to this degree. She attributed the demise to the relocation of a majority of the naval fleet to San Diego after World War II and to the emergence of suburban shopping malls, which drove the decline of the downtown area. Sato said, "I think those two things really were outside the realm of our control, but it happened to Long Beach and nothing was really done to make a correction, so it just deteriorated from year to year to year."[46] Other city officials cited factors such as Long Beach simply being an old city devoid of a new younger population to sustain its health, or blamed the lack of incentive for developers to buy land in the subsidence area for fear of long-term loss. With its high vacancy rates, poor housing accommodations, deteriorating commercial structures, and stagnant urban scene, the downtown bore the burden of this unsightly image. The city needed a jump-start to get rolling again.

In response to the downward spiral, the city developed the 1978 Downtown Plan, which comprehensively addressed the issues of growth and the outdated physical condition of the area. Long Beach received federal grants for a multimodal transportation project. Along with the $14 million in federal funds came $8 million in state and local money to support the construction of a state-of-the-art downtown transit and pedestrian mall. Called the Promenade, it was envisaged to fuse foot traffic and commerce, connecting the Long Beach Plaza shopping center with the Shoreline Village retail and restaurant center. In 1980, the Redevelopment Agency implemented a plan to assemble blighted properties for sale to developers, as well as to provide land write-downs and other financial incentives to attract new development off and around the Promenade. Unfortunately, the Promenade lacked several key factors: a strong street presence, accessibility, a high concentration of shops, and infrastructural planning for parking. Except for random events and the weekly farmers' market, it never brought large amounts of sustained activity or drew crowds like Santa Monica's Third Street Promenade.

In contrast, the Convention Center, an addition to the Arena and Terrace Theater (later renamed the Long Beach Performing Arts Center), was revealed as the new cornerstone of the local tourism industry. Completed in 1978, the $51.1 million project included a 100,000-square-foot exhibition hall, 22 major meeting rooms, and a 1,600-seat ballroom. Adding to the existing 13,600-seat arena and 3,141-seat theater, the entertainment and business-meeting possibilities multiplied. And unlike the Los Angeles Convention Center, Long Beach's facility offered accommodations and

1./ Long Beach Performing Arts Center (Terrace Theater), c. 2000

left/ Long Beach Performing Arts Center (Terrace Theater), c. 1980

restaurants within easy walking distance. After the success of its first 15 years, the Convention Center was expanded and renovated in 1994, to include a promenade area along the building and a parking structure. The $111 million enlargement encompassed more than 334,000 square feet. Capturing the grandiose and flashy design of the late 1980s/early 1990s, the massive structure stands as a beacon to thousands of convention-goers.

In the 1980s, the Redevelopment Agency, acknowledging that downtown's layered history and ideal scale welcomed both foot and vehicular traffic, invested $100 million, which in turn produced more than $3 billion in private-sector investment. Economic stimulants included the construction of more than 3 million square feet of office space, the creation of a 30-acre park along the shoreline, and the erection of four hotels. These efforts combined with the Convention Center to

2./ Long Beach Convention Center, c. 2000

3./ Pine Square, 2004

4./ Riot, 1992

create more than 15,000 permanent jobs downtown, establishing a shopper base that led to the successful Pine Avenue revitalization.[47] Several multi-million-dollar condominium developments along the ocean corridor were folded into the building campaign. Other developments such as the Downtown Harbor, a nucleus for boating, fishing, and sightseeing charters, which opened in the early 1980s, and the World Trade Center, which anchored the west end of downtown in 1989, also played a pivotal role in the transformation of the city's core. From an architectural standpoint, however, many of these projects lacked design integrity. Clouded by the overwhelming need to achieve economic success, the incorporation of enduring visual monuments slipped through the cracks.

The traditional staples of the local economy were still in place prior to 1990. The Naval Station, home to 38 warships and 16,000 home-ported sailors and officers, had fully recovered from its 1974 shutdown at the end of the Vietnam War and boasted $130 million worth of improvements. The adjacent Naval Shipyard employed 4,000, while McDonnell Douglas's 40,000-plus workers turned out commercial and military jets.

But between 1990 and 1994 California entered into another period of economic stagnation. This time, Long Beach could not rest on its laurels. The end of Communism as symbolized by the fall of the Berlin Wall in 1989 marked the close of the Cold War and contributed to defense cuts in the early 1990s, resulting in the loss of a Naval presence in Long Beach. McDonnell Douglas and other Southland contractors also suffered. In 1994, the Navy announced that it would shut down and declare surplus the Long Beach Naval Station and Naval Hospital. The Pentagon wiped out 16,000 military and 6,000 civilian jobs. Then the Naval Shipyard closed, taking 4,000 more employees with it.

In contrast, housing prices rose dramatically in the early 1990s. The city witnessed an apartment and condo building boom in Belmont Heights, Alamitos Beach, and the East Side, encompassing hundreds of eight- and 10-unit complexes on small lots that once held single-family houses. But, as Navy families moved, it immediately affected the local market, as well as aid for schools, which the children of military had attended. Vacancy rates in apartment complexes rose as the city emptied of the people who once sustained it.

Then, on April 30, 1992, the already bleak tone took a turn for the worse when an all-white jury in Simi Valley found three white Los Angeles police officers not guilty in the 1991 beating of African-American motorist Rodney King. From sunset until dawn on May 1, looters ransacked the Anaheim corridor, the Wrigley District, and areas in downtown, central, and north Long Beach. The night ended in one fatality, hundreds of injuries, the destruction of 30 businesses and residences, and the damage and looting of another few hundred. On national television, the country repeatedly viewed the horrific spectacle of people destroying their own landscape. Observed Congresswoman Maxine Waters in her essay "Unheard," featured in Anna Deavere Smith's book *Twilight: Los Angeles, 1992*: "The fact of the matter is, whether we like it or not, riot is the voice of the unheard."[48] As the after-effects of fear added to increased ethnic tension, many longtime residents fled or resisted venturing into the once-safe areas.

During this time, reports of gang activity erupted in Long Beach's blighted neighborhoods, and public safety became a major concern. Unemployment became widespread and added to the economic decline. Even one year after the traumatic unrest, little reconstruction of city streets and businesses occurred. Adding salt to the wound, the economy plunged downward.

But the 1990s also saw its share of successes. The Metropolitan Transit Authority (MTA) began operation of its first light-rail train in 1990. Called the Blue Line, it linked Long Beach and downtown Los Angeles. The Long Beach Terminus consisted of a loop at the Transit Mall. About a year later, the city established a shuttle service called the "Runabout" in response to the downtown business congestion. As dependency on this alternative transportation grew, the city decided to subsidize the shuttles by offering free fares downtown. Annual use increased from 200,000 to over 1.5 million customers in just three years. The Runabouts evolved into a more comprehensive system called the Passports. The fleet grew from 10 to 28 and service expanded to connect downtown with Belmont Shore, the Queen Mary, Catalina Landing, the Aquarium of the Pacific, and CSULB. As of 2003, the Passports carried nearly 3 million passengers a year, lightening the load of automobile traffic in congested areas.[49]

In addition to advances in transportation, two major building projects materialized in the downtown core in the 1990s: Pine Square, a 16-screen movie-theater complex featuring shops and restaurants, opened in 1992 and the Aquarium of the Pacific broke ground in 1995. These two projects presented a polar-opposite juxtaposition of design choices, with Pine Square harking to a past era and succumbing to theme-park mediocrity, and the aquarium embracing a unique architectural vision.

5./ Metropolitan Transit Authority, Blue Line, 2004
6./ Pedestrians on the Promenade at farmers' market, 2004

WHERE DO WE GO FROM HERE?

*Authentic knowledge of space must address
the question of production.*[50]
Henri Lefebvre

During the latter half of the 1990s the U.S. economy rebounded strongly from the recession, creating more than 17 million jobs and increasing payroll employment levels by 15 percent between 1994 and 2000. Nowhere was this felt more strongly than in California.[51] Long Beach benefited from this recovery, infused with new life in the form of housing, employment, and development.

Residential-housing market prices accelerated and lack of space continued to be a crisis, not just locally, but everywhere in the state of California. With land at a premium, empty, buildable parcels ceased to exist in Long Beach. By 2004, investors turned to interesting, older neighborhoods in hopes of quick, profitable turnarounds, and once affordable neighborhoods of houses with character—such as California Heights, Rose Park, and Wrigley—were simply beyond the means of those with less than $450,000 to spend on a two bedroom, one bath.

As the appeal of living in a bucolic suburb tapered off, prospective buyers looked to the multitude of convenient benefits in urban cores. Many developers invested in the rehabilitation of historic buildings; others worked from the ground up on rare open or recently razed lots. Downtown living added tremendous cachet to Long Beach, not to mention vitality to the neighboring street scene. What initially extended to the first three blocks of Pine Avenue eventually crept up and spun outward with new residential projects dotting the landscape as far north as 9th Street and east past Alamitos Avenue. The Kress Lofts, an adaptive reuse project offering units for sale in 1995, set the ball in motion. Local design firm Interstices served as the architect on the Kress Building as well as the conversion of Walker's Department Store to residential lofts, producing plans both sensitive to the historic fabric and forward thinking in regard to new additions and interiors. Bill Lindborg, the developer of the successful Walker project explained the challenge:

> It is a blending of the bottom line and creating something of substance. When you get into rudimentary devleopment, you can cut corners and deliver the bare essentials. When you do an adaptive reuse, you are put on a higher platform. You are basically giving the building another life, another chance."[52]

Similar projects ensued. As of 2004 the Lofts on 4th, Courtyard Lofts, Temple Lofts, and Insurance Exchange Lofts, among others, were in various stages of completion. Yet, as loft living proliferated to become the "flavor of the month" for housing alternatives, individuality and quality often decreased.

Two massive housing projects spoke to the other end of the design spectrum. A simulacrum of urbanity, The Park at Harbour View includes 538 apartment units above 25,000 square feet of commercial space built on the 9.5 vacant acres of the former Pike property. Of his project, Peter Cossavella, the former vice president of the real-estate development company Camden, said, "We wanted to create a St. Tropez style, staying within a Mediterranean theme … the image of a small village cascading."[53]

1./ Interior view of Walker building loft, 2003
left/ Aerial view of Port of Long Beach, c. 2000

The resulting product is a pseudo-Mediterranean village so far removed stylistically from the rest of the city's landscape that it is difficult to imagine its inspiration. While the project enjoys economic success, one is left to question the design-review process and whether the developer grasped the true spirit of the city. Headquartered in Houston, Texas, Camden does not possess the same long-term stake in the success of the downtown as Long Beach developers and architects. But even local entrepreneurs are at the mercy of governmental agencies to a degree, forced to follow imposed guidelines or integrate a certain style. The nearby Ocean Villas developed by Genesis Real Estate Group includes two 17-story towers with 556 residential units. Initially appearing to be Eastern-bloc worker housing tenements, the design now exploits historic impulses with an exaggerated Art Deco pastiche. In instances like these one is reminded of Jane Jacobs's astute observation on trying to manufacture place: "Neighborhoods in cities need not supply for their people an artificial town or village life, and to aim at this is both silly and destructive."[54]

Similarly compromised design standards apply to commercial ventures. CityPlace sits on the former Long Beach Plaza mall and International Elementary School sites. After the previous mall project failed, new developers transformed it into an open-air shopping center that includes 454,000 square feet of retail space.

A 125,500-square-foot Wal-Mart anchors the complex on the corner of Long Beach Boulevard and 6th Street.

The large-scale project is not without merit. It reintroduces streets and defines the block structure with broad, pedestrian-friendly sidewalks. If nothing else, the Wal-Mart and its discount-oriented neighbors such as Ross Dress for Less and Sav-on help maintain a diverse community by offering a vast variety of products at affordable prices. However, the insertion of Wal-Mart into the existing downtown infrastructure places smaller retailers at risk and simply creates a scenario found anywhere in suburbia, USA.

Stylistically, CityPlace symbolizes the trend of many commercial redevelopment undertakings. Employing an abstract deco motif throughout, the design, once again, attempts to extract a look from the city's historic fabric. However, the downtown area is composed of an eclectic mix of styles, including Italian Renaissance Revival, Streamline Moderne, Craftsman, Brutalist, and Corporate, among others. No one expects a city to be of strict modernity, but romanticizing about the past is not the solution either. As complexities and contradictions go in architecture, Robert Venturi said it best: "I am for messy vitality over obvious unity. I include the non sequitur and proclaim the duality."[55]

The Pike at Rainbow Harbor represents yet another attempt to infuse the downtown core with new life. Encompassing approximately 18 acres on the downtown Long Beach waterfront, the development includes chain restaurants and entertainment venues such as a 14-screen Crown Theater and GameWorks. Los Angeles-based Ehrenkrantz Eckstut & Kuhn Architects, known for its Hollywood and Highland multimillion-dollar entertainment center, designed the complex. The city lauded the project for its signature elements including a pedestrian bridge over Shoreline Drive reminiscent of the Cyclone Racer and the 2,200-space parking structure. The project personifies stage-set architecture, again anemic in originality and strength. For its significant site, the Pike lacks a more obvious relation to the waterfront, again a failure of the key players to connect the dots in its actualization.

Between the monolithic structures of CityPlace and The Pike at Rainbow Harbor reside more independently oriented businesses. Some owners along this five-block stretch of Pine Avenue reported revenue losses of up to 50 percent in 2003, something largely attributed to the absence of a unified vision and long-range thinking among city planners.[56]

ACTION: REACTION

In 2003, a group of concerned architects and urban planners formed the Long Beach Design Forum in reaction to developments such as CityPlace and The Pike at Rainbow Harbor. Observing the trend of tearing down old buildings and replacing them with new ones that mimic the previous structures, the forum advocates for quality design, which improves the physical, social, and economic vitality of Long Beach.[57]

2./ Ocean Villas, 2004
3./ Long Beach Plaza, JCPenney, 1992
4./ CityPlace, 2004

Critiquing the process for developing new projects as unhealthy and largely driven by economic interests, the group analyzed the city planning structure and found deficiencies. Among them was a lack of a formal design-review process, which resulted in projects emerging piecemeal. The role of the Design Forum is evolving, but its infiltration into the city's first Design Review Subcommittee meeting of the Redevelopment Agency in 2004, which addressed proposed projects in the concept phase, represented a move toward realizing the group's agenda.

The first official directive of the Design Forum involves the idea of form-based code. Transcending typical planning codes that are vague and not site-specific, the proposed standard focuses on uses and site connections. The code dictates facade conditions that address how buildings relate to sidewalk and pedestrian traffic, scaled cornice lines, and the location of openings, while allowing flexibility in style and use.

Another mission of the Design Forum is to cultivate the historic corridors, building up main thoroughfares to create transitional streets that are welcoming and offer services. Though Long Beach has developed strong neighborhoods such as Carroll Park and California Heights, the forum seeks to connect and create a unified city whole. Facade-improvement programs submit a relatively inexpensive way to revitalize an entire city block. The city supports such ideas and commissioned Moule & Polyzoides Architects and Urbanists in 1995 to execute the first corridor improvement on Pacific Avenue between 7th and 8th streets.

Local attorney Douglas Otto is equally concerned about the future of Long Beach and expands on the idea of urban arteries. According to Otto, the future of the city lies in the rich tapestry of residential and commercial areas unique to Long Beach.[58] He facilitated the Long Beach 2010 Strategic Plan, which identifies five areas of commitment: neighborhoods, youth and education, safety, economic opportunity, and the environment. Of particular relevance to the topic of architecture is the focus on neighborhoods as centers of community life. With all the attention on the downtown and seaport areas of Long Beach in recent decades, neighborhoods felt the neglect. The sheer size of the city necessitates a comprehensive yet targeted approach. Also integrated in the strategic plan is an earnest attempt at sustainability. By 2010 or before, all new construction and additions of municipal buildings more than 7,500 square feet will follow the LEED (Leadership in Energy and Environmental Design) Green Building Rating System.[59]

THE UNBUILT REALM

It is impossible to separate the built realm from the unbuilt realm. Open or green space and natural features of the landscape are as integral to a city's framework as its structures. Long Beach boasts a wealth of green patches, from one to 800 acres, totaling 94 parks. When acre for acre is calculated, however, the city actually falls short. Calculations from the Trust for Public

5./ Parking structure, The Pike at Rainbow Harbor, 2004
6./ Night view of The Pike at Rainbow Harbor bridge, 2004
7./ Pacific Avenue facade improvement, 1995

Land revealed Long Beach to be at 8.9 percent of total green space, much lower than other high-density cities such as New York (25.7) and Boston (15.7).[60] These cities have national, county, or state parks that serve their residents, but nothing similar exists in Long Beach. Green patches in the crowded downtown, namely Victory, Santa Cruz, and Lincoln parks, all established in the city's early days, were virtually erased by commercial and civic development in the 1970s.

Of equal consideration is the beach area. The lingering question remains of how removal of the breakwater would affect Long Beach. Consisting of three sections, the breakwater's easternmost 2.6-mile section is the target of concern. The Federal Breakwater protects the Los Angeles Harbor, and the Middle Breakwater protects the Port of Long Beach. Environmental organizations, such as the Surfrider Foundation, and many residents support the removal of the breakwater's third section. Poor tidal-driven circulation has led to excessive levels of pollution, which are only exacerbated by Long Beach's geographical placement between the San Gabriel River and the Los Angeles River, two of the most polluted rivers in the Western United States.

Certainly there are major costs involved in the removal and city council members put forth security concerns as a hindrance in the process. But have residents become complacent with the status quo? While the coastline is ideal for biking, Rollerblading, walking, running, and gentler sand-borne activities, the water is hardly desirable for those interested in more adventurous ocean sports. Economic benefits from removing the breakwater could be immeasurable. With the majority of wave energy currently dissipated, the increase in water-related activities alone could add new life to the community, not to mention the soaring property values and increased tourism inherent in normal beach cities. But the outlook remains grim. Breakwater removal is a difficult process, and many residents living in the pricey enclaves of Naples and the Peninsula are opposed to the removal for fear of flooding and erosion. Ironically enough, the breakwater intervened with the natural flow of sand that created this peninsula in the first place, and the city continually replaces the sand with taxpayer dollars.[61]

In terms of building along the coastline, Long Beach confronts an added step, albeit a safeguard, not present in noncoastal zones. The California Coastal Commission, established by voter initiative in 1972 and later made permanent by the legislature through adoption of the California Coastal Act of 1976, tends to both land and water uses in Long Beach. Holding control over the construction of buildings, divisions of land, and activities that change the intensity of land use or public access to coastal waters, the commission's involvement and effect on architecture cannot be understated.

EVENTUALITIES

As of 2004, approximately 4,000 residential units were under construction or in the planning pipeline in greater downtown Long Beach. When fully inhab-

8./ Park at Harbour View and the remains of Santa Cruz Park, 2004

9./ Aerial view of the breakwater, 1958

ited, the occupants will inject great economic and social vitality into the downtown area.

The flurry of activity is not relegated to residential work. Moule & Polyzoides Architects and Urbanists proposed a plan to restore the civic heart of the city. Their Long Beach Civic Center/Lincoln Park Renovation reinstates the pedestrian-friendly block composition of the historic city, placing City Hall, the Main Library, and Lincoln Park back into individual city blocks, and giving each facility functional upgrades and a prominent, readable face.

Other promising architectural insertions include: a Long Beach Unified School District public elementary school situated in the west end of downtown designed by the architecture firm LPA, Inc.; a new corporate headquarters for the Port of Long Beach, for which many high-profile firms have submitted proposals; and a proposed master plan for the Aquarium of the Pacific, which includes enhanced exhibits, expanded facilities, and structures that meet LEED standards. Another future project is the Art Exchange designed by Studio One Eleven at Perkowitz + Ruth Architects and modeled after the Torpedo Factory in Alexandria, Virginia. Bound by Broadway, Elm Avenue, Long Beach Boulevard, and 3rd Street, connecting to the East Village hub, the project proposes lofts, art studios, and event spaces. It is hoped that the complex will achieve LEED certification, which is in accordance with the new goals of the city's Green Building Policy.[62]

Ambitious building efforts extend far beyond the reaches of downtown. The largest project on the drawing boards in 2004 is the Boeing site, which involves developing 200-plus acres with mixed commercial and residential uses. Other projects include the new MacArthur Park Neighborhood Library on Anaheim Street and Gundry Avenue. These endeavors can potentially propel a course for design excellence citywide, but at this stage it is too early to reach a verdict.

Many attempt to compare the revival of Long Beach to revitalizations in Santa Monica and Pasadena. But City of Long Beach redevelopment officer Robert Zur Schmiede noted, "I think people ask, why can't we be more alike? But Long Beach is a larger city and has some real problem neighborhoods. We are starting from a point further back and those areas have very high income areas that support the retail. While we have the beginnings of that, like Belmont Shore, we just have to keep adding to the mix. There is not one project that is going to save it. We have a mosaic of various things but overall it is moving forward. There are a lot of gaps to fill in."[63] A better analogy is San Diego, Zur Schmiede suggests, with its similar coastal topography, demographics, and historical occurrences. But all comparisons can end in frustration, and Long Beach must find its own position in order to flourish and bloom as a thriving metropolis in the 21st century.

10./ Rendering of proposed Art Exchange, exterior, 2004
11./ Rendering of proposed Art Exchange, interior, 2004
12./ Construction of new LBUSD Elementary School, 2004

INTO THE UNKNOWN

It is here on the edge of the periphery that we should observe how things take shape. The contemporary city, the one composed of these peripheries, ought to yield a sort of manifesto, a premature homage to a form of modernity, which when compared to cities of the past might seem devoid of qualities, but in which we will one day recognize as many gains as losses.[64]

Rem Koolhaas

As Long Beach positions itself in the 21st century, it cannot ignore the impact of growth. The influx of people is an inevitable reality, and it is imperative to develop a future plan that deals with the economic, social, and cultural ramifications of an evolving community. In 2002, Long Beach had an estimated population of 472,412 according to the U.S. Census Bureau. By 2010, Long Beach is expected to be a community with a balance of four major ethnic groups: 36 percent Hispanic, 31 percent Caucasian, 19 percent Asian, and 12 percent African-American.[65] Many large cities such as San Francisco and New York boast thriving ethnic communities that contribute greatly to the fabric of the city and play a larger role than simply existing as corralled enclaves formed out of necessity. It is critical to foster, not isolate, this diversity and to encourage the richness that results.

Growth is also expected in commercial areas and this must be factored into the visual equation. Long Beach has the largest container port in the nation, and the combined Long Beach-Los Angeles Port is the third largest in the world, behind Hong Kong and Singapore. The ports' contribution to the economic viability of the city is undeniable. Throughout history, international trade carried the Long Beach economy while other industry sectors were battered by recession. As the gateway to the Pacific, the port handles trade from the Pacific Rim and beyond, and it supports more than 260,000 jobs in the region. The recently completed Alameda corridor, a direct port-rail link to the Los Angeles rail yards and one of the largest public works projects in the nation, further increases the efficiency of the trade. However, with that success come drawbacks. The growth of the ports causes gridlock, pollution, and heavy vehiclular traffic on the 710 Freeway, with 92,000 truck trips a day projected for 2020. As the terminus of this activity and crossroads of consumerism, Long Beach must absorb and respond to the growth of the entire state and country.

Long Beach sits in a privileged position in 2004. The current energy is infectious and it is difficult to immerse oneself in the scene without feeling a sense of possibility as critical mass builds. Concurrently, the State of California has a tremendous need for housing. The increasing head count continues to affect the region's economy and redefine lifestyles. In the past, even though Long Beach has effectively dealt with the disappearance of space by fabricating buildable ground through landfills (hence The Pike at Rainbow Harbor, Queen Mary, and other areas for ships to dock and industry to grow), it doesn't seem probable that the city will continue to patch together an ersatz coast. Thus Long Beach provides a case study, a microcosm of what has happened statewide, even nationwide, yet it remains singular in its examples and its possible legacy.

The necessity of occupiable space both limits and challenges new and insightful developments. Many baby boomers and Generation Xers yearn to live in an urban core. Long Beach is in an inimitable situation as a city that has the infrastructure to support this type of exponential growth. A demand for quality housing exists in the downtown nucleus, affording not only the adaptive reuse of historic structures, but also allowing the ingenuity of contemporary firms to address demands for untraditional modes of housing.

1
1./ Landfill, c. 1970
left/ International Elementary School, c. 2000

A need to reconcile the issue of providing low-income housing while also maintaining an atmosphere of respect and pride within the community also persists. The key is to find a solution that nourishes mutual stewardship and integration rather than reinforce isolated environments.

It is important to build a sustainable urbanism that adopts a multilingual approach to architecture, a strong sense of permanence, and adaptability to many uses. The need for city planning was apparent in the earliest days. In a 1920 address to the Long Beach Chamber of Commerce, consultant Thomas R. Adams warned, "You must remember that you will have to compete with other places. Unless you act wisely you will soon overflow, grow stale, and other cities will take what you might retain by planning well."[66] Although this advice has not always been heeded, it is not too late to intervene, to establish Long Beach as a unique metropolitan area among its neighbors.

The residents of Long Beach are at a point where they can demand more from those in charge of land-use decisions. The market is tested and proven. Risks to local government entities are not as high as they were 10 years ago. Because of the strong role of preservationists, groups such as the Design Forum, and positive

2./ "We Love Our Community," 1992
3./ Downtown cityscape, 2004

those of the next generations. This includes the built realm, but also extends to protecting and restoring natural resources. Nurturing the city's aesthetics will guarantee the viability of Long Beach. An improved image is central to promoting the city in the long term, as impressions can transcend economic forces. This ongoing ability to draw attention or incite curiosity will continue to build upon the notion of Long Beach as a metropolis that is, in fact, unexpectedly resonant and inspiring in terms of its architectural catalogue.

A true change to ensure longevity cannot occur without educating the public and gaining its support. Without the awareness of possibilities, people often succumb to the influence of dumbed-down cable television design and decorating shows. While average and common work has its appeal, it does nothing to motivate, nor does it symbolize the essence of timelessness inherent in well-conceived architecture. Tolerance of mediocrity lingers because of lack of foresight to invest in the future. Involvement requires great energy and commitment from all those affected. Without provocation, developers and planners address the least common denominator instead of striving for the visceral reaction. Generating excitement and anticipation can modify this bleak outlook. It is not necessary to attain the "Bilbao effect," although a few signature buildings could prove to be a magnetic force.

The city boasts an embedded history of trailblazing design and proud architectural achievements from Morphosis to Greene & Greene to Killingsworth, Brady & Smith. Why shut down history now and not press along the continuum that established Long Beach? Will the city become vapid or can it retain and reinforce its vibrant multiplicity?

It is crucial to face an expanding unknown rather than look to the past as a palette, revealing Long Beach as a leader and innovator rather than a mimic. The goal is to build on the city's incomparable history and create a collective inventory of architecture to show progress, a presentation that evolves organically rather than appearing overwrought, uninspired, or unjustified. A sole expression does not embody Long Beach. This metropolis is highly versatile, diverse, and livable with potential that exceeds beyond the reach of most cities, and to invite a sense of presence without shame or apology will constantly breathe new life into the architectural manifestations of tomorrow.

changes in the local government structure, the age of making aggressive concessions to prompt action can shift into the past. Long Beach witnessed the erection of projects that often sacrificed architectural integrity for the promise of economic prosperity. Suffering from an inferiority complex, leaders made numerous decisions with a less than confident approach, unable to commit to a vision. The city needs to raise the bar and erase the image of itself as an ugly port town. Inability to take risks and establish an identity that is solely Long Beach results in deflated architectural statements, in essence a vacuum of standards. But the veritable power and influence of strong watchdog groups, coupled with the willingness and openness of the city to evaluate its procedures, will help guide a new course and ensure higher standards.

Simultaneously, new developments should be conceived to meet the needs of the present without compromising

ENDNOTES

1. Calvino, *Invisible Cities*, 11.
2. Bidwell, *A Journey to California*, 51.
3. McCawley, *The First Angelinos*, 27.
4. Smith, *Adobe Days*, 64.
5. Krythe, *Port Admiral*, 50.
6. Case, *Long Beach and Vicinity*, 80–81.
7. *Los Angeles Times*, advertisement, April 8, 1883, 1.
8. Drake, "Life Just Long, Sweet Song," February 12, 1925, 3.
9. *Daily Telegram*, advertisement, July 21, 1905, 3.
10. Poe, *Naples: Its History*, 20.
11. *Daily Telegram, Industrial and Development Number*, "Religious Life A Civic Factor," April 1922, 13. The Volstead Law forbade the manufacture, distribution, and sale of alcoholic beverages. Politician Andrew Volstead lobbied to have this proclaimed in 1918. The law was repealed in 1933 by the 21st Amendment.
12. *Daily Telegram*, "Craig Ship Plant," April 4, 1910, 3.
13. *Daily Telegram*, "Long Beach Is Home," November 18, 1915, 11.
14. Kenneth G. Walker, (president, Farmers & Merchants Bank), interview by Cara Mullio and Jennifer M. Volland, May 2003.
15. Robinson, "Knoll Northeast of City," December 14, 1908, 1.
16. Relph, *Modern Urban Landscape*, 55.
17. Robinson, "Suggestions for Municipal Improvement," January 1909.
18. *Daily Telegram, Industrial and Tourist Edition*, "Our Building Activity," November 1917, 23.
19. *Long Beach Press*, "Setting Nation's Style in Homes," November 5, 1922, 6.
20. Sinclair, *Oil!*, 25.
21. *Daily Telegram, Industrial and Development Number*, "No 'Closed Season' Here," April 1922, 17.
22. Olmsted Brothers and Bartholomew and Associates, "Parks, Playgrounds and Beaches," 23.
23. Roosevelt, address at Oglethorpe University, Atlanta, Georgia, May 22, 1932.
24. Hinkey, *Federal Art in Long Beach*, 13–15.
25. Mumford, *City in History*, 490.
26. *Press-Telegram*, advertisement, October 31, 1937, A13.
27. Howard, *Tomorrow: A Peaceful Path*, 131.
28. Omohundro, "Carmelitos Project is Under Way," August 27, 1939, A5.

29. Kelley, "New Lease on Life," January 3, 1988, IX:1.
30. University City Business Center, marketing brochure, circa 1950.
31. Members of Los Altos Association, "Protective Restrictions for Tract," September 14, 1953.
32. Griswold, "Last Crop Being Planted," April 25, 1957, P20.
33. Waldie, *Holy Land: A Suburban Memoir*, 41.
34. *Press-Telegram*, "Cerritos Circle to Open," June 7, 1964, R4.
35. Clifton S. Jones Jr. (owner, The Jones Company), interview by Cara Mullio and Jennifer M. Volland, May 2004.
36. Strohmeier, ed., *Urban Ideal: Conversations with Paolo Soleri*, 133.
37. Starr, *Endangered Dreams: The Great Depression*, 323.
38. *Independent*, "Long-Range Plan Bright," July 23, 1959, C5.
39. Murray, "LBSU reflects—and affects," September 24, 1972, A1.
40. *Harbor Highlights Magazine*, "Where Oil and Water Do Mix!," 7.
41. Davis, "End of the Cyclone," July 21, 1968, 5.
42. Whyte, *Social Life of Small Urban Places*, 93.
43. Ivy, "Long Beach's Developing Controversy," October 28, 1973, LS1.
44. The following individuals contributed information regarding the preservation movement in Long Beach: Karen Clements (local preservation advocate), interview by Cara Mullio, March 2004; Peter Devereaux (restoration contractor), interview by Cara Mullio and Jennifer M. Volland, March 2004; Ruthann Lehrer (former Historic Preservation Officer, City of Long Beach), interview by Cara Mullio and Jennifer M. Volland, March 2004; Douglas W. Otto (attorney and facilitator, Long Beach Strategic Plan Task Force), interview by Cara Mullio and Jennifer M. Volland, March 2004.
45. Poelzig, "Third German Exhibition," 14.
46. Lumley, "Redevelopment—More Than Tearing Down," 2.
47. Armstrong, "Long Beach: Livable Places Profile," 9.
48. Waters, "Unheard," 160.
49. Long Beach Transit, "Long Beach: A New Wave in Transit," http://www.lbtransit.com/history6.html.
50. Lefebvre, *Production of Space*, 69.
51. Fogg and Harrington, "Growth and Change," May 3, 2001, 10.

52. Bill Lindborg (president, Borg Development Corporation), interview by Cara Mullio and Jennifer M. Volland, May 2004.
53. Peter Cossavella (former vice president, Camden Property Trust), interview by Cara Mullio and Jennifer M. Volland, May 2003.
54. Jacobs, *Death and Life*, 117.
55. Venturi, *Complexity and Contradiction*, 16.
56. Jergler, "Planning Pine Avenue," January 23, 2004, A17.
57. Michael Bohn, John Glasgow, Gary Lamb, and Alan Pullman (members, Long Beach Design Forum), interviews by Cara Mullio and Jennifer M. Volland, April and June 2004.
58. Douglas W. Otto (attorney and facilitator, Long Beach Strategic Plan Task Force), interview by Cara Mullio and Jennifer M. Volland, March 2004.
59. City of Long Beach, *Green Building Policy*, 6.
60. Harnik, *Excellent City Park System*, 38.
61. Light, "Shore Wars," http://www.laweekly.com/ink/99/26/news-light.php.
62. Marie Jones Consulting, *Art Exchange Feasibility Study*, 11.
63. Robert Zur Schmiede (redevelopment officer, City of Long Beach), interview by Cara Mullio and Jennifer M. Volland, April 2004.
64. Koolhaas, "Toward the Contemporary City," 15–16.
65. Long Beach Strategic Plan Task Force, *Long Beach 2010 Strategic Plan*, January 2001, 4.
66. Adams, "City Planning," 1.

PROJECTS

Bixby Ranch House

01
MAP 1, C4

LOCATION
11 LA LINDA DR.
DATE
1890
ARCHITECT
COXHEAD & COXHEAD
ADJACENT
HOWARD CDM (96)
KILLINGSWORTH, BRADY & SMITH
OFFICE BUILDING (63)
CAMBRIDGE OFFICE BUILDING (67)

1./ View of lily pool
2./ Exterior view through gate,
c. 1930

In the late 1800s George H. Bixby, a prominent Long Beach rancher, managed the sprawling Rancho Los Cerritos and surrounding land, then about 23,000 acres. The Bixby Ranch House acted as the headquarters and home for the ranch hands. In 1904, 14 years after the first dwelling was completed, Bixby commissioned the San Francisco-based architects Almeric Coxhead and Ernest Coxhead to reconstruct the existing house. Classically trained, they rejected overly ornate styles for simple designs in their residential and religious projects in the Bay Area. At the time of hiring the firm, a series of buildings including the main house, barn, bunkhouse, gardener's home, carpenter's shop, wagon shed, tank house, and slaughterhouse occupied the site.

The architects enlarged the house from approximately 3,000 to 6,996 square feet, transforming it into a beautiful and stately Shingle Style residence. In the years 1910 to 1919, the ancillary structures on the property were gradually removed and, in 1922, the 10-acre lot was subdivided. The 33 neighboring parcels now are all privately owned and the cul-de-sac is gated.

An unusual feature of the two-story ranch house is the exterior sheathing material of cedar shingles that runs from the roof to the base of the structure. The interior spaces include eight bedrooms, seven bathrooms, and six fireplaces. The dining room, with curved oak columns and solid, white-oak ceilings, walls, and floors, is the most elaborately constructed room in the house.

Sitting as the *grande dame* on La Linda Drive, the Bixby Ranch House maintains a strong presence amongst the newer residences. Five owners have occupied the property during its lifetime; in 1989, the third owners commissioned architect Blake Stephens, who conducted Coxhead research and organized a set of plans for restoration. Peter Devereaux Construction, a local firm involved in the preservation of historic structures, executed a meticulous renovation. The current owners continue to retain the house's character. Acquiring several adjacent parcels, they re-created the lily pool and garden according to the original plans.

First National Bank

The home of First National Bank opened in 1900 on the prominent corner of 1st Street and Pine Avenue. Designed by Los Angeles-based architects Robert F. Train and Robert E. Williams, it was Long Beach's second bank, and its original directors included James B. Heartwell, W. W. Lowe, and C. J. Walker. The first tent school in Long Beach occupied this site prior to the bank.

In 1906, the bank added three stories. Inspired by Renaissance Revival and rectangular in plan, the load-bearing masonry and steel structure climbs a total of six stories. Yellow pressed brick is used on floors two through six and common red brick wraps the north and west elevations. Accentuating the influence of classical design, the building's ornamental character includes pedimented entries, bays with shaft fenestration, paneled pilasters, a star-patterned open frieze, blocks adorned with lion heads and garlands, and scrolled corbels. The main lobby entrance showcases grand decorative elements while the north and west elevations (delineated with red brick) include less detailing due to the lack of visibility and public use.

A distinctive element of this building is its well-known clock tower from 1907. Standing 12 feet in height with a clock face six feet in diameter, the tower is angled to face the street junction. In addition to serving pedestrians in need of telling time, the clock also played an important role as a bright emblem of the city's financial prosperity.

The building housed a series of banking tenants, including Bank of America, California National Bank, and Security Bank. The shadow of the word *Bank*, a remnant of one of the financial occupants, can be seen on the top of the north wall. In the 1950s, the structure was modernized with the addition of blue ceramic tile covering the ground floor and the removal of the decorative cornice. In the 1980s, the building and clock tower underwent a major refurbishment and were brought back to an approximation of their original look, marking the first project in the city to use federal income-tax credit incentives for historic rehabilitation.

LOCATION
101 PINE AVE.
DATE
1900; 1906
ARCHITECT
TRAIN AND WILLIAMS
ADJACENT
SECURITY PACIFIC NATIONAL
BANK (25)
MASONIC TEMPLE (3)
BIKESTATION LONG BEACH (90)

1./ *Exterior view with clock tower, c. 1925*

First National Bank Building

Winstead
Photo
L.B.

1

Masonic Temple

The construction of the Masonic Temple marked the beginning of tremendous growth and development in downtown Long Beach, affirming Pine Avenue as the city's "Main Street." This meeting hall and private club counted many prominent citizens among its members. The top floor of the three-story rectangular brick building was reserved for the lodge's activities and the ground floor housed retail stores.

One of the oldest remaining structures in downtown, the temple is thought to be the only surviving work by Henry Fletcher Starbuck. Born and educated in Massachusetts, Starbuck practiced architecture in many U.S. cities throughout his prolific career, including Chicago, Milwaukee, San Diego, Los Angeles, Oakland, and Fresno. It was mid-career, in 1899, that he moved his office to Long Beach and designed many of the city's turn-of-the-century buildings. Although he specialized in church architecture, Starbuck's work also included residential, commercial, and civic structures.

The building blends Masonic iconography and Romanesque influences. Columns on pedestals define the three-bay facade. Above the bull-nosed cornice, raised piers articulate the second- and third-story bays. The top of the roofline is decorated by three steeply pitched gables with tin molding pressed into an egg-and-dart motif. These gables signify the equality of the trinity, a Masonic principle.

The Masons moved out in 1951 and the two upper floors sat largely unused for three decades. New owners restored the building in 1986, and the interior was subsequently remodeled for a retail- furniture store in the early 1990s. Although the interior walls no longer exist and many alterations were made, the second floor retains the large-scale mural of the sun that is part of Masonic symbolism. Finely detailed woodwork from the original architecture also remains.

03
MAP 1, C9
MAP 2, C3

LOCATION
230 PINE AVE.
DATE
1903
ARCHITECT
HENRY FLETCHER STARBUCK
ADJACENT
FARMERS & MERCHANTS BANK
AND TOWER (18)
INSURANCE EXCHANGE BUILDING (24)
SECURITY PACIFIC NATIONAL BANK (25)

1./ *Exterior view*
2./ *Gable detail, 1974*
3./ *Interior meeting hall, 1985*

Adelaide A. Tichenor House

04
MAP 1, D10
MAP 2, E3

LOCATION
852 E. OCEAN BLVD.
DATE
1905
ARCHITECT
GREENE & GREENE
ADJACENT
VILLA RIVIERA (39)
INTERNATIONAL TOWER (79)
LONG BEACH SKATING PALACE (42)

1./ *Garden with Japanese bridge,*
   c. 1920
2./ *Aerial view of house on bluff,*
   c. 1920

Occupying a choice position on the ocean bluffs, the Adelaide A. Tichenor House is one of three in Long Beach designed by architects Charles Greene and Henry Greene. Known for their prolific residential work in Pasadena, in particular the 1908 Gamble House, the Greene brothers first explored combining Japanese elements with Craftsman-style bungalow architecture in the Tichenor House, foreshadowing a major theme in their later work. The house also claims the distinction of being one of only two designed by the Greenes that is sited on a coastal property (the other is the 1918 James House in Carmel Highlands).

The Tichenor House was commissioned by Long Beach philanthropist Adelaide Alexander Tichenor. Considered the "mother of Long Beach," Tichenor focused her attention on altruistic advocacy and helped establish the Long Beach Carnegie Public Library and the Ebell Club, the area's oldest women's organization. Tichenor played an integral role in the design of her house while giving the Greenes latitude to demonstrate their own emerging architectural vocabulary.

Significant elements displayed in the architecture include pronounced half-timbering construction with wood beams framing clinker-brick panels, and exposed beams that connect to vertical members with round pegs. The Greenes organized the house in a U shape anchored by a two-story central mass with one-story wings. Broad, low-pitched roofs with railings accentuate the dramatic ocean views and allow for sun decks. The pitch and design of the green-tiled roof and the garden teahouse stemmed directly from the Greenes' interest in Asian architecture, which dovetailed with Tichenor's passion for Oriental design and furnishings. The house was one of the first projects for which the Greenes created a significant number of interior furnishings, including furniture, stained-glass lighting fixtures, and windows. In addition to the teahouse, the Greenes also landscaped the property with an arched bridge over the pond and steppingstone patterns throughout the gardens. An owl-themed door handle, especially devised for Tichenor, exemplifies the extent of Charles Greene's personal attention to detail and craftsmanship.

Changes to the house occurred early on in its history. Tichenor commissioned the Greenes to add a low clinker-brick wall and garage in the second decade of the 20th century. After Tichenor vacated, the residence became a rooming house for several years, then was left unoccupied in the 1940s. In the 1950s, the primary entrance was moved to the back from its original position facing the ocean, and a new concrete motor court replaced the Japanese garden. Following this, the Tichenor House experienced a series of owners and extreme renovations. A second story was added to the garage wing in the 1990s. Though that addition is reversible, many irreversible changes have been made to the Greenes' architectural intentions and the original meaning of the house.

1

2

Bembridge House

LOCATION
953 PARK CIRCLE DR.
DATE
1906
ARCHITECT
UNKNOWN
ADJACENT
PHYSICAL TESTING AND CHEMICAL
LABORATORY (6)
YORK RITE MASONIC TEMPLE (31)
INTERNATIONAL ELEMENTARY
SCHOOL (93)

1./ *Exterior view*
2./ *Postcard of main house and
    carriage house, 1908*

The Bembridge House, designed as a grand Queen Anne Victorian, three-story, 18-room residence, is one of Long Beach's best-preserved architectural legacies. Built as a retirement house in 1906 by Seattle couple Josephine and Stephen Green, it is located across from Drake Park, a fashionable neighborhood during the early part of the 20th century.

Though there is no architect of record, tribute has been given to Josephine Green for her sense of design. The exterior materials include shiplap siding and patterned shingles, and the roof features a series of complex gabled tops. A corner polygonal-shaped tower hovers over graceful double columns that wrap around the deep front porch, which is adorned with an elaborate floral frieze band under the eave. Leaded-glass and stained-glass windows accentuate the houses's ornate design while roofing shingles soaked several times in a fire-resistant solution further exhibit Green's attention to detail. This act alone protected the house from destruction in a 1966 fire. A two-story carriage house at the back of the driveway and an octagonal aviary at the side of the yard also grace the property.

In 1918, Thomas and Hazel Rankin, a musically talented couple from Nebraska, purchased the house, and their daughter Dorothy (Mrs. Charles) Bembridge resided in the house for over 80 years. The Rankins had become familiar with the house, having admired it during their summer vacations in Long Beach. In fact, prior to purchasing the Bembridge House, Thomas Rankin commissioned a similar house in 1914 in Cambridge, Nebraska. Family oral history attributes both houses to the Gordon-Van Tine Company, a Wyoming-based outfit that manufactured kit houses.

The interiors, including the wall finishes and gas-electric chandeliers, are preserved, and the richly detailed woodwork and period furnishings evoke an era of elegance. It is an example of a supreme Victorian house, unlike any found in Long Beach. Dorothy Bembridge's knowledge of the arts, music, and culture, and her advocacy for architectural history and preservation contribute to the excellent condition. Now maintained and operated by Long Beach Heritage, the Bembridge House can be toured by appointment.

1

2

Physical Testing and Chemical Laboratory (Southern Pacific Depot)

06
MAP 1, B8

LOCATION
1475 SAN FRANCISCO AVE.
DATE
1907
ARCHITECT
UNKNOWN
ADJACENT
BEMBRIDGE HOUSE (5)
YORK RITE MASONIC TEMPLE (31)
HANCOCK MOTORS (34)

1./ Exterior view
2./ Jelly vendor at municipal market
  in front of depot at Broadway
  location, 1908

In the early 1900s, great locomotives brought passengers into the heart of downtown Long Beach. The Santa Fe station was located on Ocean Avenue near the Pine Avenue Pier and the Pike. The Southern Pacific Depot was placed adjacent to city hall, on Broadway between Pacific and Cedar avenues, across from Lincoln Park.

After train service was discontinued, the Southern Pacific Depot building served as a Railway Express station. During the 1930s, the city moved the building to its current location, for use as a physical testing and chemical laboratory. A massive piece of machinery tested materials for tensile strength, following the 1933 earthquake.

The Mission Revival-style building features three distinct elements co-joined under a series of red-tiled, hipped roofs. Wood trusses project from under the roof overhang and wooden arched windows line the sides of the modestly scaled structure. One arched window (now boarded) highlights the central mass and a scalloped-ribbon border wraps the parapet-wall edge. The Mission Revival style was favored for railroad depot design because of its association with the traditions and ambience of old California. Its romantic architecture still resonates.

Weathered and worn, the building is in a quiet industrial area, positioned between nondescript machinery buildings. Owned by the Long Beach Department of Public Works, it requires a structural retrofit for seismic safety and is currently used for storage.

1

2

Hotel Virginia

07
MAP 1, B10
MAP 2, B3

LOCATION
DEMOLISHED
DATE
1908
ARCHITECT
JOHN C. AUSTIN AND
FREDERICK G. BROWN

1./ Rear view of hotel, c. 1928
2./ Postcard of gardens, c. 1920

In November 1904, the owners of the land at the foot of American Avenue (now Long Beach Boulevard) set out to erect a great hotel, which would be a source of local pride and draw people of influence and prestige. The Long Beach Hotel and Land Company was thus established with Colonel Charles Rivers Drake as president. A hotel to rival the world's best, it created a buzz as shipments of the finest woods and interior furnishings were gathered at the site. Originally called the Hotel Bixby, named in honor of Jotham Bixby, the "father of Long Beach," it was the first high-class resort hotel on the Pacific Coast. It stood on Ocean Boulevard just east of Magnolia Avenue.

Shortly after construction began, catastrophe struck when a section of the hotel collapsed, leaving 10 workmen dead and injuring many others. An investigation concluded that the supports were removed before the concrete was completely dry. In order to avoid adverse publicity, the company changed the name to the Hotel Virginia.

Despite the tragedy, the hotel was erected at a cost of $1,250,000. The reinforced-concrete structure stood six stories high and was built in the shape of a large *H*. The south front overlooked the Pacific Ocean and a veranda lined the perimeter. The north front faced Ocean Avenue with a distant view of the San Gabriel Mountains. The ground floor provided dressing rooms and direct access to the beach and promenade. Massive marble pillars and a grand marble staircase welcomed guests in the lobby. One of the architects, John C. Austin, also built Los Angeles City Hall and Griffith Park Observatory, among other landmarks. Broad lawns and gardens surrounded the building and three large concrete tennis courts offered a recreational diversion. Mrs. Walter Lewis Burn, one of only a few female landscape designers employed in the United States at the time, created the elaborate gardens.

For decades the Hotel Virginia was a social center of Southern California. It served as the gateway to the Pike, Long Beach's thriving beach amusement park. Touted as the ultimate in luxurious accommodations and service, it drew many distinguished guests, including William Howard Taft and early film stars Ruth Roland and Jackie Saunders. Operated in conjunction with the Maryland Hotel in Pasadena, guests could hop on the hotel's specially commissioned Pacific Electric Car to shuttle between the two retreats.

Following the stock market crash of 1929 and an increase in tax rates, the Hotel Virginia could not attract enough guests and finally closed its doors in October 1932. In 1933, the structure was razed.

1

2

Carnegie Public Library

08
MAP 1, C10
MAP 2, C3

LOCATION
DEMOLISHED
DATE
1909
ARCHITECT
F. P. BURNHAM

1./ *Renovated library, c. 1940*
2./ *Postcard, c. 1910*

Opening on May 29, 1909, with much fanfare, the Carnegie Public Library was an impressive formal structure made possible by renowned philanthropist Andrew Carnegie and his gift of $30,000. In the early part of the 20th century, Carnegie contributed over $50 million to help fund public library buildings across the nation. The stipulation accompanying Carnegie's financial support stated that the donation could only be used for the building, leaving it up to the city to contribute a site and supply the library with books and general maintenance. Many Carnegie-endowed libraries between 1886 and 1917 introduced a classical architectural vocabulary, including the nine designed by architect F. P. Burnham.

Positioned in Lincoln Park (today the Civic Center), the centerpiece of the city, the library was the first educational facility in the area to offer free privileges to the general reader. Long Beach ranked as a city of industrious readers, and few cities equaled it in the per capita circulation of books due to the large leisure class and influx of numerous vacationers.

The stately design of the library featured granite columns with wide stone steps that led up to the entrance. Though the effect was monumental, the building was surprisingly small in size. Symmetrical with few angles or projections, the library's roofline was unadorned. At the time, the library was lauded as one of the most modern library buildings in Southern California with an up-to-date book-filing system and an elevator that transported reading materials to the stacks. The layout consisted of reading and reference rooms, a lecture room, and an art gallery for rotating exhibitions.

In the 1930s, a remodeling of the library added a double height space and the Work Projects Administration incurred the cost. The library had an important existence until 1972, when a fire destroyed its collection. Deemed inhabitable, even though the concrete structure didn't burn, the building closed and a temporary facility was located near the Traffic Circle. In the meantime, the Civic Center, a major downtown development in the 1970s, received approval and a library design was formalized in this proposal. The 1909 library building was demolished in 1973.

1

PUBLIC LIBRARY.   LONG BEACH, CALIFORNIA.

2

Long Beach Museum of Art

LOCATION
2300 E. OCEAN BLVD.
DATE
1912; 2000
ARCHITECT
MILWAUKEE BUILDING COMPANY;
FREDERICK FISHER AND PARTNERS
ADJACENT
RAYMOND HOUSE (12)
LIFEGUARD HEADQUARTERS,
CHERRY AVENUE (50)
GALAXY TOWER (77)

1./ Aerial view, c. 1925
2./ Exterior view, c. 1940
3./ New museum addition, 2000

The Long Beach Museum of Art was built as the summer home of Elizabeth Milbank Anderson, a wealthy philanthropist and art collector. She was an heiress to Jeremiah Milbank, a financier, founder of the Chicago, Milwaukee & St. Paul Railroad, and co-founder of the Borden Company. Situated on a bluff overlooking the ocean, Anderson's home represents an early phase in the residential development of Long Beach. The Milwaukee Building Company produced a number of significant California Craftsman residences in Long Beach and Santa Monica, and later became the Los Angeles architectural firm of Meyer and Holler.

A grand example of Craftsman style, the museum consists of a 15-room mansion and a carriage house with a five-room apartment on top. The structure displays prominent triple gables on the facade, projecting rafter beams, horizontality, and clinker-brick columns that frame the front entrance porch. Clad in concrete, the first story was later refaced with brick. Wooden shingles cover the upper floor, which features a small protruding balcony. A two-story carriage house and servants' quarters match the residence and originally faced Ocean Boulevard.

The property's succession of uses mirrors important stages in the history of Long Beach. The home was transformed into the Club California Casa Real, Long Beach's first social and athletic club, in 1926. However, its popularity was eclipsed three months later by the million-dollar Pacific Coast Club. Oilman Thomas A. O'Donnell bought the property at auction for $200,000 in 1929. When gun emplacements consumed the bluffs in the first years of World War II, the O'Donnells abandoned the site and retreated to their other residences. During the ensuing war years, the home served as the Navy Chief Petty Officer's Club. In 1950, the city purchased the property for $100,000 and remodeled it as a Municipal Arts Center. It officially became the Long Beach Museum of Art in 1957.

In 2000, Frederick Fisher and Partners completed an addition to the museum after a lengthy proposal process and an in-depth dialogue with the community. Charged with the task of balancing traditional design with contemporary function, the firm created a separate structure that complements the historic residence and carriage house. To make room for the structure, the carriage house was moved to the rear of the site. The new, 12,000-square-foot, two-story pavilion incorporates elements of Craftsman style such as dark wood shingles, a gable roof, brick, and overhanging eaves. Yet it is simplified, modern, and scaled to properly showcase the museum's collections and exhibitions. The most dramatic features are the glass-enclosed lobby on the north side of the building and the second-story gallery windows that frame the ocean.

First Congregational Church

The First Congregational Church is one of the oldest surviving churches in Long Beach. Located at the center of the city, the structure has been a landmark since pioneer and church benefactor Jotham Bixby laid the cornerstone.

Designed by H. M. Patterson of Los Angeles and built by C. T. McGrew of Long Beach, the building combines Romanesque and Gothic styles. McGrew constructed it of red brick manufactured by the L.A. Brick Company, one of the first and largest suppliers in California. Arranged in an Italianate pattern, the brick contrasts with ornamental elements in a white terra cotta. Two intersecting gables form the roof, and three 16 1/2-foot, stained-glass rose windows set with white terra-cotta tracery consume a large portion of the three-and-a-half-story elevation. A 110-foot bell tower anchors the corner of 3rd Street and Cedar Avenue. A simple cornice with dentils surrounds the tower's flat roofline as well as the fifth-floor level.

Wood double entrance doors are flanked by spiral columns and capped with an elaborately carved semicircle frieze. The inside opens to a large sanctuary with balconies on three sides. The 4,074-pipe Moeller organ, one of the finest in Southern California, is an interior focal point. Other noteworthy features include the mahogany paneling, leaded glass, wooden beams, and painted decoration on the plaster walls and ceilings.

When the building needed structural rehabilitation in the 1980s, the extensive decoration on the interior and exterior walls posed a dilemma. Traditional methods of configuring a strengthening system would have been difficult and expensive. Thus, the city, with the support of the National Science Foundation, tested a new technology called the CenterCore system. This allowed for vertical drilling from the top of the structural walls, the insertion of a single bar of reinforcing steel, and the pouring of a special grout that migrated into pores and cracks of the existing masonry. This innovative step enabled First Congregational Church to adhere to the earthquake safety ordinance without disturbing the architectural and decorative integrity of the building.

Dominy + Associates Architects of San Diego designed an addition for classroom space, which opened in 2004. Connected to the southern end of the existing structure, it complements the church with brick detailing, arched windows, and a similar sense of scale.

10
MAP 1, B9
MAP 2, C3

LOCATION
241 CEDAR AVE.
DATE
1914; 2004
ARCHITECT
H. M. PATTERSON;
DOMINY + ASSOCIATES
ARCHITECTS
ADJACENT
THE WILLMORE (26)
CALIFORNIA VETERANS MEMORIAL
STATE OFFICE BUILDING (86)
LONG BEACH CITY HALL AND PUBLIC
LIBRARY (82)

1./ Exterior view with new addition
2./ Capital detail
3./ Exterior view, c. 1990
4./ Column and arch detail

1

2

4

3

Harnett House

LOCATION
730 SUNRISE BLVD.
DATE
1918
ARCHITECT
UNKNOWN
ADJACENT
CHENEY/DELANEY HOUSE (49)
OLIVE COURT (98)
ATLANTIC AVENUE WORKFORCE
HOUSING DEVELOPMENT (97)

1./ *Exterior view*

The Harnett House was the home of one of Long Beach's pioneer families, who emigrated from England in 1889 and first settled on a nearby farm. Julia Sarah Harnett, the matriarch of the family, built the house on Sunrise Boulevard in 1918. This "pocket" neighborhood developed adjacent to the Pacific Electric Railway line that ran diagonally through Long Beach to Newport Beach in 1902. The lots vary significantly in size and contain a high concentration of Craftsman bungalows and Spanish Colonial Revival homes. The curving streets are reminiscent of other Long Beach historic districts such as Carroll Park and Drake Park.

A visually prominent contribution to the Sunrise Boulevard Historic District, the large two-story Tudor Craftsman reflects the family's English ancestry. The wood-clad exterior features clapboard siding on the lower floor and shingles on the upper floor. A front gable with Tudor half-timbering and projecting gable ends, offset from the side gable roof, punctuates the facade. A deep front porch extends two-thirds of the way across the front and rectangular brick piers support a balcony faced with brown shingles. An outdoor staircase at the rear once led to the second story and an enclosed sleeping porch.

Two important local architects are associated with this residence. Hugh Gibbs and his family, related to the Harnetts, lived in the house. In 1944, Kenneth S. Wing performed an extensive remodeling of the kitchen, rear bedrooms, and living-room fireplace. Wallpaper from this era still lines the walls of the interior.

Many of the Harnett family members contributed to the civic, educational, and cultural development of Long Beach. As a result, the clan's history equals in importance to the architecture. The house has remained in the Harnett family for three generations.

Raymond House

12
MAP 1, E10
MAP 2, H4

LOCATION
2749 E. OCEAN BLVD.
DATE
1918
ARCHITECT
IRVING J. GILL
ADJACENT
GALAXY TOWER (77)
MARINA TOWER MODEL APARTMENT (68)
LONG BEACH MUSEUM OF ART (9)

IMAGES
1./ *Exterior view*

Relatively unknown—even to architecture aficionados—the Raymond House is one of a few residential projects by Irving J. Gill in the Los Angeles area that remains intact. In his book *Irving Gill and the Architecture of Reform*, historian Thomas Hines writes: "Gill radically redefined the architectural landscape of Southern California and set the stage for a later, more widely celebrated generation of modernists who would continue his experiments with new forms and construction techniques."

A retirement residence for the Oklahoma banker Samuel Raymond and his family, the house sits across from the bluff and Pacific Ocean, garnering unobstructed views. Gill's plan incorporates his quintessential vocabulary of cube and arch, the interplay of straight and curved elements, and a staggered geometric floor plan.

The flat-roofed, two-story residence is constructed of concrete and hollow tile. Comprised of abstract forms, the structure displays a primitive simplicity. Hines describes the unornamented facade as "aggressively plain," recalling the walls, arches, and patios of the Indian pueblos and Spanish missions of the American Southwest. The thick walls and white reflective surfaces adapt to the mild California climate.

The house features two main entrances at opposite sides of the building, catering to both car passengers and guests. An entrance court of concrete planters and low garden walls leads into a central stair hall. The same hall is entered from the other side through an arched porte-cochere. The generous living room lies west of the hall with large plate-glass windows overlooking the ocean. The upstairs bedrooms open onto roof decks, again reminiscent of a pueblo dwelling. Guest or servants' quarters and a sturdy garage sit beyond the back garden.

1

Markwell Building/Jergins Trust Building and Jergins Subway

13
MAP 1, C10
MAP 2, C3

LOCATION
DEMOLISHED
DATE
1919; 1929
ARCHITECT
HARVEY H. LOCHRIDGE

1./ *Exterior view, late 1920s*
2./ *Arcade, c. 1930*

Conceived by Sylvester Markwell and his three sons, the Jergins Trust Building holds both an illustrious and distressing place in the history of Long Beach architecture. Sensing the potential of Long Beach as a business center and ocean retreat, the Markwells acquired a prime site at Ocean Boulevard and Pine Avenue to construct a multiuse building. The ground floor and mezzanine contained an arcade with 60 shops. A theater occupied the third through fifth floors with the remainder of the structure designated as office space. Because it housed many uses under one roof, the building exemplified a a unique concept of urban development that was ahead of its time. A. T. Jergins, a Signal Hill oilman, acquired the building in 1925, renamed it, and hired architect Harvey H. Lochridge to add three additional floors in 1929. The penthouse floor, designed by architect Kirtland Cutter, also was added that year. The expansion accommodated the Long Beach branch of the Los Angeles County Superior Court.

The quality and richness of the terra-cotta fabrication distinguished the building from others of the period. All four facades were identical in fenestration and decorative detail, except for variations on the ground floor. Above the entablature, the shaft of the edifice consisted of pilasters separating the bays and spandrel panels separating the floors. A white-and-yellow glazed terra-cotta unit decorated the pilaster bases and white glazed brick faced the rest. Colorful "cakelike" art-stone carvings in hues of red, yellow, blue, and white girded the top two floors of the building. The parapet wall above the cornice featured particularly elaborate terra-cotta units, including a shield surrounded by scrollwork and topped by a cherubic face flanked with wings.

In the 1920s, city councilman and pedestrian-safety advocate Alexander Beck spearheaded the effort to excavate a tunnel underneath the busy intersection of Ocean Boulevard and Pine Avenue. Many tunnels ran underneath the city in the 1900s but none as well-known as the Jergins Subway, which was dedicated in 1928. Built of reinforced concrete and steel, the subway was lined with extensive tile work. From 1934 to 1940 the city allowed small booths in the subway, and combined with the shops in the adjoining Jergins Arcade, it was called Los Artesanos Village, patterned after Olvera Street in Los Angeles.

Several factors led to the demise of the Jergins Trust Building and Jergins Subway. With the federal breakwater completion in 1949 and subsequent landfills, the beach disappeared and the motivation to pass through the tunnel was all but lost. In the early 1960s, the county courts moved to a new location and the building never regained full occupancy. The subway entrances were sealed in 1967. The property was purchased in 1979 and proposals to build a new luxury hotel on the site circulated. The same year, the city council declared the building a local landmark. But economic interests prevailed. Despite efforts by preservation groups, the Redevelopment Agency decided not to fund a rehabilita-tion-feasibility study and the Jergins Trust Building was razed in 1988.

1

2

Seashell House

LOCATION
4325 E. 6TH ST.
DATE
1922
ARCHITECT
CHARLES LIBKA
ADJACENT
BELMONT HEIGHTS UNITED METHODIST
CHURCH (15)
CAPTAIN PONTO HOUSE (17)
KIMPSON/NIXON HOUSE (53)

1./ *Exterior view*

Enchantingly small and a work of folk art, this 650-square-foot house is exactly what its title implies: a house made of seashells. Local builder Charles Libka and his wife, Adena, created this fantastic structure using crushed seashells—primarily abalone—embedded in exterior plaster building material. The plasterwork includes abalone-shell fragments of pearl and iridescent colors that clad the entire volume of the house. It cost an estimated $2,500 to build and the simple plan embraces a small attached porch and wood-pergola overhang.

Libka, originally from Indiana, specialized in plasterwork in Long Beach, and his craftsmanship is evident in the delicate but sturdy coating of the Seashell House. Unusually solid, the house offers proof that seashells can be used as an inexpensive material for sheathing. Evocative of a beach city, it shimmers among the other residences of regional character.

1

Belmont Heights United Methodist Church

15
MAP 1, F10
MAP 2, J3

LOCATION
317 TERMINO AVE.
DATE
1923
ARCHITECT
PARKINSON & PARKINSON
ADJACENT
CAPTAIN PONTO HOUSE (17)
SEASHELL HOUSE (14)
GAYTONIA (41)

1./ *Exterior view, c. 1970*
2./ *Tower*

The Belmont Heights United Methodist Church was founded in an abandoned building at the corner of 4th Street and Termino Avenue in 1914. The establishment of this religious organization came at a time when city residents formed an abundance of congregations. In 1916, the church constructed a new edifice from salvaged lumber on the corner of Colorado and Termino. By 1923, it moved into its first major structure, which, at the time, looked down Mira Mar Avenue to the ocean.

John Parkinson and his son Donald B. Parkinson designed the building in a Mediterranean Revival style. The most prominent feature is a square-shaped tower that rises above the roofline, with an entrance at its base and rectangular windows with balconies at the top. The red-tile roof and a series of rectangular windows and openings on the front facade accent the white stucco surface of the walls. A colonnade lines the back of the structure following the L-shaped layout. Delicate ironwork—in the form of balconies, a tower cross, and grills to cover the lower sash and transom—provides the main ornamental detailing.

During the early years, services were held in this primary structure. It had been built for a community hall and gymnasium with the intention of developing a second unit, which would contain the nave. The church converted it into a formal sanctuary in 1943. New additions on adjacent properties have maintained the architectural integrity of the original structure.

During the years 1920 through 1945, Parkinson & Parkinson designed many of Los Angeles's landmark buildings including the original campus of the University of Southern California, the Los Angeles Memorial Coliseum, and Union Station. While the firm designed a handful of other structures in Long Beach including the 1922 Omar Hubbard Building, they have since been demolished.

1

2

Better Home Electrical

Described in a February 1923 *Long Beach Sunday Press* article as "the home which housewives have yearned for and that electrical engineers and modern home builders have dreamed of," Better Home Electrical targeted the average family. Said to contain 35 electrical appliances—including a dishwasher, an iceless refrigerator, and a range—the installed devices promised to minimize the drudgery of housework. The plan also touted numerous and strategically placed convenience outlets.

Harold E. Ketchum, structural engineer, builder, and owner of the property, collaborated with the Long Beach Electric Club to exhibit a furnished model to the public for several weeks. The model had seven rooms: a living room, dining room, and kitchen on the first floor; two bedrooms, an enclosed sleeping porch, and bathroom on the second floor. Nine similar structures followed on the property, ranging in price from $9,000 to $13,000. Ten units in total are arranged with five units on each side and a central drive down the middle.

Unattached, the two front units face the street while the others, paired in two, face the drive. Lined side-by-side, the resulting structures create narrow passageways along the exterior walls. The modest and compact two-story Spanish design bears little ornamentation, barring coved doorways and a few arched windows. The exterior finish, a magnesite stucco, was guaranteed not to leak, crack, stain, or require paint. It also was reputed to repel the heat of summer and retain the warmth of winter. Some of the original wood-framed windows have been replaced.

Hundreds of people visited the model home and Thomas Edison sent a telegram that read: "Congratulations on Long Beach progressiveness, and the fact that she is interested in Better Homes [sic] Electrical."

16
MAP 1, D10
MAP 2, F3

LOCATION
1715 AND 1721 E. 1ST ST.
AND 100–116 EDISON PLACE
DATE
1923
ARCHITECT
HAROLD E. KETCHUM
ADJACENT
ROSE TOWERS (36)
LIFEGUARD HEADQUARTERS,
CHERRY AVENUE (50)
GRACE UNITED METHODIST CHURCH (78)

1./ *View of central drive*
2./ *Front unit and view down Edison Place, 1925*
3./ *Individual unit*

1

2

3

Captain Ponto House

17
MAP 1, F10
MAP 2, J3

LOCATION
254 MIRA MAR AVE.
DATE
1923
ARCHITECT
MINER R. SMITH
ADJACENT
BELMONT HEIGHTS UNITED
METHODIST CHURCH (15)
CASA GRANDE APARTMENT
BUILDING (33)
APARTMENT BUILDING ON 1ST (52)

1./ *Exterior view*

Miner R. Smith designed and built many speculative houses that were dictated by his architectural visions versus client demand. "Bungalow mansions," as Smith referred to them, extended beyond the imagery of a simple small house and encompassed grander sizes and scales. Smith designated his houses as "Miner R. Smith superior standard" and planned them as "healthful" homes.

As the owner, designer, and builder, Smith placed advertisements in the local paper and featured his "enchanting" bungalow mansions, furnished or unfurnished, by a chronological number indicating the date of completion. Fine appointments included three-mirror, built-in dressing tables in the bedrooms, cedar closets, lavatory with hot and cold water, and conveniences to aid "a woman in the kitchen." He even installed an electric refrigerator, an uncommon appliance in the 1920s, and wiring and heating systems. Smith acknowledged the worth of spending the budget on minutia in a 1923 *Long Beach Press* article: "My houses are priced higher because they cost a great deal to make. But the buyer is getting good value for his money." To maximize the allure, he provided an electric Chickering piano recital at open houses and even gave the instrument to new buyers when they purchased one of his creations.

For 254 Mira Mar Avenue, Smith approached the house as he had his others—with brash enthusiasm. Melding Victorian intricacy with Craftsman style, Smith spared no expense. A play of steep roof slopes makes the front facade read as an active elevation. Raising the ground floor of the house so that the floorboards kept dry and well ventilated reinforces Smith's reference to his houses as healthy. Expensive cast stone is used throughout the exterior on the stairs, columns, porch, and chimney. The front door—elegantly constructed of gumwood with a beveled glass *M* insert—is a standard element in many of Smith's residences in the area. The interior is equally ornate with a large spacious living room, moldings, and carved-wood built-ins. Smith appeared to have constructed many of his houses from a plan book, a popular offering in builders' trade journals. Clusters of Smith's mini-mansions, unique to Long Beach, emerged in the Belmont Heights vicinity at 212 and 244 Mira Mar Avenue, 310 and 343 Loma Avenue, and 301 Euclid Avenue.

After moving to Long Beach in 1919, Smith worked on wartime housing. He started his career as a stonecutter, but since high-quality stone was difficult to obtain in Southern California, he experimented with his own molds, casting artificial stone as a substitute. Smith owned M. R. Smith Stone and Mantel Company and in 1912 was listed as a dealer of artificial stone in Los Angeles. He worked in Long Beach on and off for years, establishing his office at 1219 Euclid Avenue.

1

Farmers & Merchants Bank and Tower

18
MAP 1, C9
MAP 2, C2

LOCATION
302 AND 320 PINE AVE.
DATE
1923; 1925
ARCHITECT
CURLETT & BEELMAN
WITH W. HORACE AUSTIN
ADJACENT
MASONIC TEMPLE (3)
WALKER'S DEPARTMENT STORE (40)
INSURANCE EXCHANGE BUILDING (24)

1./ *Exterior view*

Determined to create a sound financial institution that would serve the people of Long Beach, C. J. Walker and his wife Carrie founded Farmers & Merchants Bank in 1907. The structure has served as the bank's headquarters since its completion in 1923 and continues to be operated by the Walker family.

Although the bank is not a designated landmark, the family treats it with respect and care. The building maintains the atmosphere of a bygone era. The teller cages, desks, and hardware are all original. Interior marble columns and exterior columns support the two-story atrium space, which is covered with a massive skylight. When the bank opened, a 1923 article in the *Long Beach Press* touted the magnificent use of Verona Red marble: "Its surface is so highly polished that photographs of the interior show reflections of objects from the pillars and wainscoting." Numerous terra-cotta relief panels and gold-leaf ornamentation add to the highly decorative interior.

Alexander Curlett and Claud Beelman, the premier practitioners of period-revival building in Southern California, designed the two-story bank in an Italian Renaissance Revival style. The first level has eight fluted composite columns on each side of the building separating the windows, topped by a row of dentils and a narrow frieze. Located on a corner parcel, an angled entrance punctuates the convergence. Urn and scrollwork detailing adorn the space between the second-floor windows. The building survived the 1933 earthquake with only minor cosmetic damage.

The 10-story steel and terra-cotta office tower was constructed adjacent to the bank in 1925 and follows the same aesthetic along the second and 10th floors to ensure continuity between the two structures. The roof of the tower is crowned with a historic neon sign displaying the F&M letters in blue and red on one side and the bank's full name on the opposite side. The structure was Long Beach's first "skyscraper," introducing the modern era of building design to the city. The bank sold the tower in 1945.

1

Kress Building

LOCATION
100 W. 5TH ST.
DATE
1923; 1995
ARCHITECT
THOMAS FRANKLIN POWER;
INTERSTICES
ADJACENT
WALKER'S DEPARTMENT STORE (40)
FARMERS & MERCHANTS BANK
AND TOWER (18)
INTERNATIONAL ELEMENTARY
SCHOOL (93)

1./ *View of steel staircase and
    penthouses*
2./ *Exterior view, c. 1930*

The Kress Building was the 152nd store in the Kress's empire of variety stores. One of the most prosperous merchants in the first part of the 20th century, Memphis-based Kress & Company represented a new way of selling goods at inexpensive prices. The guiding force behind this unique concept was department-store magnate and major art collector Samuel H. Kress.

The Kress five-and-dime stores proliferated during the early 20th century, and at the company's peak in the 1920s more than 250 dotted the nation. Founder Kress believed in good store design and realized his vision in the architecture and interiors of the buildings. Unlike other retail stores at the time, Kress employed an in-house architecture division to facilitate the design of all details, from lighting fixtures to popular window displays and exteriors. He believed that it was important to create a layout to fit into the context of the surrounding buildings.

Thomas Franklin Power, who designed Loyola Marymount University in Los Angeles, conceived the aesthetic of the Kress Building. Made out of cement stucco scored to resemble terra cotta, the building stood seven stories high on the main retail street of Pine Avenue. Unusual for a department-store plan, two stories served as retail space while the rest was rented for commercial use. Tenants of the building included the noted commercial photographer Lawrence Inman and the architecture firm of Hugh Gibbs. In 1928, a three-story addition was built on the side facing Pine Avenue to accommodate more retail space and food services.

The Kress Building suffered years of vacancy and neglect after its close in the late 1960s. The property was purchased in the 1980s by a developer who stripped the exterior and gutted the interiors, leaving a skeletal structure behind as he exited the scene.

Soon after, Interstices, a group of young architects interested in making something of the dilapidated Kress, began discussions about rehabilitating the building for loft living. Though the Kress faced demolition to make way for a surface parking lot, Interstices saved the edifice with its determined foresight. The firm involved funders and completely transformed the building to accommodate 49 units, sparking a renaissance in the downtown core. Two steel-and-glass penthouses, known as jewel boxes crowning the roof, feature their own private decks, fireplaces, and landscaping. Communal outdoor spaces between the fifth and sixth floors serve all residents. An ingenious architectural move produced the addition of a steel staircase that offers both seismic support and a circulation connector for the two wings. Several exemplary architectural details from the original building still exist such as the frieze ornamentation and the large ground-floor display windows.

1

2

Art Theater

20
MAP 1, E9
MAP 2, G2

LOCATION
2025 E. 4TH ST.
DATE
1924; 1933; 1947
ARCHITECT
R. C. ALDRICH; SCHILLING AND
SCHILLING; HUGH GIBBS
ADJACENT
GRACE UNITED METHODIST CHURCH (78)
ROSE TOWERS (36)
THE SKINNY HOUSE (45)

1./ Marquee detail
2./ Floor detail
3./ Exterior view, c. 1935
4./ Ticket booth
5./ Exterior view

The Art Theater is the last remaining neighborhood movie theater in Long Beach. When it opened, the 636-seat theater showed silent films and contained an orchestra pit and a pipe organ. Originally called the Carter Theater, it became the Lee in 1935 and the Art in the 1940s.

The structure is a composite of architectural design revealing three successive eras of development. Plans indicate that the first building was constructed in a modest vernacular style with "Orientalizing" touches reminiscent of Grauman's Chinese Theater in Hollywood. Two storefronts flanked the theater. The one on the east side survives, with its original transom windows intact.

Schilling and Schilling extensively remodeled the building in an Art Deco style after the 1933 earthquake. The structure's main architectural features date from this era including the ticket booth, black ceramic tile, and colorful geometric terrazzo floor inscribed with then-owner's name "Lee." Zigzag elements include the stepped piers, vertical fluting, and the central-stepped vertical tower that unfolds as a fern. The horizontal stringcourses wrapped around curving corners of the central mass project a more streamlined approach.

Another local architect, Hugh Gibbs, completed a renovation in 1947. Keeping in tradition with the earlier Art Deco style, the marquee was remodeled, the glass-block wall inserted, and new poster boxes built.

The Art Theater exemplifies movie-theater architecture, with its richly decorative facade and ornamental sidewalk, highly visible and designed to attract. In the 1940s and early 1950s, Long Beach possessed dozens of downtown and neighborhood movie houses. In 2004, such theaters are a dying breed. The Art Theater is one of only a few from this era remaining in the Los Angeles region.

1

2

3

4

5

Community Hospital of Long Beach

The Community Hospital of Long Beach first opened its doors to the public on July 15, 1924. When it was built, the hospital was surrounded by farmland and located on a hill in the outskirts of Long Beach. It started with 100 beds and a staff of 175 surgeons and physicians. Founded by then-Mayor Fillmore Condit, the hospital offered nonprofit, nonsectarian, and low-cost healthcare. The initial ward costs of $3 per day catered to the "middle-class" citizen.

The Community Hospital is indicative of Long Beach architect Hugh R. Davies's early work, drawing from period-revival styles popular in the first decades of the 20th century. Designed in a Spanish Colonial style, the building has smooth, stucco walls and a red-tile roof. It consists of two stories and a basement. Visitors enter through a red-brick-and-tile courtyard featuring an octagonal-based, tiled fountain. The fountain was not part of the original design but seamlessly blended into the surroundings when it was added in the 1970s. Arcades flank three sides of the courtyard. A two-story arch in relief and large wooden door mark the main entrance, and rectangular windows rhythmically punctuate the facade. The grounds are richly landscaped with mature trees and flowers. The hospital is decidedly warm and intimate in stark contrast to the cold, clinical environments of today's hospitals.

In 1959 the hospital dedicated a new east wing with an additional 148 beds and 34 bassinets; however it is largely concealed by the original structure. Likewise, subsequent expansions and additions have had negligible effect on the overall character of the building.

Over the years, the hospital continued its commitment to a high standard of medical care and personalized service. It remained in operation 24 hours a day at the same location until it briefly closed in September 2000 when a new owner bought the hospital and systematically began to reduce services and cease operation. But doctors, volunteers, staff, and concerned citizens organized a grass-roots movement to reopen the historic institution, and in June 2001, their efforts were rewarded. Today the hospital continues to serve the local community.

21
MAP 1, F8

LOCATION
1720 TERMINO AVE.
DATE
1924
ARCHITECT
HUGH R. DAVIES
ADJACENT
TICHENOR ORTHOPEDIC CLINIC
FOR CHILDREN (51)
JAVA LANES BOWLING ALLEY (64)
ALEXANDER HOUSE (59)

1./ *Courtyard through arcade*
2./ *Exterior view, 1930*

1

2

Cooper Arms

LOCATION
455 E. OCEAN BLVD.
DATE
1924
ARCHITECT
CURLETT & BEELMAN
ADJACENT
BROADLIND HOTEL (32)
LAFAYETTE COMPLEX (35)
LINDEN TOWER (75)

1./ Exterior view

Based on the cooperative plan of ownership first conceived in New York in the second decade of the 20th century, the 160-unit Cooper Arms targeted individuals who preferred the convenience and simplicity of apartment-style accommodations. Its erection reflected the building boom in Long Beach after World War I and the discovery of oil. At the time, the Cooper Arms was the epitome of elegant resort living. The beachfront was visible across Ocean Boulevard and since landfill had not yet occurred, the shore was closer and easily accessible. With units ranging in price from $3,800 to $17,000, owners were able to request variations in the individual floor plans and built-in amenities. Although it was the sixth cooperative built in Long Beach, it was the largest and most expensive to date. Unlike others executed at the same time, the Cooper Arms remains a cooperative.

Alexander Curlett and Claud Beelman designed the Cooper Arms in Italian Renaissance Revival style. Similar to other period-revival structures, the Cooper Arms is composed in an ordered tripartite pattern, with a distinct base, shaft, and a terminating cornice. The 12-story, L-shaped building consists of one narrow, deep wing along Linden Avenue, and one smaller, shallow wing extending westward. The plan incorporates a ground floor arcade containing commercial space, a fenced garden fronting Ocean Boulevard, a Spanish loggia, a palm promenade, and a rooftop domed ballroom and solarium.

The arched Ocean Boulevard entrance, with a decorated tympanum and central keystone, is flanked by tall, arched windows, also with central keystones. This neoclassical window treatment, the most visually prominent feature, is repeated throughout the ground-floor spaces. Variation in the window arrangement pattern on the nine stories of the shaft lends to the building's rhythmic composition. Wrought-iron balconies accessed by French doors punctuate the smooth stucco facade. The terminating cornice carries a row of decorative brackets below a rolled-edge parapet.

The Cooper Arms building possesses remarkable integrity with minimal alterations to the interior and exterior historic features.

1

Ebell Club and Theater

23
MAP 1, D9
MAP 2, E3

LOCATION
290 CERRITOS AVE.
AND 1100 E. 3RD ST.
DATE
1924
ARCHITECT
C. T. MCGREW
ADJACENT
LONG BEACH SKATING PALACE (42)
THE KOFFEE POT CAFE (43)
VILLA RIVIERA (39)

1./ Exterior view

The Ebell Club was an important American institution founded by Dr. Adrian Ebell, an advocate for educating women. Established in 1896, the Long Beach chapter is the city's oldest civic and philanthropic institution. The founding president was Adelaide A. Tichenor, a prominent leader in the city.

The clubhouse and theater are an example of Spanish Renaissance architecture, a popular period revival style of the 1920s. The most salient features are the highly decorated doorways, made of cast cement in its natural sand color. The lavish sculptural facade verges on the Churrigueresque style. Named after the 17th-century Spanish architect Jose de Churriguera, the look is characterized by rich and lavish Baroque ornamentation.

A low-pitched, red-tile hipped roof tops the two-story rectangular clubhouse. The two wings are connected by a projecting cast-stone entryway of elaborate design with a central escutcheon bearing the initials *EC*. The large single arch is framed with decorated pilasters, framed in turn by narrow, twisted column shafts. The clubhouse is arranged around a central patio that was originally open but, after the 1933 earthquake, received a roof.

A firewall several feet thick connects the clubhouse to the theater. The rectangular three-story theater was built as a companion facility at the same time as the club. A short flight of stairs leads to the entryway, where an arched doorway contains a semicircular window with a multipaned wood sash. The ornamental facade tiers up the front, with arches, foliate scrolls, niches, and piers. The side and rear walls are plain and utilitarian. The interior once held seating for 1,000.

The designer and builder, C. T. McGrew, had a large firm that erected several hundred residences and some of the city's larger structures. When the Ebell Club was under construction, outsiders repeatedly told club members that they were overbuilding. The edifice was, in fact, damaged in the 1933 earthquake, but not to the severity of other local structures. Since it was rebuilt and repaired in 1934, it has passed all earthquake tests. No other large building of the same age shares this distinction in Long Beach.

The Ebell Club sold the buildings to two different entities in 2001. Since that time, the Ebell Club has been restored and now is leased back to its members as one of several uses, which also include special events and offices. The Ebell Theater is being adaptively reused for 11 loft units. The theater interiors were removed.

1

Insurance Exchange Building
(Middoughs' Boys' Shop)

24
MAP 1, C9
MAP 2, C3

LOCATION
205 E. BROADWAY
DATE
1924
ARCHITECT
HARVEY H. LOCHRIDGE
ADJACENT
BIKESTATION LONG BEACH (90)
MASONIC TEMPLE (3)
U.S. POST OFFICE
AND FEDERAL BUILDING (47)

1./ *Exterior view, c. 1930*

Commissioned by Way and Lorne Middough, well-known business brothers in the community, the Middoughs' Boys' Shop was designed by architect and engineer Harvey H. Lochridge. Local attorney Clyde Doyle also played a major role in facilitating the building's erection. It housed the Boys' and Men's Shop, a retail shop for "boys from 1 to 100." The names "Middoughs' Men's Shop" facing the Promenade and "Middoughs' Boys' Shop" on Broadway are still carved in stone on the building.

The $400,000, eight-story brick building, realized at the height of the Long Beach building boom, is clad in polychrome terra cotta and features a three-part Beaux-Arts organization. The first floor and mezzanine levels form a visual base, the repeating floors compose a shaft, and the ornamental cornice acts as a cap. The exterior details include light-colored walls, decorative terra-cotta tiles, bas-relief panels, foliated swags at the cornice lines, and colonettes with ornamentation between the pivot windows. The relief decoration portrays tridents, sea serpents, and griffins, which refer to the local water life. The frieze above the mezzanine level, depicts playful scenes of children running, boating, and playing tennis. These vignettes recall the original function of the building.

From the beginning, the building housed a mixed commercial program that included a restaurant in the basement, retail spaces on the first and second floors, a spacious mezzanine, office spaces, and a gymnasium on the rooftop. For a short period the municipal court and a branch of the superior court occupied the top floors, adding the interesting presence of law mingling with youth.

In 1930, Wayne H. Fisher bought the building and embarked on an ambitious interior renovation, which included changing the name to Insurance Exchange, relocating the entrance, modernizing the elevators, and outfitting spaces with electrical outlets. The Art Deco remodel maximized the rental space for a total of 80 offices. When the building reopened, a 1930s *Press-Telegram* article heralded it as one of the most modern edifices in the city. On the rear brick walls, painted commercial signage of former tenants still exists.

The building is currently undergoing construction as an adaptive reuse for loft development.

1

Security Pacific National Bank
(Security Trust and Savings Bank)

25
MAP 1, C10
MAP 2, C3

LOCATION
110 PINE AVE.
DATE
1924
ARCHITECT
CURLETT & BEELMAN
ADJACENT
FIRST NATIONAL BANK (2)
BIKESTATION LONG BEACH (90)
MASONIC TEMPLE (3)

1./ *View of entrance with traffic
policeman and female pedestrian
in foreground, c. 1925*

The Security Pacific National Bank still retains much of its original décor and grandeur. Built in 1924 as a result of a bank merger, the Security Trust and Savings Bank was an icon of commercial and financial prosperity in the 1920s. Under the leadership of P. E. Hatch, vice president of the bank, the building was designed by the Los Angeles architecture team Curlett & Beelman. Solidly constructed of brick and concrete, the edifice symbolized security, a goal for banking institutions. The bank occupied the first and second floor of the 12-story building, while professional offices leased the upper floors.

Dressed in varying shades of red brick cladding with white-marble detailing, the building incorporates classical architectural motifs. Adorning the front entrance of the building, two full and two half classical Corinthian columns stand tall and strong, stretching three stories. The building's symmetry along with the columns and window treatments provide a vertical rhythm extending the entire facade. Marble facing is used as the cladding material at the entrance.

Elegant interiors include a vast two-story main space with the original carved mahogany wall and column treatments. When the bank underwent adaptive reuse to become a restaurant, a dropped ceiling was removed, revealing a stenciled beamed ceiling two stories high. The finely crafted work displays a timber grid with a painted heart motif. Another authentic feature of the building is the reinforced concrete bank vault that extends underneath the entire length of the first floor. A solid-steel vault door and bronze gate lead up to the cavernous space.

1

The Willmore

26
MAP 1, B9
MAP 2, C2

LOCATION
315 W. 3RD ST.
DATE
1924
ARCHITECT
FISHER, LAKE & TRAVER
ADJACENT
FIRST CONGREGATIONAL CHURCH (10)
CALIFORNIA VETERANS MEMORIAL
STATE OFFICE BUILDING (86)
LONG BEACH CITY HALL
AND PUBLIC LIBRARY (82)

1./ Exterior view c. 1930s

The Willmore was erected during a prolific building campaign of luxury high-rise apartment-hotels. The Stillwell Hotel Corporation developed the property as an "own-your-own" and the structure originally bore the name "The Stillwell." When the company lost control of the property after a land-title dispute in 1928, the name was changed to "The Willmore," after Willmore City, the original town of Long Beach. In 1934, the new ownership converted the building to an apartment-hotel for permanent owner-residents and short-term and long-term guests as rentals.

The 11-story edifice is constructed of reinforced concrete and tile. Italian Renaissance Revival characteristics include a spacious, tile-paved entry court, arched ground-floor windows, twisted colonnettes around major windows and door openings, wrought-iron light fixtures, and Renaissance-inspired ornamentation on the exterior. The design follows the Beaux-Arts organizational model: the first story forms a base, which consists of a colonnade and a series of retail storefronts; an undifferentiated series of eight floors with paired windows and smooth stucco wall surfaces compose the shaft of the building; and the 11th floor forms the capital and houses the solarium.

The original 117 apartments were small and affordable with relatively little upkeep, offering an ideal respite from harsh East Coast winters. The immense public areas compensated in grandness. The lobby features a large skylight, terrazzo floors, and fireplace, creating an elegant space to receive guests. The Willmore was originally designed as a U-shaped structure but only the central unit and one wing were completed, leaving the building in an L-shaped configuration. An underground parking garage provided a rare amenity at the time. The solarium, an important center for social gatherings and card playing, retains its original hanging light fixtures, card tables, and chairs. A series of symmetrically placed full-length casement windows with arched headers dominate the room. A large industrial kitchen off the sun terrace provided for the hotel's needs.

Own-your-own apartment hotels were a Long Beach phenomenon resulting from the economic boom of the 1920s. Borrowing from East Coast cooperative precedents, the Willmore offered hotel amenities and the security of home ownership.

The firm of Fisher, Lake & Traver, also designed the Hollywood Roosevelt Hotel.

The Breakers Hotel

27
MAP 1, C10
MAP 2, C3

LOCATION
210 E. OCEAN BLVD.
DATE
1925
ARCHITECT
WALKER AND EISEN
ADJACENT
OCEAN CENTER BUILDING (38)
BIKESTATION LONG BEACH (90)
COOPER ARMS (22)

1./ *Exterior view*
2./ *View of Wilton Hotel marquee, 1952*

Developer Fred B. Dunn commissioned the prominent architects Albert R. Walker and Percy A. Eisen to design the Breakers Hotel. Known for many noteworthy commercial buildings in Los Angeles in the 1920s, the firm's work included the Beverly Wilshire Hotel, Fine Arts Building, and Oviatt Building. Positioned on the bluff overlooking the shoreline, the Breakers Hotel debuted as one of the exclusive resorts for Long Beach tourists. Its prime location on Ocean Boulevard, architectural detailing, and sweeping circular drive added to the hotel's feeling of a luxury escape.

Designed in a Spanish Colonial Revival style, the Breakers Hotel reaches 15 stories high with a tower and incorporates 320 rooms. Constructed during a one-year period and costing $1 million, the hotel was the largest structure built during the 1920s in Long Beach. Distinctively slender in its side elevation, the building not only extends lengthwise, it also gradually steps down the sloping hill in the rear. The most eye-catching element is the entrance design. Sculpted in concrete and ornate in detail, the slightly recessed opening showcases a floral motif and bas-relief with a mermaid bust. Even with this elaborate decoration, the Spanish tile roof and stucco walls lend simplicity to the architecture. A spacious lobby and ballroom add grandeur to the plan. An arcade under the Breakers Hotel once featured a passageway of shops.

Hotel magnate Conrad Hilton purchased the Breakers in 1938, the eighth in his chain of hotels and his first on the West Coast. He spent $200,000 to renovate the facilities with the addition of his Art Deco penthouse (now the Sky Room restaurant) and operated the hotel until 1947. During the Hilton years, a Streamline Moderne entrance marquee adorned the motor court. Subsequent owners, including the Wilton Hotel, have managed the building and, in the 1980s, it became a residence for senior citizens.

1

2

YWCA

28
MAP 1, C9
MAP 2, C2

LOCATION
DEMOLISHED
DATE
1925
ARCHITECT
JULIA MORGAN

1./ Pool, 1928
2./ Side view of building, 1926

One of the preeminent architects of her generation, Julia Morgan was all the more remarkable due to the fact that she practiced at a time when men overwhelmingly dominated the profession. She was one of the first women to graduate in civil engineering from the University of California, Berkeley, and was the first woman ever to earn a certificate in architecture from the prestigious École des Beaux-Arts in Paris. Newspaper titan William Randolph Hearst selected Morgan as the architect for his "castle" at San Simeon, and she designed and built more than 700 structures during her prolific career.

The first Young Women's Christian Association (YWCA) was established in Long Beach in 1904. In 1924, after outgrowing several locations, the Long Beach YWCA launched a campaign to erect a new building at 6th Street and Pacific Avenue. The national YWCA recommended Morgan. By this time, she had already completed numerous YWCA residence halls up and down the coast.

Utilizing the academic design principles of her Beaux-Arts training, Morgan designed a building of symmetry, proportion, and structural integrity based on a classical architectural vocabulary. The five-story Italian Renaissance building plus basement used red brick as the main material with a steel-reinforced framework. The facade, an austere and minimally ornamented surface, displayed elegant window spacing and framing in a balanced order. A low-pitched tile roof capped this simple, yet highly engineered structure. A large dining room, gymnasium, and clubroom dominated the first floor of the building. Below the street level were the swimming pool and kitchen. About 100 residential rooms lined the corridors of the third, fourth, and fifth floors. The fifth floor featured a covered loggia, and a tennis court was situated on the roof.

Pools were a prominent feature of Morgan's structures but this one met a tragic end. In 1976, the swimming-pool ceiling collapsed, killing one woman and injuring four other people. The YWCA had renovated the building in 1958, installing a suspended cement-and-acoustical-tile ceiling over the pool area. The cause of the accident was never determined, but fire department officials speculated that moisture and humidity from the pool might have gradually weakened the materials over the years.

The YWCA board of directors had contemplated vacating the premises even before the accident. Their decision was sealed when city officials rejected the Y's application for a one-year extension to bring the building up to modern earthquake standards. The board was ordered to either upgrade the entire facility at a cost of about $1.5 million or tear it down. For financial reasons they chose the latter. As if defying its fate, Morgan's structurally solid YWCA did not succumb to demolition without a fight. It took crews close to a year to finally level the structure and clear the grounds.

1

2

Pacific Coast Club

29
MAP 1, D10
MAP 2, D3

LOCATION
DEMOLISHED
DATE
1926
ARCHITECT
CURLETT & BEELMAN

1./ *Large crowd gathered at opening ceremony, 1926*

The Pacific Coast Club was a prominent feature of the shoreline and a prestigious building when it opened in 1926. Built on land purchased from philanthropist Adelaide A. Tichenor, the club sat next door to her estate and commanded a panoramic view of the ocean. The architecture team of Alexander Curlett and Claud Beelman created a gigantic castlelike structure based upon 16th-century Norman architecture. Builder C. T. McGrew was instrumental in realizing this one-of-a-kind edifice.

The club featured modern and luxurious amenities leaving no expense behind at a cost of $2 million for construction and $250,000 for furnishings. The huge undertaking included securing the structure by extending large pilings below sea level and building 14 floors of poured concrete. Touted in its inaugural volume as being "fully equipped for training and competitive contests in all the ordinary gymnasium sports," the club offered a gym and five handball and squash courts. Another grandiose element included the 77-foot pool with filtered and sterilized water. An accumulation of 15,000 pieces of silver, 20,000 pieces of china, and 9,000 yards of carpet, along with countless objects of fine furnishings completed the lavish dining appointments.

The Pacific Coast Club, with its ultraluxurious atmosphere, listed many wealthy Long Beach patrons as lifetime members on its roster. In the first years of operation, the club ranked as one of the largest places of exercise, relaxation, and repose in California. The club's edict recognized keeping fit and the importance of involving the entire family. In 1928, the club merged with the Los Angeles Athletic Club and remained in operation until the early 1980s.

The club was placed on the National Register of Historic Places in 1980 but because of the city's seismic safety ordinance, the building closed. In 1984, it was demolished to make way for a 16-story condominium. With the loss of this iconic building, the preservation movement ignited. The Long Beach Foundation for Architectural and Cultural Heritage, a nonprofit advocacy group for the preservation of Long Beach's architecture, ensued and continues under the name of Long Beach Heritage to protect and monitor the fragile state of historic buildings in the city.

1

Pray/Dawson House

This English Tudor mansion in the exclusive Virginia Country Club area is one of the grandest residential structures in Long Beach. At two-stories and 4,321 square feet, its scale, size, and detail are unmatched.

The house was designed and constructed by William E. Babb with the architectural help of Clarence Aldrich in 1927. Once a prominent businessman in Long Beach, Babb became a building contractor. Working with other local builders, Babb completed plans for an exclusive residential project, but the development was abandoned when oil was discovered on Signal Hill. A believer in the city's future, Babb received large oil royalties and invested extensively in Long Beach real estate. Russell H. Pray, a well-known and successful lawyer of Long Beach, purchased the house from Babb in 1929. His widow, Leonie Pray, lived in the house through the 1980s.

The house features a shake-covered gable roof, and multicolored brick-and-stucco siding with decorative half-timbering. Multisash, multipaned, irregularly shaped leaded-glass windows appear on both levels. A conical tower with a weather vane tops the gable dormer. Molded stone frames the main entry. Arches at the garages and in the wing facing the rear yard are of cement plaster, reproducing the stone effect in a different manner. An oversized brick chimney extends from the roof. The living room is the most prominent interior space, rising two stories in height and featuring the original trusses.

The current owners restored the house during 1991 and 1992 and, at the same time, expanded the kitchen and added an architecturally sensitive second-story master suite.

30
MAP 1, B4

LOCATION
4252 COUNTRY CLUB DR.
DATE
1927
ARCHITECT
WILLIAM E. BABB AND
CLARENCE ALDRICH
ADJACENT
HENRY CLOCK HOUSE (46)
CRAIG/MCLEOD HOUSE (54)
BIXBY RANCH HOUSE (1)

1./ *Exterior detail*

1

York Rite Masonic Temple

Under the Masons' directive, the Long Beach architecture and engineering firm of Parker O. Wright and Francis H. Gentry designed the immense York Rite Masonic Temple in Greek Revival style. Constructed of concrete and masonry with a steel frame, the vast rectangular building was one of the largest Masonic temples in Southern California. Serving as an assembly hall and gathering place for the York Rite Masons fraternal organization, it offered a monumental presence on Locust Avenue, a low-scale, residential neighborhood street.

The building is designed as a replica of a Greek temple using Indiana limestone. Six Doric columns dominate the facade, and two friezes of varying width, adorned with a decorative relief, wrap the front. The central doorway features Greek designs, and a square panel blazons a Masonic insigne. The side and rear walls take on red brick cladding.

Accentuated by the double-height entrance, the interior spaces of the lobby particularly stand out with 25-foot-tall ceilings and columns and Swanton black, Columbia white, and Kasota yellow marble floors. The decorative black-and-white diamond flooring patterns bounce off the grand scale of the foyer. The interior originally housed several large meeting halls, all decorated in varying period styles depicting Egyptian and Roman themes.

In 1955, with the decline of Masonic activities, the temple changed over to Morgan Hall and was used for large social gatherings. In the 1970s, Long Beach passed a seismic safety ordinance, which the temple did not meet; it was therefore abandoned. The building sat vacant for years, suffering acts of vandalism to the interior and exterior.

In 2002, a developer bought the entitlements from another developer for adaptive reuse as loft living. The Santa Monica-based architecture firm Frederick Fisher and Partners was commissioned as design architect to revive the structure with a new program. HKS Architects acted as executive architect for the project. The firms restored the building to include 50 loft units. Two new buildings adjoin the temple with 16 lofts each, totaling 150,000 square feet. The lobby's original stenciled walls and diamond floor patterns still remain in good condition. Historical photographs aided in restoring the lobby space back to its former splendor.

31
MAP 1, C9
MAP 2, C1

LOCATION
835 LOCUST AVE.
DATE
1927; 2005
ARCHITECT
PARKER O. WRIGHT AND FRANCIS H. GENTRY; FREDERICK FISHER AND PARTNERS AND HKS ARCHITECTS
ADJACENT
INTERNATIONAL ELEMENTARY SCHOOL (93)
KRESS BUILDING (19)
WALKER'S DEPARTMENT STORE (40)

1./ Exterior view
2./ Foyer, 1928
3./ Exterior view, 1928

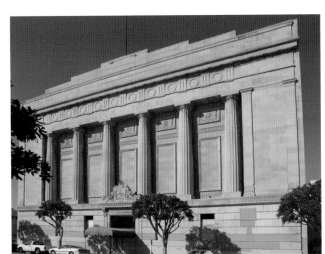

Broadlind Hotel

32
MAP 1, C10
MAP 2, D3

LOCATION
149 LINDEN AVE.
DATE
1928
ARCHITECT
PIPER & KAHRS
ADJACENT
LAFAYETTE COMPLEX (35)
LINDEN TOWER (75)
COOPER ARMS (22)

1./ Exterior view, c. 1930
2./ Exterior view

Perfectly proportioned, the Broadlind Hotel gracefully sits at the intersection of Broadway and Linden Avenue. The name is derived from its position on these two streets. The Long Beach architecture firm Piper & Kahrs, also known for its drive-in market in Long Beach, was hired to design the hotel in 1928. This year was a prosperous time for development in the neighborhood; other buildings included the Lafayette Hotel across the street and the Villa Riviera on Ocean Boulevard.

The square plan and four-story height of the Broadlind contribute to the fine look of the building. Constructed of thin, dark-red brick, the 20-room hostelry also included a manager's unit. Unusual in its use of brick, the building is reminiscent of old structures seen in Midwestern towns. The red-brick and cream terra-cotta detailing emits Italianate elegance.

History notes that the Broadlind appealed to a male clientele as a place for temporary accommodations. Apartments were rented by working men on a short-term basis. A spacious penthouse peers out above the rooftop. A wrought-iron overhang of intricately jeweled metalwork suspends over the entrance and exudes classic New Orleans style. Decorative features include square marble columns with braided concrete ornamentation that reach alongside the capitals.

The original painted sign advertising the hotel is still stenciled in tall letters on the side of building. The Broadlind, which sat vacant for years, was recently renovated into 17 apartment units and retail spaces on the first floor.

1

2

Casa Grande Apartment Building
(La Casa Grande)

The Casa Grande Apartment Building is an excellent example of Spanish-style courtyard housing. Popular in Southern California for multifamily housing during the 1920s and 1930s, the plan offered many amenities of single-family residences. The developer, Ernest G. Toms, appealed to an exclusive clientele with design schemes that offered one to three bedrooms, a living room on a separate level from the other rooms, mahogany floors and doors, and individual color treatments in each apartment.

Prominently situated on an elevated corner lot, the building originally commanded views of the Belmont Pier and the ocean. It consists of 12 units configured in a U-shape around a central concrete courtyard. The focal point of this area is a white cast-concrete fountain, containing a statue of a draped female supporting a shell on her head. The landscaped setting and varied size and placement of the individual units evoke a picturesque hillside village.

The exterior is finished in irregularly textured white stucco with black-painted woodwork and a low-pitched, red-tile roof. The structure is an assemblage of asymmetrical, diverse shapes: rounded corner towers, blocky masses, projecting turrets and chimneys, exterior balconies and staircases, cantilevered second stories, and recessed doorways.

The building reflects a strong Andalusian influence, yet it also incorporates other styles. A Baroque curvilinear arch crowns the east tower entry while other doorways are accented by shell contours. Elements of modernism also are apparent in the use of metal casement windows, a rectangular bay with extensive glass, and the use of abstract geometric ornamentation.

The firm of Schilling and Schilling is best known for its Art Deco commercial buildings in Long Beach. The Casa Grande Apartment Building is one of the few remaining examples of its Spanish Colonial Revival designs.

33
MAP 1, F10
MAP 2, I4

LOCATION
3717 LIVINGSTON DR.
DATE
1928
ARCHITECT
SCHILLING AND SCHILLING
ADJACENT
APARTMENT BUILDING ON 1ST (52)
CAPTAIN PONTO HOUSE (17)
GAYTONIA (41)

1./ Exterior view
2./ Rectangular bay and rounded
   corner tower
3./ Construction view, 1928

1

2

3

Hancock Motors

LOCATION
500 E. ANAHEIM ST.
DATE
1928
ARCHITECT
SCHILLING AND SCHILLING
WITH W. HORACE AUSTIN
ADJACENT
LONG BEACH POLYTECHNIC
HIGH SCHOOL (48)
YORK RITE MASONIC TEMPLE (31)
OLIVE COURT (98)

1./ *Detail of stone bas-reliefs*
2./ *Exterior view*

The Hancock Motors building, the city's first Art Deco structure, stylishly displayed its product: the Hupmobile. Named after its designer, Robert Hupp, this automobile was mass-produced with a sleek, streamlined frame, aluminum pistons, and elongated headlights. Used as a model showroom for the latest and greatest car designs of the Hupmobile, Hancock Motors' modern appearance complemented its product.

Lemuel A. Hancock, a business adventurer, started Hancock Oil Company in 1922 and then changed gears to sell Hupmobiles. Hancock hired the Long Beach firm of Schilling and Schilling, who worked closely with consulting architect W. Horace Austin. The Schilling team, known for attention to detail and use of fine materials in building, originated and pioneered the Art Deco style in Long Beach.

The Hancock building's highly detailed exterior accentuates the stone bas-reliefs in stepped patterns of floral and geometric motifs with bandlike ribbons of ornamentation running along the facade. The showroom's interior is unusually stylized with a mezzanine that overlooks chandeliers of hard-edged geometric shapes and a wrought-iron banister with triangular bracing detail. With one foot in modernism and one in consumerism, Hancock Motors' architecture straddles both categories to show off its wares.

Situated on Anaheim Street, the structure sat in the midst of auto row, a popular dealership thorough-fare during the 1920s and 1930s. Throughout Hancock Motors' history, it stayed true to its function with a string of car and auto-body businesses leasing the space. Today, restoration of the show windows is complete, and the building still operates as an auto-body shop.

Lafayette Complex

35
MAP 1, C10
MAP 2, D3

LOCATION
130 LINDEN AVE.
AND 140 LINDEN AVE.
DATE
1928; 1929; 1948
ARCHITECT
PARKER O. WRIGHT AND FRANCIS H.
GENTRY; SCHILLING AND SCHILLING;
THEODORE H. CRILEY
ADJACENT
BROADLIND HOTEL (32)
LINDEN TOWER (75)
COOPER ARMS (22)

1./ Exterior view
2./ Detail on Campbell Apartments
3./ Campbell Apartments, 1928

The Lafayette Complex is comprised of three separate buildings, each displaying a distinct architectural style. The Broadway Land Company acquired the lot for the earliest structure of the complex from the Southern Pacific Railway Company, and local investor and capitalist Reginald E. Campbell developed the Campbell Apartments. The 1928 completion of the 11-story deluxe apartments with hotel service marked the first major step of an important new business district and contributed to the emerging cosmopolitan skyline of Long Beach. The Spanish Renaissance building is constructed of steel frame with reinforced-concrete walls. Symmetrical in design, the facade features scroll and swag terra-cotta decorations beginning at the second floor and pyramiding up to the fourth floor. Ornamentation resumes at the ninth-floor balcony.

The Lafayette Hotel, developed a year later by the Broadway Land Company, is constructed of reinforced concrete. Although the architectural firm of Schilling and Schilling would later work extensively in the Art Deco style, this building is an original interpretation of modern architecture, drawing inspiration from French Moderne. The seven-story building consists of a centerpiece with projecting piers, flanked by lower and setback corners. Two art-stone friezes with pronounced zigzags line the second story. A canopy with art-stone and wrought-iron designs topped by a neon sign originally graced the front entrance.

In 1948, the hotel added an eight-story structure facing Broadway. Campbell made an inspection tour of all leading U.S. hotels before drafting his final plans. Built in the International Style, it is constructed of reinforced concrete and displays symmetry and austerity in the design.

Hilton Hotel Corporation purchased the group in 1952 and joined the three buildings. Hilton commissioned the architects Killingsworth, Brady & Smith to design a lanai addition in 1956 to be erected as a separate building behind the hotel. This instead became the Inn of Long Beach.

In its heyday, the Lafayette Complex housed several renowned restaurants and clubs, which were frequented by Hollywood celebrities, business tycoons, and politicians. It also hosted the first Miss Universe pageants in the early 1950s.

In 1968, Hilton turned the complex back over to Campbell's heirs and a year later the whole complex was converted to condominiums. The Lafayette Association of Homeowners (LAHO) was the first condominium association in the state of California. In 1990, the LAHO undertook a $3.5 million, three-year retrofit and restoration effort; in 2004 it continues to sensitively restore and renovate the interior and exterior of the building.

1

2

3

Rose Towers (El Cordova Apartments)

36
MAP 1, D10
MAP 2, F3

LOCATION
1728 E. 3RD ST.
DATE
1928
ARCHITECT
GEORGE D. RIDDLE
ADJACENT
GRACE UNITED METHODIST CHURCH (78)
BETTER HOME ELECTRICAL (16)
EBELL CLUB AND THEATER (23)

1./ Exterior courtyard view

The dwellings of Rose Towers are clustered around a lushly landscaped space that is open to the street, providing a tranquil outdoor respite for residents. The romantic, picturesque qualities of Spanish Revival courtyard housing flourished in Southern California in the 1920s as a result of several factors, including the interchange of ideas between movie-set construction and architecture, a growing nostalgia of the mission-rancho heritage, and the foreign travel of young architects to the Andalusia region of Spain and the subsequent transplantation of ideas.

While the 20 units vary in size and design, the overall composition of the building is symmetrical. It is arranged as two separate wings facing the central garden. A concrete meandering path traverses the courtyard, culminating in a tiled fountain set into a wall. The wall supports a raised rear terrace that is accessed by twin stairs flanking the fountain.

The terra-cotta, stacked-tile roof is intact and the exterior surface is currently being restored to its original handtroweled stucco finish. Other distinctive features include exterior stairways, wood balconies with turned posts, wrought-iron balconies, cantilevered second stories with embellished corbels, recessed entryways, pointed and parabolic arches, inset wood-casement windows, and decorative multicolor tile accents on stairs and window areas.

George D. Riddle designed several other courtyard housing complexes in the vicinity—The Barcelona, Casa Del Patio, Alvarado, Casa Nido—creating a unified architectural theme. In 1955, El Cordova Apartments was converted to own-your-owns and renamed Rose Towers.

1

Engine Company No. 8

This Italian Renaissance Revival public building was originally the Belmont Fire and Police substation, the city's first police substation sharing a structure with two fire platoons. It represents the expansion of city services to outlying neighborhoods. The building is constructed with a two-story, frame-and-brick-veneer exterior and a red-tile roof. Art stone accents the archways, windowsills, and the base. The choice of a period-revival style at this date indicates a conservative choice for a public edifice, as well as a compatible blend with the character of the homes in the surrounding neighborhood. Although the police department no longer occupies the space, the fire department is still active. It is one of the few remaining 1920s commercial structures in Belmont Shore, and the only one operating with its original use.

The Long Beach Department of Public Works recently completed renovation work, adding new lanterns to flank the entry door and replacing the windows.

37
MAP 1, G10

LOCATION
5365 E. 2ND ST.
DATE
1929
ARCHITECT
DEPARTMENT OF ENGINEERING,
CITY OF LONG BEACH
ADJACENT
PORTOFINO (71)
OPDAHL HOUSE (65)
FRANK HOUSE, CASE STUDY #25 (73)

1./ *Exterior view with fire platoon,*
   c. 1930
2./ *Exterior view*
3./ *Front and side view, c. 1940*

Ocean Center Building

LOCATION
110 W. OCEAN BLVD.
DATE
1929
ARCHITECT
MEYER AND HOLLER
ADJACENT
THE BREAKERS HOTEL (27)
FIRST NATIONAL BANK (2)
SECURITY PACIFIC NATIONAL
BANK (25)

1./ *Exterior view*

One of the first modern office towers on the bluff, the Ocean Center Building rose to the city's height limit at the time it was built. It remains an emblem of the Long Beach skyline.

The architecture conveys an image of picturesque romanticism, blending various period-revival styles. The stucco exterior and red-tile roofs display Mediterranean Revival design. Italianate detailing is apparent in the distinctive quoining on all the corners and the decorative use of pediments, escutcheons, and crenellations. The steel-sash casement windows are the only element of modernism.

The overall image is one of asymmetrical massing. The south elevation cascades down the bluff, taking advantage of the ocean view. A small tower sits over the seventh floor at the rear. An arcade at the base of the building under the bluff provided direct access to the Pike. The north elevation, whose massing also is broken up with a series of stepped setbacks, rises 13 stories. There is a balcony at the seventh floor under a pediment supported by brackets. The front entry, on Ocean Boulevard, is crowned by a broken pediment, the center of which is adorned with a shield of seashells and the face of Neptune. The penthouse consists of two stories topped by an octagonal tower. The tower originally held another 50-foot concrete tower and lantern, but these were removed following the 1933 earthquake.

The building remains essentially unchanged and still has many of the original site features such as the exterior stairs with railings and the large palm tree. It is also the only vintage office building in the city with its interiors largely intact, including the large display windows in the lobby, corridors lined with terrazzo floors, and mahogany office doors with glass and transoms.

Construction of Meyer and Holler's other Long Beach landmark, Walker's Department Store, occurred the same year.

1

Villa Riviera

LOCATION
800 E. OCEAN BLVD.
DATE
1929
ARCHITECT
RICHARD D. KING
ADJACENT
INTERNATIONAL TOWER (79)
ADELAIDE A. TICHENOR HOUSE (4)
COOPER ARMS (22)

1./ *Exterior view*

The Villa Riviera is an icon of the Long Beach skyline. Based loosely upon the style of 16th-century French châteaux, the design combines elements from the Gothic and Renaissance periods. At 15 stories, the Villa Riviera was for many years one of the Southland's tallest buildings, second only to Los Angeles City Hall. It is prominently sited at the juncture of two major streets, Alamitos Avenue and Ocean Boulevard.

The building is clad in smooth stucco accented with cast stone. Completely symmetrical in plan, massing, and fenestration, the central section of the Villa Riviera is organized in a classical tripartite composition. The facade features a relatively plain one-story base, a slightly more detailed shaft, and a highly elaborate capital that consists of a 20-foot, steeply pitched copper roof with a green patina, which in turn is crowned by a prominent 60-foot hexagonal pinnacle. Steel-casement windows open to sweeping views of the coastline and city. Approximately 30 gargoyles molded from poured concrete and rebar originally perched along the roof. The building's two wings form an obtuse angle. In addition to the 132 apartments and two penthouses, the building originally featured a ballroom, lounge, roof garden, restaurant, shops, and a parking structure.

Lionel V. Mayell, a developer of multifamily housing in the city and a tireless promoter of the own-your-own apartment concept, developed the Villa Riviera after similar Long Beach projects such as the Artaban and Cooper Arms. The distinctive architecture, luxurious amenities, and oceanfront location proved to be a winning combination, drawing movie stars and some of the city's elite to its tenant roster. Among the illustrious residents were Charlie Chaplin and silent-film star Norma Talmadge, who briefly owned the building in the 1930s with her movie producer ex-husband Joseph M. Schenck. The Villa Riviera experienced many incarnations over time, serving as apartments, a luxury hotel, and Naval housing during World War II. In 1991, the building was converted to condominiums.

Richard D. King appears to have been a little-known architect. The Villa Riviera represented a high point of his career and attests to his advanced engineering skills, as the steel skeleton, held together by triple layers of rivets with thick poured concrete, survived the 1933 earthquake.

1

Walker's Department Store

Walker's Department Store is a vestige of the retail development that occurred in Long Beach's downtown commercial district during the economic boom of the 1920s. The facility first housed the Hugh A. Marti Company. Hugh A. Marti opened his business at 411 Pine Avenue in 1923 and quickly sought to expand. A January 1924 article in the *Press-Telegram* depicted plans for a new eight-story home by the architect W. Horace Austin. However, Marti eventually retained Meyer and Holler. He may have been influenced by the firm's design of the West Coast Fox Theater that was erected on Ocean Boulevard in 1925 and has since been demolished.

The architecture blends two traditions—Renaissance Revival and Art Deco—bridging historicism with a new modern style. Renaissance Revival characteristics include the rectangular building profile, the balance between verticals and horizontals, and a distinct ground-floor base. The vertical ground pilasters, grouping of windows, and decorative motifs are Art Deco in nature.

Constructed of reinforced concrete, the original building consists of four stories and a typical commercial arrangement. Large display windows line the street level along the busy intersection of Pine Avenue and 4th Street. Continuous fluted piers define the second through fourth story bays. Each bay contains three double-hung sash windows, separated by pilasters. The massive square structure features decorative facades on the east and south elevations, while the west and north elevations consist primarily of flat concrete wall surfaces articulated by irregularly placed windows. A plain frieze, accented by cast-stone panels, wraps the building above the first floor. The panels contain floral and fauna designs. Some have an Egyptian-influenced art motif using the lotus, while others have stylized peacocks and palm trees. This design scheme is also carried out on the parapet crenellations.

Ralf H. Walker purchased the building shortly after it survived the disastrous 1933 earthquake and renamed it accordingly. The structure underwent a major renovation program during a subsequent ownership in the 1960s, resulting in the removal of the parapet. When Walker's, dubbed "The Friendly Store" for its dedication to customer and community service, closed in 1979, it marked the end of an era in downtown.

A group of investors purchased the landmark in 1999 and the architectural firm Interstices transformed it into 39 loft condominiums and seven two-story penthouses. During this process, the original crenelated parapet was re-created, using fiberglass molds and referencing historic photographs. The roof-level penthouses sit back from the cornice of the building, clearly differentiated as new construction, preserving and highlighting the original architecture.

LOCATION
401–423 PINE AVE.
DATE
1929; 2002
ARCHITECT
MEYER AND HOLLER;
INTERSTICES
ADJACENT
KRESS BUILDING (19)
FARMERS & MERCHANTS BANK
AND TOWER (18)
MASONIC TEMPLE (3)

1./ *Exterior view*

1

Gaytonia

41
MAP 1, G10

LOCATION
212 QUINCY AVE.
DATE
1930
ARCHITECT
REGINALD FREEMONT INWOOD
ADJACENT
CASA GRANDE APARTMENT
BUILDING (33)
CAPTAIN PONTO HOUSE (17)
ENGINE COMPANY NO. 8 (37)

1./ *Exterior view, c. 1948*
2./ *Exterior view*
3./ *Entrance*

Positioned on a hilltop in Belmont Heights, the Gaytonia is a beautiful yet eccentric four-story, 27-unit apartment complex. Local contractor George Thomas Gayton spearheaded the Gaytonia project, which catered to Naval officers stationed in Long Beach. Amenities of this fashionable apartment building included maid and valet service as well as a stock of linens and dishes for each unit. Reginald Freemont Inwood, architect of the project, is recognized in the annals of Long Beach architecture as designer of the Belmont Theater.

A medieval revival fantasy, the Gaytonia has a steep roof, turrets, battlements, chimney pots, coats of arms, and a series of arched and square windows with heavily paned glass. Stone quoins on the building's corners, window details, and decorative half-timber patterns are applied to the front facade. The massive front door sits under a pointed arched and is flanked by stained-glass windows.

The interior's decor remains intact and in excellent condition. Much of the original elements in the lobby still exist such as wood-paneled floors and a Batchelder tile fireplace. A series of corbel arches line the hallways.

The Gaytonia neon rooftop sign in Gothic script can be seen from afar, a beacon for this unique complex nestled in its residential neighborhood. The building has been carefully preserved and restored, appearing today just as it did when it first opened.

1

2

3

Long Beach Skating Palace

42
MAP 1, C9
MAP 2, E2

LOCATION
278 ALAMITOS AVE.
DATE
1930
ARCHITECT
UNKNOWN
ADJACENT
EBELL CLUB AND THEATER (23)
THE KOFFEE POT CAFE (43)
VILLA RIVIERA (39)

1./ *Exterior view*
2./ *Exterior view, c. 1970*

The Long Beach Skating Palace played an important part in the city's recreational history. As a roller rink, the building served as a social center for several decades. The subsequent closure reflects the changes in the leisurely activities of Americans and the decline in the economic profitability of such ventures.

Constructed of masonry walls and a concrete facade faced with brick, the two-story structure remains relatively unchanged on the exterior since its early days. The architecture represents a pure example of zigzag Art Deco, with stepped pilasters, chevrons, and geometric ornamentation. The four symmetrically balanced bays of the facade are further subdivided into three parts. Stepped brick piers that rise above the roofline to create pyramidal caps define the two focal bays. Panels decorated in sunburst motifs and topped by stepped parapets are centered over the interior bays.

The most distinctive feature of the building is the roof. It signifies a major engineering innovation used for spanning large spaces. Described as "lamella" in the construction drawings, the ceiling consists of a wooden arched roof uninterrupted by interior supports, pierced by skylights. The arches are composed of a web of diamond-shaped wood supports surmounted by planking and anchored at the base by slender metal tie rods. This method of open-span roof design looks like a precursor of the geodesic dome.

In 2000, the Robert Gumbiner Foundation converted the former roller rink into 19 live-work spaces as part of a large-scale adaptive reuse project. The units were constructed inside the formerly open interior, but views up to the lamella ceiling were retained, and the marquee was replicated.

The adaptive reuse of this building follows the precedent established by Robert Gumbiner, who converted another vacated roller rink (The Hippodrome) a few blocks north at 6th Street and Alamitos Avenue into FHP, a medical-services provider. Subsequently, this building held yet another use when the Robert Gumbiner Foundation founded the Museum of Latin American Art.

1

2

The Koffee Pot Cafe

43
MAP 1, D9
MAP 2, E2

LOCATION
955 E. 4TH ST.
DATE
1932
ARCHITECT
UNKNOWN
ADJACENT
LONG BEACH SKATING PALACE (42)
EBELL CLUB AND THEATER (23)
ROSE TOWERS (36)

1./ *Detail of stained-glass window*
2./ *Detail of signs*
3./ *Exterior view*

The Koffee Pot Cafe is the only remaining example of programmatic architecture in Long Beach. Programmatic buildings were popular in the 1920s and 1930s, when businesses tried to attract passing motorists with whimsical forms and shapes that resembled the product sold inside. This roadside vernacular architecture responded to the rising popularity of the automobile. Because the size and scale of signs were regulated, fantasy architecture offered a novel advertising alternative. This building type has vanished with redirected land uses.

The small octagonal café is wood frame and stucco, with brick piers. A giant octagonal metal coffeepot with a knob of colored mosaic tile surmounts the two-tiered roof. Beside the centrally located door are paired large windows with stained-glass clerestories. Some original elements have been altered. Old photographs indicate that the composition roof had a decorative pattern insert in each roof section. They also show that the separation between the two roof levels consisted of windows; this has since been covered by stucco.

Although the name and ownership changed over the years, the structure continuously operated as a restaurant-café. The structure is currently vacant, awaiting a sensitive restoration.

1

2

3

Municipal Auditorium

44
MAP 1, C10
MAP 2, C3

LOCATION
DEMOLISHED
DATE
1932
ARCHITECT
J. HAROLD MACDOWELL
AND W. HORACE AUSTIN

1./ *Aerial view of auditorium, c. 1940*
2./ *Detail of promenade, c. 1935*

Constructed under a $2.8 million bond issue, the Municipal Auditorium constituted Long Beach's biggest civic endeavor during the Great Depression. It was set on sand fill amid an eight-acre park, surrounded by a 32-acre still-water lagoon that was in turn enclosed by the 3,800-foot Rainbow Pier.

The auditorium rested on a foundation of 1,600 wooden pilings. Concrete piers placed on top of the clustered pilings acted as a foundation for the structural steel frame. The Italian Renaissance-style building loomed nine stories and was faced with blending shades of sandstone. A large Roman arch 35 feet across and 40 feet high marked the front facade. An 18-foot promenade encircled the third-floor level, commanding views of the city, beach, and harbor.

The auditorium contained three principal meeting halls: convention hall, concert hall, and exhibit hall. A 1930s *Press-Telegram* article described its multipurpose function: "It was designed to meet all the requirements of social, educational, religious, industrial and political functions of the city and to act as a magnet to draw in the outside world from the many convention groups." During the Depression years, the space was often offered to conventions for free in an effort to boost the local economy. Over the years, the halls welcomed many famous performers including Liberace, Judy Garland, Elvis Presley, and Bob Hope.

Two gigantic works of art graced the complex. Norwegian-born artist Martin Syvertsen was commissioned to complete a 40-by-77-foot mural for the ceiling of the main concert hall. Entitled *To Music*, the painting represented Orpheus on a cloud entering Elysium in search of his wife Eurydice. Henry Allen Nord originated the concept for the second artwork entitled *Long Beach Recreation*. The cost to the city was prohibitive but, with funds made available by the Work Projects Administration, an $11 billion program initiated by President Franklin Delano Roosevelt that provided public work for the unemployed from 1935 to 1943, the project was revived and redesigned by Albert King and Stanton Macdonald-Wright. The resulting piece is a large mosaic mural consisting of 462,000 brilliantly colored glazed semivitreous tiles set in waterproof cement on a reinforced-concrete wall. The mural depicts the recreational activities of ordinary folk as seen along the shores of Long Beach. The 38-by-22-foot mosaic mural, one of the nation's largest, was installed in the 12-foot-deep recess under the building's exterior arch in 1938.

In the 1975, the auditorium was knocked down to make way for the Pacific Terrace Theater and Convention Center. The mosaic mural was saved from demolition and today stands at the East 3rd Street terminus of the downtown promenade.

1

2

The Skinny House
(Newton P. Rummond House)

45
MAP 1, E9
MAP 2, H2

LOCATION
708 GLADYS AVE.
DATE
1932
ARCHITECT
NEWTON P. RUMMOND
ADJACENT
ART THEATER (20)
GRACE UNITED METHODIST CHURCH (78)
SEASHELL HOUSE (14)

1./ *Exterior view*

The Skinny House is one of the quirkiest structures in Long Beach. The three-story, 860-square-foot building is compressed onto a 10-by-50-foot residential lot, gaining the distinction of the nation's narrowest home in Ripley's Believe-It-Or-Not. Over the years, its fame drew thousands including Walt Disney.

The unusual size lot was created by an oversight in a real-estate transaction. Acquired by Newton P. Rummond in payment for a $100 debt in 1931, it was presumed to be useless. Challenged by friends, Rummond declared he could build a home on the site and set out to prove his case. He enlisted the help of unemployed craftsmen who, due to the ensuing publicity, found other work after finishing the Skinny House.

Designed in an English Tudor revival style, the exterior originally featured half-timbering (it has since been covered with stucco), flower boxes under the windows on the second floor, and a gable dormer on the third floor. The structure occupies every inch of the lot except for an enclosed front yard 18 inches deep from the sidewalk. French doors open directly into the living room and offer a secondary source of light. Despite the narrowness, the space is efficiently divided to permit room sizes comparable to that of a regular house. With no garage and little storage space, the house relies on built-in conveniences for organization, as in a ship. But Rummond spared no cost on the finer details. The house features handcarved and ornamented beams, an Art Nouveau tiled bathroom, a mahogany stairway, wrought-iron sconces, and groove-and-dowel wood floors.

Successive occupants have routinely praised the house as comfortable. One individual, who incidentally ran for president against Ronald Reagan, used the house not only as his residence but also as his law offices.

1

Henry Clock House

LOCATION
4242 PINE AVE.
DATE
1933
ARCHITECT
KIRTLAND CUTTER
ADJACENT
PRAY/DAWSON HOUSE (30)
CRAIG/MCLEOD HOUSE (54)
BIXBY RANCH HOUSE (1)

1./ *Exterior view*

This two-story, Monterey-style house was built for Henry Clock, an attorney and outstanding leader in Long Beach. The residence sprawls over a large triangular-shaped lot in the Virginia Country Club area. Asymmetrical in design, the plan emphasizes horizontality with its low-pitched gables and shallow roof overhangs. A shady loggia marks the front of the house. Mexican character can be seen in the heavy wooden-door entry. However, the double-hung windows with stationary shutters retain American Colonial Revival influences.

The house is characterized by large expanses of plain white stucco and a red-tile roof. This red accent is carried through the brick wall that conceals the garage. The upper story extends beyond the first-floor wall breaking the monotony of the front exterior. The first floor looks onto patios and the second-floor master bedroom opens on two sides to Monterey-style balconies. A generously sized living room projects from the core of the plan to offer views and garner light from its three sides. The original garden scheme, designed by Ralph R. Cornell, is largely intact with many massive pepper trees. The residence and grounds maintain beautiful proportions.

Architect Kirtland Cutter is best known for his body of work in Spokane, Washington. As the city transformed from a frontier settlement to a modern city in the years 1887 to 1923, he developed an eclectic form of architecture that reflected the rich regional and historical influences present at that time. After a long and prolific career in the Northwest, Cutter moved to Long Beach and set up offices in the Farmers & Merchants Bank Tower. From 1923 to his death in 1939 at age 79, he designed numerous residences in the finer neighborhoods of Long Beach, Palos Verdes, San Marino, Balboa Island, and Beverly Hills. Several other Cutter-designed homes exist in the Virginia Country Club vicinity, ranging in styles from Monterey to Colonial to English Cottage.

1

U.S. Post Office and Federal Building

Stately in appearance and size, the U.S. Post Office and Federal Building is one of Long Beach's finest public structures. The local post office began in 1885 as part of a general store, but the city's tremendous growth demanded a larger facility by the 1920s. Conceived during the late 1920s as part of the national expansion of the U.S. Postal Service, the building underwent a series of planning and property negotiations and was not completed until 1934, one year after the deadly 1933 earthquake.

It is a magnificent example of Moderne classicism. Constructed out of granite and terra cotta, the building encompasses seven floors plus a penthouse. Its geometries of scale, proportion, and design present an austere formalism of classical revival influenced by Moderne abstraction. The stepped building shape is traditional in its symmetry and order, with fluted pilasters and decorative marble, concrete, zigzags, and wrought iron. Beautiful large iron lamps sit on the entrance stairs offering a civic welcome. The interior of the building is dignified, as befits a federal structure.

Although newspaper articles during the time note several different design architects, a framed photograph in the post office shows several men in front of the cornerstone that reads: "A. W. Mellon Secretary of the Treasury, James A. Wetmore Acting Supervising Architect, 1932." Another intriguing fact about the authorship appeared in a 1934 *Press-Telegram* article, which stated that the Long Beach Architectural Club, under the direction of president Hugh R. Davies, instituted modifications to the original design.

In 1980, the U.S. Department of the Interiors placed the property on the National Register of Historic Places. The post office is in excellent condition, and its existence memorializes the importance of a burgeoning Long Beach during the 1930s. It is the last remaining public building exemplifying Moderne classicism in the city; all others have been demolished.

47
MAP 1, C9
MAP 2, C2

LOCATION
300 LONG BEACH BLVD.
DATE
1934
ARCHITECT
UNKNOWN
ADJACENT
INSURANCE EXCHANGE BUILDING (24)
LINDEN TOWER (75)
BROADLIND HOTEL (32)

1./ *Exterior view, c. 1930s*
2./ *Exterior view*

1

2

Long Beach Polytechnic High School

48
MAP 1, C8

LOCATION
1600 ATLANTIC AVE.
DATE
1936
ARCHITECT
HUGH R. DAVIES
ADJACENT
HANCOCK MOTORS (34)
OLIVE COURT (98)
MACARTHUR PARK NEIGHBORHOOD
LIBRARY (99)

1./ *Exterior view of auditorium*
2./ *Exterior view, c. 1940*
3./ *Exterior view, c. 1940*

The schools of Long Beach suffered a devastating blow with the 1933 earthquake. At Long Beach Polytechnic High School, nearly all of the buildings were destroyed and reconstruction efforts were estimated at $1 million. The rebuilding plan called for 10 new major structures.

A photograph of the proposed new plan by Hugh R. Davies appeared in an October 1933 *Press-Telegram*. It depicted a two-story building with low, flat roofs and solid bands of windows wrapping each floor. A series of stepped geometric planes that rose above the roofline demarcated a glass entrance, emphasizing verticality.

The actual design differs from the published plan. The buildings lost some of their streamlined elements, adopting a more simplified, rectangular geometry. The predominance of windows gave way to alternating bands of glass and concrete. Davies simplified the entrance and marked it with a didactic message in green copper: "Enter to learn, go forth to serve." The buildings are symmetrically laid out around an open landscaped courtyard. They are interconnected by covered walkways. The school has steel construction and a low center of gravity to mitigate earthquake hazards.

The auditorium, designed by W. Horace Austin, was the only building to withstand the earthquake and thus served as the anchor for future reconstruction. It underwent rehabilitation and design modification by Davies to blend in with the new campus scheme. It is monumental, almost severe, with a dramatic copper crown.

The school displays a wonderful selection of Work Projects Administration artwork. Ivan Bartlett and Jean Swiggett, both alumni of the school, designed the mural in the stairwell of Building 300. Dedicated in 1939, the 18-by-32-foot mural depicts the commercial and recreational activities at the city's harbor. The east face of Building 300 features a painted tile arrangement with the image of Mercury, the fleet messenger of the gods. Finally, cast-concrete relief panels line many of the doorways on the Polytechnic campus.

1

2

3

Cheney/Delaney House

Long Beach has only a few examples of pure Streamline Moderne architecture, and the Cheney/Delaney House is an exceptional representation of this design aesthetic. Constructed in 1937 by an unknown architect, this house stands apart from its more traditional neighbors showing a progressive modernism that heralds the future. Suggestive of a ship in motion, this house reacts to the quaint concept of home.

Consistently executed in a streamline mode with pure curves and linearity, the residence is sleek and clean in appearance. The design emphasizes exterior curving corners, strips of horizontal window bands, a flat roof with a pronounced overhang, and projecting horizontal cornices that curve around the roofline. The windows are steel-sash casement. With a band of wraparound windows and one circular, porthole-like window divided into four parts, the window treatment is a prominent visual feature of the house.

The interiors are largely intact with the original details of moldings and built-in lights.

49
MAP 1, B6

LOCATION
2642 CHESTNUT AVE.
DATE
1937
ARCHITECT
UNKNOWN
ADJACENT
HARNETT HOUSE (11)
PAUL EDWARD TAY OFFICE
AND APARTMENTS (76)
LIVABLE PLACES COMPETITION (95)

1./ Exterior view

Lifeguard Headquarters, Cherry Avenue

50
MAP 1, D10
MAP 2, F4

LOCATION
2100 E. OCEAN BLVD.
DATE
1938
ARCHITECT
CITY ENGINEER, CITY OF LONG BEACH
ADJACENT
LONG BEACH MUSEUM OF ART (9)
BETTER HOME ELECTRICAL (16)
RAYMOND HOUSE (12)

1./ *Exterior view with oil-drilling island in background*
2./ *Exterior view*

Long Beach once boasted the West Coast's best surf, and each summer thousands flocked to the city's seven miles of sandy beaches. In 1908, the city became the first in the state to offer an organized lifeguard service. This service pioneered the operation of power rescue boats, a radio communication system, and the use of dories and paddle boards.

A Work Projects Administration project, the building was first constructed at the foot of Linden Avenue to replace the lifeguard headquarters that a bad storm washed away along with the Pine Avenue Pier. In the early 1960s, the building was moved to its current location at the beach below the intersection of Cherry Avenue and Ocean Boulevard. Many of the city's vintage lifeguard towers have been replaced with new, more portable structures, but the city refurbished the Cherry Avenue station after it received a historic landmark designation in 1981.

The two-and-a-half-story clapboard structure rests on a raised foundation that stores life-saving equipment. The building is rectangular in shape and its low-pitched gable roof supports a hexagonal lookout and clock tower. The east and west facades are distinguished by the shiplike portholes, catwalks, and an entrance ramp that leads to the working quarters. This site continues to serve the community as the main lifeguard headquarters.

1

2

Tichenor Orthopedic Clinic for Children

Based on personal experience, influential civic leader and philanthropist Adelaide A. Tichenor was a firm believer in the treatment of orthopedic problems during childhood. Her dream to help children with chronic orthopedic disabilities, regardless of their ability to pay, was realized with the opening of the Tichenor Orthopedic Clinic for Children in 1926. Since that time, the clinic has helped children affected by polio and infantile paralysis, operated the city's premier bone bank, and developed some of the first metal implants for joint replacement in children.

The facility opened at its current location in 1938. The interior plan included five treatment rooms, two swimming pools in the basement, and playrooms and a gym on the first floor. Designed by Long Beach architect W. Horace Austin, the building reflects the Streamline Moderne style with its flat roof, horizontal bands of windows, and sleek surfaces. The entry, however, nods to Art Deco, with its stepped setbacks and vertical striations. During the 1960s, the front of the building was covered with a metal-grate facade, masking its period characteristics.

In 2000, WDM Contracting, J. H. Leff and Associates, and Huston & Partners began a three-year process to restore the exterior of the existing building to its original architecture and complete a compatible 2,800-square-foot addition for a new program and computer lab. The clinic celebrated the completion of the project in June 2003.

51
MAP 1, F8

LOCATION
1660 TERMINO AVE.
DATE
1938
ARCHITECT
W. HORACE AUSTIN
ADJACENT
COMMUNITY HOSPITAL OF
LONG BEACH (21)
JAVA LANES BOWLING ALLEY (64)
ALEXANDER HOUSE (59)

1./ *View of front entrance*

1

Apartment Building on 1st

52
MAP 1, F10
MAP 2, I4

LOCATION
3511 E. 1ST ST.
DATE
1939
ARCHITECT
UNKNOWN
ADJACENT
CASA GRANDE APARTMENT BUILDING (33)
CAPTAIN PONTO HOUSE (17)
MARINA TOWER MODEL APARTMENT (68)

1./ *Staircase detail*
2./ *Exterior view*

This two-story building is one of the best examples of Streamline Moderne in Long Beach, perfectly intact and outstanding in both scale and design. Typical of this architectural style, it reflects the public fascination with speed and travel in the 1930s, with its nautical motifs and sense of movement. Consisting of five units and totaling more than 6,000 square feet, the structure spreads over a double lot. The elegant design is set far back from the street, leaving a wide expanse of grass and landscape free of structure. The result evokes an ocean liner slicing a pathway through the water.

The five units are unified in a design that resembles a large single-family home. A horizontal composition and abstract, simplified forms characterize the building. Banding above the first and second floors wraps around the structure. Corner windows pull the focus to the edges and further emphasize the horizontality. The asymmetrical facade is stepped back on the west side and is balanced on the east by a semicircular projection. Circular forms are also evident. A curving exterior staircase leads to a rounded bay, with banded windows on the ground floor and an open balcony above. Three porthole windows, one on the first floor and two on the second floor, punctuate the facade and add to the nautical theme. A curved metal handrail attaches to a supporting wall with a circular hole at the entrance to one of the units. Other typical stylistic features include the flat roof, glass blocks, and a front porch marked by slender metal supports with disks.

1

2

Kimpson/Nixon House

53
MAP 1, G9

LOCATION
380 ORLENA
DATE
1940
ARCHITECT
RAPHAEL SORIANO
ADJACENT
SEASHELL HOUSE (14)
VA LONG BEACH HEALTHCARE SYSTEM (57)
CALIFORNIA STATE UNIVERSITY,
LONG BEACH (58)

1./ *Rear view, 1940*
2./ *Front view*
3./ *Side view*

This striking modern house is one of the purest expressions of early modernism in the city. Raphael Soriano began designing this house for Dean and Marion Kimpson during a six-month stay in the hospital after being struck by a speeding car. During construction, he traveled on crutches via the old Red Car line to Long Beach to oversee the project. The bank appraisers were initially reluctant to lend because they were not familiar with progressive architectural styles. It seems that the Kimpsons too were not ready for this drastic adjustment. They only lived in the house a year, at which point Howard and Gladys Nixon purchased the property for $10,000 in cash. Gladys Nixon has lived in this house for over 60 years. In fact, she claims to have made the initial introduction between the Kimpsons and Soriano.

The compact, two-story house is situated on a flat lot overlooking the Colorado Lagoon. A pure example of the International Style, the design consists of rectilinear volumes punctuated by a continuous band of windows. The facade is simple and unadorned, finished in stucco with silver-painted redwood trim. The metal-casement windows that extend across the front culminate in an unassuming entrance. Narrow steel posts support a slender rectilinear canopy over the doorway. The second story is set back and to one side, and the roof cantilevers in the front section. The flat roofs on both floors emphasize the geometric forms of the structure. The floor plan embraces the Southern California indoor-outdoor lifestyle with its interconnected spaces and transparent windows and doors. The living area opens to a spacious backyard concrete terrace protected by a windbreak of sandblasted glass. The second story, with its inset lights, cantilevers over this rear terrace. The second-floor bedrooms sit adjacent to a large roof deck.

Soriano was one of Los Angeles's leading progressive architects. Born in Rhodes, Greece, Soriano moved to Los Angeles in 1924 at the age of 20. After graduating from the University of Southern California, he worked in the offices of Rudolph Schindler and Richard Neutra. He started his own practice in 1935 and participated in the Case Study House program, always advocating new building materials and construction techniques. Like many of his contemporaries, he was interested in novel solutions for middle-class housing in postwar America. Soriano designed 150 buildings in his career of which 38 were built; however, only about a dozen remain standing.

Craig/McLeod House

54
MAP 1, B4

LOCATION
4223 COUNTRY CLUB DR.
DATE
1941
ARCHITECT
ROLAND E. COATE SR.
ADJACENT
PRAY/DAWSON HOUSE (30)
HENRY CLOCK HOUSE (46)
BIXBY RANCH HOUSE (1)

1./ Rear view
2./ Front view

Designed for the shipbuilding industrialist James Craig and his family, the Monterey Colonial Craig/McLeod house grants a position of prominence and authority on the cul-de-sac road off Country Club Drive. Developed 10 years after the older residential estates along this street, the plot, initially owned by the Virginia Country Club, was the first to be sold in the late 1930s. Completed during World War II, a time of material shortages and decreased residential-building expenditures, the house still maximized design and craft.

Craig commissioned Los Angeles-based Roland E. Coate Sr., former partner of the acclaimed architecture firm of Johnson, Kaufmann, and Coate, known for his investigations of Mediterranean-style residential architecture in South Pasadena and Beverly Hills. Coate designed the Craig/McLeod house shortly before he closed his Los Angeles office in 1941 and defined it as modern architecture.

The house, secluded from the formal street entrance, connects to a detached two-story guesthouse over a breezeway. The partite, reminiscent of other Coate residential designs, produces an indoor/outdoor relationship. Simplicity of form, composition, and informal openness exemplifies Coate's later work blending early California architecture with Colonial-style details. Large glazed areas articulate the rear elevation and overlook the golf course, with additional vistas of Los Angeles and the Palos Verdes Peninsula.

The original exterior features are virtually intact. The geometry of shutters and horizontal wood-slat siding accentuate the house plan as it steps and undulates along the site. Distinguishing Coate elements include the entrance porch with slim column supports, bay-window details, and a low pitched-roof angle. Coate, in keeping with his client's profession of sea transport and large vessels, integrated a shipbuilding language throughout the residence. Examples include interior doors with dual cabin locks on both sides, cabin lighting, and a porthole window that once graced the swinging door of the galley kitchen. There is also speculation that the carved woodwork on the living room fireplace and stairway banister was fabricated at the shipyard. The study, one of the most authentic and highly crafted cabinlike rooms in the house, is finished with teakwood, a difficult material to obtain at the time.

The current owners purchased the house from the Craig family in 1997. Kelly Sutherlin McLeod Architecture, Inc., referred to original documents and scrupulously restored the property to Coate's intention and beyond, melding contemporary needs with historic formalities. A typical 1940s service kitchen was renovated for a more family-oriented area. The restoration also included the cultivation and intensive landscaping of 33,000 square feet of grounds resulting in the resurrection of the rose garden and the introduction of a series of winding pathways, a water feature, and dedicated entertainment spaces.

1

2

Long Beach Airport

55
MAP 1, G5

LOCATION
4100 E. DONALD DOUGLAS DR.
DATE
1941
ARCHITECT
W. HORACE AUSTIN AND
KENNETH S. WING
ADJACENT
RUTH BACH NEIGHBORHOOD
LIBRARY (66)
FARMERS & MERCHANTS BANK,
LOS ALTOS BRANCH (94)
COMMUNITY HOSPITAL OF
LONG BEACH (21)

1./ Exterior view
2./ Floor mosaic detail

Long Beach played a prominent role in the early history of aviation. In 1910, only seven years after the Wright brothers' 1903 feat, Long Beach witnessed the flight of the first airplane built in the city. In 1911, Calbraith Henry Rodgers completed the first transcontinental journey from New York to Long Beach. Through the efforts of Earl S. Daugherty, a prominent aviator of his day, the Long Beach municipal airport was founded in 1924, thus becoming the oldest municipal airport in Southern California, preceding Los Angeles International Airport by three years. Because of the presence of the city's airport, Douglas Aircraft Company made a key decision in 1940 to locate in Long Beach.

The present terminal building was constructed from 1940 to 1941. Designed by two of the city's most eminent architects, W. Horace Austin and Kenneth S. Wing, it is one of the most significant public buildings in the city both architecturally and historically. Incorporating elements from the Streamline Moderne style of the 1930s and glimpses of early International Style, the plan consists of a three-story structure with a control tower, curved like an arc to convey a sense of dynamic movement.

All architectural elements—windows, doors, railings—reinforce this idea with a sleek, modern approach. The design also alludes to sea transportation through its sweeping horizontality and stepped elevation, as well as the use of metal ship's railings and round porthole windows, making it particularly relevant to Long Beach's identity as a port and beach town. The most salient feature of the first floor is the concourse that extends the length of the building. The second floor is dedicated to offices, a terraced restaurant and bar, and open decks for viewing the airfield.

The building is equally noted for its synthesis of architecture and the decorative arts. As part of the nation's Work Projects Administration program, Los Angeles-based Grace Clements designed an extensive ceramic-tile mosaic. Originally covering 4,300 square feet of the first and second floors, the decorative artwork interpreted the subject of aviation and sea transportation. Carpets now cover much of the mosaic on the first floor.

1

2

Roosevelt Naval Base, Terminal Island

56
MAP 1, A11

LOCATION
DEMOLISHED
DATE
1941
ARCHITECT
ALLIED ENGINEERS INC., ARCHITECTS
AND ENGINEERS (DONALD R. WARREN,
S. B. BARNES, ADRIAN WILSON, AND
PAUL R. WILLIAMS)

1./ Administration building
2./ Swimming pool
3./ Auditorium/gymnasium

In the late 1930s, President Franklin D. Roosevelt directed millions of New Deal public works dollars toward military construction. Funding from this initiative went toward the 400-plus-acre Naval Operating Roosevelt Base development on Terminal Island, a man-made, dredged landmass in the Long Beach harbor. These buildings provided support for the training and recreational activities of the Pacific Fleet, the country's largest fleet operating base in 1941. While many temporary structures occupied the Navy site during World War II, approximately 27 permanent buildings and adjacent properties made up the core base site.

The original complex of buildings was designed by the collaborative team Allied Engineers Inc., Architects and Engineers, which included engineers Donald R. Warren and S. B. Barnes, and architects Adrian Wilson and Paul R. Williams. The most well-known architect of the collaboration is Williams, a leading African-American architect during the 1920s through 1950s. Williams had a varied practice of residential projects and major commercial developments. The integrity and excellence of the base's design was attributed to Williams's unsurpassed talent as a gifted architect.

Rushed to completion after the Japanese attack on Pearl Harbor, the 60-acre base contained a campus of buildings linked along an axis. The buildings exhibited a formal, spatial, and hierarchical relationship to one another that embodied traditional town-planning principles. The structures, encompassing administration, officers' club, naval legal services, fire station, heating plant, child center, bowling alley, gymnasium, veterinarian office, swimming pool, and arcade made up the permanent compound of the Roosevelt Naval Base campus. Standard foundations could not be used due to the landfill, and a series of cast-in-place concrete piles were emplaced.

Many of the buildings embraced a similar architectural aesthetic with reinforced-concrete construction, flat and low-pitched roofs, steel-ribbon treatments, cantilevered elements, and simplified geometry. The base's look presented clean and strong lines of an International Style architecture, which symbolized the power of a military presence in California. The smooth unadorned surfaces appeared as rectilinear forms chiseled to enhance the architectural uniformity. Landscape was instrumental in integrating the structures into a unified plan, which included courtyards, lawns, rows of palms, and mature trees that traversed the architecture with connecting vistas of roads and pathways.

When the base closed in 1991, the land was turned over to the city and the facilities were slated for demolition. Even though preservation advocates waged a strong battle, the entire site was razed in 1999 to make way for terminal-cargo usage.

1

3

2

173

VA Long Beach Healthcare System (Navy Hospital)

The VA Long Beach Healthcare System serves approximately 40,000 veterans in the Long Beach area and has an operating budget of over $192 million. The compound, located at the intersection of 7th Street and Bellflower Boulevard, contains dozens of structures that were named numerically according to the order in which they were realized.

The original administration building, Building 1, was constructed for the United States Navy in 1943. At this time, the facility operated as a navy hospital. VA Long Beach Healthcare System, the current tenant, moved onto the deactivated site in 1950. In 1958, Building 122, a major surgical ward comprising over 300,000 square feet and containing 558 beds, was erected. Attributed to Welton Becket & Associates, the design featured a series of five wings projecting off a main hall. The repetition of form in these concrete, rectangular units reinforced the institutional nature of this facility and marked it as a model of efficiency and mass treatment. However, this section's configuration ceased to be effective for the changing needs of the hospital due to outmoded technology and outsourcing, and it was demolished in 2004.

Towering over the other structures, Building 126 has dominated the campus since 1967. Placed directly in front of Building 1, the 11-story concrete building was dedicated to accommodating 692 inpatients, making the VA Long Beach facility, at the time, the largest VA system hospital in the country. Designed by Adrian Wilson Associates, the massive cubical form remains an enduring visual reference point. A building campaign ensued throughout the years producing additional structures such as the 170-bed Nursing Home Care Unit in 1975, the Ambulatory Care Building in 1979, and the Spinal Cord Injury Unit in 1988.

The medical center is recognized for its contributions to seismic technology. The main tower was completely retrofitted in 1997 using a technique known as "base isolation." The process involved completely cutting through the building and installing seismic cushions to allow for the structure to withstand major-magnitude earthquakes. During this complex undertaking, the building remained in full operation.

57
MAP 1, H9

LOCATION
5901 E. 7TH ST.
DATE
1943 TO PRESENT
ARCHITECT
VARIOUS ARCHITECTS INCLUDING
WELTON BECKET & ASSOCIATES
AND ADRIAN WILSON ASSOCIATES
ADJACENT
CALIFORNIA STATE UNIVERSITY,
LONG BEACH (58)
PYRAMID, CALIFORNIA STATE
UNIVERSITY, LONG BEACH (89)
MOORE/HAFLEY TWIN HOUSES (62)

1./ Building 122, 1958
2./ Building 126, c. 2000
3./ Aerial view of site, c. 2000

1

2

3

California State University, Long Beach

58
MAP 1, H8

LOCATION
1250 BELLFLOWER BLVD.
DATE
1949; 1962
ARCHITECT
HUGH GIBBS; KILLINGSWORTH,
BRADY & SMITH
ADJACENT
PYRAMID, CALIFORNIA STATE
UNIVERSITY, LONG BEACH (89)
VA LONG BEACH HEALTHCARE
SYSTEM (57)
MOORE/HAFLEY TWIN HOUSES (62)

1./ Aerial view, c. 1955
2./ Exterior view of bookstore,
    c. 1965
3./ Detail of bookstore, c. 1965

Strolling through the grounds of the California State University, Long Beach, campus, one would be surprised to realize that more than 30,000 students attend classes daily. The lush, parklike intermesh of greenery and buildings belies this fact. The campus was purposely developed over half a century to reflect a relaxed suburban setting.

The City of Long Beach bought the land for $1 million in 1949 and contributed it to the state for the development of a college. Originally Long Beach State College, the facilities opened in temporary quarters in a remodeled apartment house during the fall semester of 1951 with an enrollment of 200 students. Prominent Long Beach architect Hugh Gibbs designed the first master plan and permanent buildings in January 1955, accommodating 5,000 full-time students. However, education demands were so great that the plan soon required augmentation.

Edward A. Killingsworth served as master planner and principal design architect since the completion of his seminal 1962 study that set the stage for the transformation of Long Beach State College into a California State University. His design incorporated the best features of the existing campus, established an easily recognized central entrance, excluded automobiles from the academic core, located sites for new facilities or expansion of existing facilities, and inserted parking for what was to become the most populated student university in the system.

Killingsworth's architecture, veiled in greenery, was constructed over decades to create a total building program, rather than one of parts. To that end, buildings of a simple basic design were sought to provide a timeless architecture. Similarities in scale, proportion, massing, and a common vocabulary of materials provide a collegial relationship amongst the edifices. Buildings are thoughtfully sited. An exemplary instance is the location of the student union at the juncture between upper and lower campuses. This social heart of the university is terraced into a steep hillside so that its roof does not block the northern view toward a majestic winter backdrop of snow-covered mountains.

Edward Lovell acted as landscape architect. Forty-five percent of the 324-acre site is given over to landscaping. Eighty species of ornamental plants thrive on campus, while 7,000 trees of 40 different varieties have grown to maturity. Helen Borchers peach trees suffuse the site with a profusion of pink blossoms in springtime. Another landscape highlight is the poignant, secluded Earl Burns Miller Japanese Garden designed for quiet contemplation.

In 1965, the school organized a sculpture symposium, the first such annual international gathering of sculptors to be held in the United States. As an outgrowth of this seminar, nine monumental site-specific sculptures were commissioned from artists such as Andre Bloc and Claire Falkenstein. Each artist personally selected the location for his or her artwork on the campus.

1

3

2

Alexander House

LOCATION
5281 EL ROBLE
DATE
1950
ARCHITECT
JOHN LAUTNER
ADJACENT
MATLOCK HOUSE (61)
MOORE/HAFLEY TWIN HOUSES (62)
CALIFORNIA STATE UNIVERSITY,
LONG BEACH (58)

1./ *Exterior view*
2./ *Roof detail*
3./ *Rear view*

The Alexander House was among the first houses in the exclusive residential tract of Park Estates. In an effort to "preserve the attractiveness" of the property, the Neighborhood Association enforced strict guidelines that were carried out by an architectural board. Although all designs were required to conform to the general feel of the neighborhood, architect John Lautner left his mark.

Lautner applied a practical approach to the design process and engaged the Alexanders in an extensive dialogue about their lifestyle and requirements. He said, "As long as you know how you live, I can build it for you. It's when you don't know that I have problems." Growing up on a ranch in the San Joaquin Valley, Grace Alexander did not want to feel boxed in or restricted. She insisted on an element of openness and stipulated no enclosed halls. She also sought informality and comfort. Lautner always remained wide open to these suggestions, sketching several iterations and building a scale model. Finding a local builder to take a chance on this unconventional plan proved challenging so they finally hired someone who had worked with Lautner on a previous project.

The resulting house is a relaxed composition. From any position in the structure, one is granted views of several outside garden areas. Moored to the site, the footprint of the house follows the contour of the lot including the sunken living room. This square pavilion is set at an angle to the rectangular body. A bedroom wing juts out from the primary mass, originally positioned to frame a backyard pool. Many elements are reminiscent of Frank Lloyd Wright's architecture, including the use of narrow red brick and horizontal wood siding, the flat roof of the Usonian house, and the incorporation of built-ins throughout the interior. Lautner's defining element is the roof plane, which glides from one end of the house to the other, dipping daringly low and enveloping the entire program, even the driveway.

Lautner absorbed much from his training under Wright at Taliesin, but he went on to develop his own architectural language. Creating residences tailored to each individual client, Lautner constantly pushed the conventional boundaries of home design. In many of his projects he mastered the art of engineered architecture by using structure to define form, exploiting the malleable qualities of materials and creating open space through structural expression. Successful architecture is a delicate balance between art and science, and Lautner's Alexander House is a prime example of this fusion. It is the only Lautner work in Long Beach.

1

2

3

George's Fifties Diner

60
MAP 1, C3

LOCATION
4390 ATLANTIC AVE.
DATE
1950
ARCHITECT
WAYNE MCALLISTER
ADJACENT
HENRY CLOCK HOUSE (46)
KILLINGSWORTH, BRADY & SMITH
OFFICE BUILDING (63)
BIXBY RANCH HOUSE (1)

1./ *Exterior view, evening*
2./ *Interior view*

The drive-in is a distinctly American building type that was prevalent from the 1930s through the 1950s and 60s. Synonymous with the consumption of hamburgers and milkshakes, drive-ins attempted to capture the attention of the car-loving generation. Thus, fresh and appealing structures from which to serve populist products emerged along the American roadside. Termed "Googie," this type of architecture implied dynamism with fast-food service and easy automobile access.

Changing land uses and corporate marketing led to the demise of the drive-in. George's Fifties Diner is one of the last surviving examples of this type of commercial architecture that originated and flourished as part of America's infatuation with the automobile.

Built of ordinary materials such as stucco, brick, glass, and tile, the diner has a free-form, curvilinear shape. Located on the corner of two major streets, Atlantic and San Antonio, the restaurant is intended to attract passing motorists with its visually dramatic elements. Large, contiguous plate-glass windows allow passersby to see the brightly lit and colorful interior. The curved, flat roof canopy with a deep overhang appears to float over the structure, emphasizing horizontality and dynamic movement. A prominent rectangular tower anchors the building and marks the entrance.

The building is sited at the center of a large parking lot where customers would park and be served in their cars by waitresses. The restrooms are a separate accessory building fashioned as an abstract geometric cube. Originally built as Grisinger's Drive-In, the building has remained in use as a coffee shop under different names since.

Architect Wayne McAllister was known for his design of hotels and casinos in Las Vegas as well as for roadside architecture in the Los Angeles area. He designed the first Simon's drive-in in Los Angeles in 1935, originating a new type of streamline circular design with central pylon. His 1950s coffee shops are classics of that genre.

1

2

Matlock House

61
MAP 1, H8

LOCATION
1560 RAMILLO AVE.
DATE
1952
ARCHITECT
RICHARD NEUTRA
ADJACENT
ALEXANDER HOUSE (59)
MOORE/HAFLEY TWIN HOUSES (62)
CALIFORNIA STATE UNIVERSITY,
LONG BEACH (58)

1./ *Intersection of indoor and
outdoor space*
2./ *Exterior view*

Nicknamed "pill hill" because of the doctors residing in the elite area, Park Estates was Long Beach's most fashionable community to live in during the 1950s. Looking for land to build, Dr. and Mrs. Richard Matlock located a large site and commissioned Los Angeles-based Austrian émigré Richard Neutra. Inspired by Neutra's 1940 Palos Verdes Beckstrand residence, the Matlocks hired him to design their domestic environment. The Matlock's was the first of three Neutra houses in Long Beach.

The Matlock program and property, rather spacious in comparison to other residences designed by Neutra, occupy a one-acre lot. Constructed of wood frame and stucco, the house consists of eight rooms plus a three-car garage. Absence of walls allows for an open floor plan and built-in birch bookcases become part of the architecture. Pivoting around the intersecting point of the expansive sliding-glass doors and the outside terrazzo terrace, the house gracefully introduces light, air, and a California living style. The tongue-and-groove wood ceiling extends beyond the interior to the exterior utilizing one continuous plane. Enhancing the indoor-outdoor feeling, a band of horizontal windows runs under the eave of the front facade and side portions of the structure. Unlike many of Neutra's other residential projects, this particular example features a pitched roof, as was dictated by the building regulations of Park Estates.

Complementing Neutra's design, local landscape architect Edward Lovell worked to create privacy in the front garden with a variety of planting materials and tall hedges. Adding a mystique to what lies beyond, the front garden has grown to hide the pathway that leads up to the entrance. Under Neutra's direction, Lovell linked together the palm trees, grass, and chameleon flowers in the backyard. Along with a pool and tennis court area, the architecture and landscape meld into one unified plan.

The house, currently owned by a Matlock descendent and family, is in excellent condition.

1

2

Moore/Hafley Twin Houses

62
MAP 1, H8

LOCATION
5551 AND 5561 LA PASADA
DATE
1953
ARCHITECT
RICHARD NEUTRA
ADJACENT
MATLOCK HOUSE (61)
ALEXANDER HOUSE (59)
CALIFORNIA STATE UNIVERSITY,
LONG BEACH (58)

1./ *View into Moore courtyard*
2./ *Exterior view of houses*

Olin Hafley recalled learning about architect Richard Neutra in a high school class in 1934. His teacher quoted from a *TIME* magazine article: "Neutra designed the only homes fit for a man to live in." Many years later in 1951, Olin and Aida Hafley decided to commission Neutra to design a residence in the exclusive tract development of Park Estates.

Almost finished with the plans for the Hafley residence, Neutra proposed to the family that they discuss with the neighboring property owner, Bethuel Moore, the possibility of commissioning him for a similar house. Neutra not only sought a cohesive plan for these twin houses, he also felt that designing two residences instead of one would justify commuting to Long Beach once a week. All agreed on the plan and the two houses were built simultaneously.

The Moore and Hafley plans vary in modest ways but also strike many similarities. Commanding a vertical presence, the Hafley house is slightly larger with a second story over the garage and separate driveway. The Moore house, on the other hand, is more horizontally directed and hovers above the ground plane. Working within the confines of the strict Park Estates building codes, which dictated pitched roofs, Neutra implemented modified, yet modern, roof angles on each house.

Both roofs use cedar-wood shingles with redwood eaves. Another wood element includes loggia-covered walkways that are slightly asymmetrical and lead up to the front doors of the houses. A subtle play of redwood facing on the garages, roof details, and white stucco walls create strong geometric patterns. In each house, rust-colored concrete floors with heating coils flow throughout, and large sliding-glass doors off the living room spaces open to private front patios.

The uniqueness of the twin-house construct is the communal backyard. No fence or gate separates the properties; only rolling grass and planting occupy the landscape of the co-joined sites. Both residences are in good condition, thanks to the current owners' genuine appreciation for their design.

1

2

Killingsworth, Brady & Smith Office Building

63
MAP 1, C4

LOCATION
3833 LONG BEACH BLVD.
DATE
1955
ARCHITECT
KILLINGSWORTH, BRADY
& SMITH
ADJACENT
BIXBY RANCH HOUSE (1)
HOWARD CDM (96)
CAMBRIDGE OFFICE BUILDING (67)

1./ *Reception area*
2./ *Exterior view*
3./ *Steppingstones and
    reflecting pool*

Glimpsed briefly from a busy, commercial boulevard, this one-story architectural office building appears as three garden pavilions set back into lush planting beyond a motor court shrouded by a group of native sycamore trees. In 1955, belying its initial modest appearance, this office building represented the first commercial structure in Long Beach to be built as a pure statement of mid-century modern architecture.

Edward A. Killingsworth illustrates many precepts of this style in the building's design. The roof is flat. The structural frame of post and beam is articulated and left open. The infill within the exposed structural frame is mainly fixed- or sliding-glass panels with occasional solid shear walls expressed as simple, geometric planes. The structure and space revealed compose the primary architectural expression of form. Elegant proportions of glazed or solid planes are spare, crisp, and nearly austere.

Such open pavilion construction allows for a blurring of distinction between indoor and outdoor spaces, an integration of landscape and space. Interior structural beams extend outdoors as cantilevered framing or engaged freestanding columns to complete outdoor, airy pergolas. Over time, the exterior structure came to serve as an armature for lush, hanging, green, and flowing vines.

Rectangular steppingstones gradually ascend through the garden and appear to float on a shallow black reflecting pool abutting an 11-foot-tall entry door. Interior doors and matching overhead panels extend from floor to ceiling. Thus interior walls are also rendered as simple, geometric planes. Continuous strip skylights cause ceilings to hover inches away from solid vertical structures awash in daylight. Interior sliding-glass doors provide access to linear interior shade gardens. In one such garden, the limb of a live California oak tree blithely passes through clerestory glazing and onward to the sky through a rectangular opening in the roof.

The overall impression is of simplicity and harmony created through the use of geometric modules and rectangular forms, all rendered on a decidedly residential scale. The appearance of such a scale is not surprising, as the architect was concurrently designing residences as part of John Entenza's Case Study House program featured in *Arts & Architecture* magazine from 1945 to 1962.

This building has been a continuous "home" to an international architectural practice for nearly half a century under the names of Killingworth, Brady & Associates and the subsequent Killingsworth, Stricker, Lindgren, Wilson and Associates.

1

2

3

Java Lanes Bowling Alley

64
MAP 1, F8

LOCATION
3800 PACIFIC COAST
HIGHWAY
DATE
1958
ARCHITECT
DALY, DEROSA AND POWERS
ADJACENT
COMMUNITY HOSPITAL OF
LONG BEACH (21)
TICHENOR ORTHOPEDIC CLINIC
FOR CHILDREN (51)
ALEXANDER HOUSE (59)

1./ *Exterior view, c. 1960*
2./ *Neon "Bowl" sign*

Known for their designs of bowling alleys, the Long Beach-based architecture firm Daly, DeRosa and Powers created Java Lanes. This bowling alley was the place to be in the 1960s, offering a variety of activities beyond the standard game. Performers such as Frank Sinatra and Zsa Zsa Gabor graced the stage at the cool Java Lounge, and limousines gathered outside the bowling alley many nights a week for chic black-tie events. Featuring a circular cocktail lounge of lush red booths and a sunken fireplace with tropical plants, Java Lanes' interior décor kept with the South Pacific look and feel.

The exterior features a 34-foot exaggerated diagonal A-frame roof that leans beyond the entrance driveway. The exposed wood-roof detail is one of the most dramatic elements of the building's architecture. Underneath the jutting form is a vertical wall of lava rocks, which vary in color and size. The architects patterned the concrete-block pilaster on the front of the building with decorative tiles. In a reverse-channel metal-lettering backlight, the "Java Lanes" sign still flashes today, and a freestanding neon "Bowl" sign pays homage to humor and playfulness with its suspended curving line connecting the floating bowling balls.

Java Lanes boasts that it was one of the first bowling centers to have electronic scoring. It is the oldest bowling alley in Long Beach and the last one of its kind in the city. It is slated for demolition to make way for a housing development as this book goes to press.

Opdahl House

65
MAP 1, H11

LOCATION
5576 VESUVIAN WALK
DATE
1958
ARCHITECT
KILLINGSWORTH, BRADY & SMITH
ADJACENT
FRANK HOUSE, CASE STUDY #25 (73)
NAPLES CANAL HOUSE (88)
PORTOFINO (71)

1./ *Exterior view of house and entry*

How might a young family be housed with adequacy, delight, privacy, and seclusion on a small, narrow lot in a well-established, older residential enclave hemmed in closely by neighbors? The Opdahl House provides a prototypical solution to this dilemma while supporting the maxim that the simplest scheme may yield the most effective and dramatic result.

A 30-by-80-foot lot divides nearly in half, with the two-story residence located to the rear of the property. An entry garden, carport, reflecting pool, and outdoor terrace are situated between 18-foot-tall sidewalls that extend beyond the living room. The front entry is half of the property and appears as an outdoor extension of the living room, giving the illusion of great space. Balcony bedrooms on the upper level overlook the living room and terraced entry.

A two-story front wall of fixed and sliding glass dematerialize the separation between indoors and outdoors. Blessed with southern exposure, the gracious entry experience involves the traversing of textured precast concrete pavers, which progress through a garden arbor, pass over a shallow reflecting pool, and lead to a sliding-glass entry door. Both paving stones and adjacent terrace are of an identical material and appear to float over a dark, reflective moat.

The main floor of the enclosed portion of the residence is a single, large, 23-foot-wide space divided only by a storage wall separating the living room from the dining area. The dining space is furnished with fixed and sliding glass providing a view and access to an enclosed patio. A single, curved steel spine painted red bears open wood treads and follows a minimal steel balustrade to the upper bedroom level. The unimpeded flow of space is abetted by kitchen cabinetry designed to appear as fine furniture hovering above the floor without the standard piping apparatus.

Although the house suffered years of neglect and abuse, it has had a rebirth with the current owner who is restoring it back to its roots.

1

Ruth Bach Neighborhood Library

66
MAP 1, H4

LOCATION
4055 BELLFLOWER BLVD.
DATE
1958
ARCHITECT
LOUIS SHOALL MILLER
ADJACENT
LONG BEACH AIRPORT (55)
FARMERS & MERCHANTS BANK,
LOS ALTOS BRANCH (94)
GEORGE'S FIFTIES DINER (60)

1./ *Elevated circulation desk, 1958*
2./ *Exterior view*
3./ *Exterior view, 1958*

Named for Long Beach's first councilwoman, Ruth Bach, this library was 10th in the city's system and the fourth one built in 1958. During the late 1950s and early 1960s, many of the city's literary facilities assumed a modern aesthetic and advanced systems. The release of Tidelands money helped to support this major building campaign.

Anchoring Heartwell Park and a local children's nursery, Ruth Bach Neighborhood Library was designed by Long Beach-based architect Louis Shoall Miller. Miller was involved with selecting the color scheme, patterning, and landscaping, and worked with local vendors to select the contemporary furnishings. According to the 1957 *Library Journal*, this facility was considered one of the most beautiful in the country at the time of its erection.

At 7,000 square feet with a capacity to hold 35,000 books, the library was large for a neighborhood facility. Planned in a T shape, the building consists of two rectangles with a reading room and service areas. California redwood is used inside and out, and glass, steel, and brick materials mingle to exude a West Coast aura and relaxed learning atmosphere. The front facade is painted sky blue. The roof plane, one of the building's most striking features, extends over the clerestory window, and is poised just above the steel columns that line the rectangular structure.

Furnished by the stylish Long Beach furniture store Frank Bros., the library exemplified a fresh approach to utilitarian architecture and functional design. A special element of the interior library fixtures is the circulation desk. Engineered as three separate interchangeable sections, it is positioned on legs to provide passage of light and air. Landscaping was integral to the library execution, and Miller created internal patios with plants for quiet reflection. Asymmetrical in plan, the outside front palms and grass suggest a play of shapes and voids.

1

2

3

Cambridge Office Building

67
MAP 1, C4

LOCATION
324 E. BIXBY RD.
DATE
1959
ARCHITECT
KILLINGSWORTH, BRADY & SMITH
ADJACENT
HOWARD CDM (96)
KILLINGSWORTH, BRADY & SMITH
OFFICE BUILDING (63)
BIXBY RANCH HOUSE (1)

1./ Courtyard garden

Bathed in sunlight, the indoor and outdoor spaces that compose the Cambridge Office Building are unique. Fifteen crystalline structural bays, delineated by 17-foot-tall, four-inch-square exposed wood columns, are centered within courtyard shade gardens sheltered behind two-story perimeter sidewalls. The exposed roof beams, which engage and support the ivy-covered perimeter walls extend through the offices to create a rhythmic spacing over the small lot.

Nothing constricts a free spatial flow between gardens and work space, as the walls consist only of single panes of quarter-inch, floor-to-ceiling polished plate glass framed directly into each structural bay. The flat roof appears as a minimal three-inch-thick membrane lightly pinned to the columns. Wood columns are sporadically replaced with structural steel tubes, which are utilized as downspouts. Square-headed, exposed-steel bolts at the intersection of columns and beams are carefully spaced as decorative adornments with all clustered bolts aligned to one another and the rectilinear geometry.

Daylight, both direct and reflected off the garden walls, creates ideal conditions for ambient task lighting. Occasional striations of shadow, which enliven the walls, subtly change the quality of light as the sun arcs across the sky. This effect mimics the beautiful and mysterious conditions often encountered in a Middle Eastern souk.

Entry to the garden environs is choreographed through the western-oriented courtyard as a series of precast steppingstones rising through greenery and floating over a shallow reflecting pool. The same steppingstones are transformed into airy treads that provide mezzanine access over a delicate, minimal steel stairway armature.

The crisp, pure geometry of design; the interweaving of interior and exterior space; flat roof; and the use of industrial materials such as steel support and glass walls are all hallmarks of the midcentury International Style, as filtered through the sensibilities of architect Edward A. Killingsworth. The look is softened and humanized through a subtle balance of residential proportions, delicate and graceful forms, clarity of spatial articulation, tall soaring spaces, and the integration of landscaping, water, and architecture.

The richness of this humane garden-style office was recognized in 1961 when an international jury at the Sao Paulo Design Biennial proclaimed the Cambridge Office Building the "top-designed new commercial structure in the world."

1

Marina Tower Model Apartment

68
MAP 1, E10
MAP 2, H4

LOCATION
3051 E. OCEAN BLVD.
DATE
1959
ARCHITECT
KILLINGSWORTH, BRADY & SMITH
ADJACENT
GALAXY TOWER (77)
RAYMOND HOUSE (12)
APARTMENT BUILDING ON 1ST (52)

1./ *Exterior view*
2./ *Image of Edward A. Killingsworth and woman with scale model*
3./ *Rendering of Marina Tower*

The Marina Tower cooperative development was a venture of MKM Projects Inc., which comprised three companies: building contractors Millie and Severson Inc.; the architectural firm of Killingsworth, Brady & Smith; and Moore Realty. With vacant land disappearing, the group felt that vertically divided space offered an obvious solution for modern living.

Situated across from the ocean bluff at 3065 E. Ocean Boulevard, the $3 million speculative project combined luxury and convenience in a unique seaside setting. The design for the 12-story, 150,000-square-foot steel-and-concrete building placed four apartments on each of the upper floors, with panoramic views of the harbor and coastline. Each unit ranged in size from 2,300 to 3,100 square feet and featured two large bedrooms, a convertible den, and two baths. Wide walls of glass separated the living room from a large outdoor terrace. The ample use of glass (33,000 square feet) and carefully thought out proportions invoked an atmosphere of lightness and carefree serenity, perfectly encapsulating the casualness and informality of a beachside environment. Amenities were to include an outdoor terrace and pool and the Marina Sky Terrace, a rooftop lounge area designated for the exclusive use of guests.

The developers began marketing the units in 1958. Priced from $57,000 to $76,000, the initial sales were weak. Feedback from prospective buyers indicated that the apartments were too large and too costly. Thus, the Marina Tower was redesigned in the early part of 1959 to incorporate a wider range of units, from penthouses to smaller, one-bedroom floor plans. The amended prices ranged from $29,500 to $82,000.

As part of the marketing campaign, a 3,000-square-foot prototype furnished by Frank Bros. opened in the summer of 1959 on the adjacent site. Within just over a month, the sales office registered more than 1,000 interested parties. The model and redesign were well received, but the developers sensed a resistance to Long Beach from out-of-town prospects. Many potential buyers also felt that the projected annual operating costs were too high. At the same time, an abundance of units at various prices saturated the own-your-own market. The developers abandoned the project in the fall of 1959 when presale goals were not met. Although they hoped to reactivate the project on another site, the plans were never realized. The model home at 3051 E. Ocean Boulevard is now a private residence, and the bluff area was subsequently protected from high-rise developments.

1

2

3

Long Beach Elks Lodge No. 888

69
MAP 1, F6

LOCATION
DEMOLISHED
DATE
1960
ARCHITECT
FRANCIS J. HEUSEL

1./ *Exterior view, c. 1960*

Long Beach Elks Lodge No. 888, in search of a new site for its growing constituency, purchased over 11 acres of land on Willow Street from the City of Long Beach for $55,000. The lodge hired architect Francis J. Heusel, known for his civic collaborations and library projects in Long Beach, to design a landmark home with all the modern conveniences. Central to Heusel's plan was a large white dome, 150 feet in diameter and constructed of reinforced concrete. The four-inch-thick shell of concrete was supported by a three-foot-10-inch tension ring at the second-floor flat slab; concrete columns in turn supported the slab.

The 476-foot circumference of the dome structure was partially encircled by a reflecting pool, which had to be traversed by one of two bridges for access to the lodge. Water from over 400 other Elks lodges around the country helped fill the pool in a symbolic gesture of brotherhood. The spacious interior unfolded in brilliant hues of emerald green, marine blue, pure white, and gold furnishings, flooring, and walls, and featured rock gardens and open-air lanais. The 190-foot bar overlooked a patio and Olympic-sized pool through sheer white drapes. The oval Lodge Hall served as the centerpiece with ideal acoustics, a domed ceiling, and seating for 1,100.

The Elks organization originated in 1868 and the Long Beach chapter was instituted in 1904. Since 1914, the group occupied a downtown building at 19 Cedar Avenue. The Elks broke ground for this new facility in 1959 and many members donated time and services to ensure a formal opening in August 1960. The Long Beach Elks Lodge No. 888 was the organization's biggest facility in the United States, serving the largest constituency of members (over 9,000 at its peak). As the years took their toll on the building and membership diminished, the lodge proved too expensive to operate. The Elks Lodge moved in 1992 and the structure was later demolished to make way for a new development.

1

Long Beach Public Safety Building and Long Beach County Building

70
MAP 1, B10
MAP 2, B3

LOCATION
400 W. BROADWAY
AND 415 W. OCEAN BLVD.
DATE
1960; 1960
ARCHITECT
FRANCIS J. HEUSEL IN COLLABORATION
WITH KILLINGSWORTH, BRADY & SMITH;
KENNETH S. WING AND FRANCIS J.
HEUSEL, ARCHITECTS ASSOCIATED
ADJACENT
LONG BEACH CITY HALL
AND PUBLIC LIBRARY (82)
CALIFORNIA VETERANS MEMORIAL
STATE OFFICE BUILDING (86)
FIRST CONGREGATIONAL CHURCH (10)

1./ Exterior view of county building
2./ Exterior view of public safety building

Similar in size, scale, and materiality, the Long Beach Public Safety Building and Long Beach County Building nonetheless house distinct functions. Designed and realized within one year of each other, the buildings served the purpose of centralizing the major bodies of power in the city. The structures present an aura of strength through their austere and imposing design but also reflect a streamlined, modern approach to the consolidation of civic activities through their sleek and orderly appearance.

The public safety building was the first of the two buildings to be opened. It serves as the emergency center for the entire Long Beach area. Designed to hold the fire and police departments, city prosecutor, and public defender, it has six floors of office space above ground, two levels of basement, and a two-story equipment penthouse on the roof. Rectangular in plan, the building is attached perpendicularly to a two-story appendage structure. Curtain walls make up the north and south facades and divide into two parts on every floor, with the upper part consisting of fixed glass and the lower part of colored porcelain-enameled steel panels. The building is currently undergoing a structural-mitigation process to strengthen the facility and significantly reduce the chances of structural failure in the case of a major seismic event. As part of this retrofit, the exterior has taken on a slightly different appearance with dark, reflective glass replacing the earlier geometric configuration.

The county building evolved within months of the public safety building and was designed to hold the municipal courts, superior courts, assessor civil service, coroner, county clerk, and other departments. Similar to the public safety building in architectural language, the structure is one large rectangular block of varying heights, with six floors on the bay side and 10 floors on the north side. Constructed of reinforced concrete slabs and concrete shear walls, it forms a rigid frame for protection against vibration and earth shocks. Curtain walls, consisting of the same colored porcelain-enameled panels set in aluminum frames, define the facades, while the solid end walls are of precast concrete inlaid with a quartz aggregate. The interior layout established separate traffic patterns for the public, judges and juries, and prisoners, the latter of which were at one time brought to the courts from the public safety building through a connecting tunnel.

1

2

Portofino (Toledo Tower)

71
MAP 1, H11

LOCATION
5400 THE TOLEDO
DATE
1961
ARCHITECT
HUGH GIBBS & DONALD GIBBS
ARCHITECTS
ADJACENT
ENGINE COMPANY NO. 8 (37)
OPDAHL HOUSE (65)
NAPLES CANAL HOUSE (88)

1./ Poolside

Striking a pose overlooking the bay front in Naples, the Portofino is a massive unit for modern living. Developer and businessman Barry Taper spearheaded the project. Entrepreneurial in his vision for the development of land parcels that he owned in Naples, Taper had plans for a housing unit and grand hotel project nearby. He opted to pursue the tower project and commissioned Hugh Gibbs & Donald Gibbs Architects in 1961 to realize this sleek residential block.

The Portofino, looking like a slim cruise liner, is one broad rectangular stroke of floor-to-ceiling glass with a series of viewpoints out to the Alamitos Bay and Pacific Ocean. Scaled only to itself, the multiunit complex carries a larger-than-life presence in the unassuming residential neighborhood. A pool straddles the communal ground-floor deck. The tower includes 60 units (30 on each side) and two penthouses that extend the full length of the building. Once a swampland, the surrounding waters were dredged to make way for the complex's three-foot-thick raft foundation that was constructed to float in position. The interior program centers around a long corridor that slices the building down the middle. Boat slips for occupants are perpendicularly situated alongside the structure.

Marking a gateway to multiple bodies of water, the tower lights up at night and reflects off the liquid blue below.

1

Duffield Lincoln-Mercury Agency

72
MAP 1, G7

LOCATION
DEMOLISHED
DATE
1963
ARCHITECT
KILLINGSWORTH, BRADY & SMITH

1./ Exterior view

No building in Long Beach set so lightly upon the ground as the showroom of the Duffield Lincoln-Mercury Agency. It consisted of a wafer-thin, flat roof plane suspended from 21-foot-long, four-inch-square steel columns. The only definition between exterior and interior display space beneath the pavilion roof was a taut, recessed, clear plate-glass scrim within minimal metal framing. Flooded with sunshine, the varied paint hues, chrome detailing, and glass of the automobiles displayed were shown to their best day-lit advantage within the simple, elegantly proportioned structural frame.

The architectural community acclaimed the classic modernism of this exquisite "display case" and considered it one of the finest works of architecture created within Southern California during the postwar years.

Lamentably, the pavilion and its attendant auto-parts and service wing were razed in the 1980s when ownership of the property transferred to another dealership.

1

Frank House, Case Study #25

A heightened sense of arrival and anticipation at entering a residential domain has seldom been expressed as artfully as at the Frank House, a bachelor pad designed for Edward Frank, co-owner of Frank Bros. furniture store. Situated on Rivo Alto Canal in the Naples section of Long Beach, this two-story structure presents its canal face as the primary entrance. All that can be seen in the front elevation are two elegantly proportioned vertical walls flanking a narrow doorway slot and a partial glimpse of living spaces through a dense leafing of tree branches.

Ascending steppingstones that rise through a garden and cross a reflecting pool, guests are deposited onto a floating platform facing a single, 17-foot-high entrance. This grand gesture of a door was engineered in aluminum by the Northrop Aircraft Company.

Access continues on floating steppingstones and a moated terrace inside a two-story, outdoor garden room. This courtyard space is enclosed on two sides by solid walls and on two sides by the rooms of the house. The "roof" consists only of beams supporting wood two-by-threes spaced one and a half inches apart, all open to the sky. A sculpture, *Jericho* by Bernard Rosenthal, backed by yet another artfully proportioned solid vertical wall, was originally placed on an axis opposite the entry door to terminate the carefully orchestrated sequence of arrival.

Most of the interior rooms overlook the courtyard through all-glass walls. The floor-to-ceiling, fixed and sliding glass is framed directly into four-by-four wood post and wall framing, blurring the distinction between indoors and outdoors. Water and glass reflections, together with the constant daylong shifting patterns of striated lath shadows on walls and floors, further diminish the demarcation between interior and exterior space.

The living room has a commanding view of the canal and the courtyard that it borders, thus providing the illusion of a 31-foot-wide room. The master bedroom, directly above the living room, overlooks the canal through foliage, giving its occupants the impression of residing in a treehouse.

Opulent, dramatic yet relaxed, the simple elegance of this residence was the brainchild of Killingsworth, Brady & Smith. This distinguished and singular design for California living was built under the aegis of the Case Study House program.

73
MAP 1, H11

LOCATION
82 RIVO ALTO CANAL
DATE
1963
ARCHITECT
KILLINGSWORTH, BRADY & SMITH
ADJACENT
OPDAHL HOUSE (65)
PENN/CROWELL HOUSE (81)
NAPLES CANAL HOUSE (88)

1./ *Aluminum 17-foot-high entrance door*

1

Hugh Gibbs & Donald Gibbs Architects Office Building

74
MAP 1, C5

LOCATION
3575 LONG BEACH BLVD.
DATE
1963
ARCHITECT
HUGH GIBBS & DONALD GIBBS
ARCHITECTS
ADJACENT
HOWARD CDM (96)
CAMBRIDGE OFFICE BUILDING (67)
PAUL EDWARD TAY OFFICE
AND APARTMENTS (76)

1./ *Exterior view, 1963*
2./ *Entrance pathway*

Hugh Gibbs founded his architectural firm in 1934, and Donald Gibbs joined his father's practice in 1960. At the time, the company was located at 441 1st Street in an old speakeasy. When they decided to move, the father-and-son team purchased a series of adjacent lots on Long Beach Boulevard because of their proximity to the elder Gibbs's house, freeway access, and the Virginia Country Club. Hugh Gibbs wanted to build a four-story structure, where the firm would use one floor and rent out the rest. However, Donald Gibbs was granted carte blanche in the design. Wanting to change the direction of the firm, he executed a building that he felt represented this new image.

Inspired by Mies van der Rohe's rational Farnsworth House, the structure extends over a concrete foundation, appearing to hover effortlessly above the earth. Constructed of a steel and wood frame and floor-to-ceiling, darkened-glass walls, the one-story building presents a simple, geometric design with a flat roof and an unadorned surface. The entrance is accessed on the side of the building, maintaining the symmetry of the straightforward design. A series of concrete squares line a path from the sidewalk to a larger landing, off which a platform leads to the door. The 6,500-square-foot interior consists of an open floor plan with one large, unobstructed room and nine-and-a-half-foot ceilings. The elegant simplicity of the structure rests gently on the site, allowing a peaceful coexistence with the lush landscaping.

1

2

Linden Tower

75
MAP 1, C9
MAP 2, D3

LOCATION
250 LINDEN AVE.
DATE
1964
ARCHITECT
JOE W. PASSERO AND VERNON WELBORN
ADJACENT
LAFAYETTE COMPLEX (35)
BROADLIND HOTEL (32)
U.S. POST OFFICE AND FEDERAL
BUILDING (47)

1./ Exterior view
2./ Curvilinear concrete awning
3./ Staircase detail

Advertised as condominium apartments "loaded with luxury items," the Linden Tower opened in 1964 as the first major full-condominium project in Long Beach. Located two blocks from the beach and close to downtown, the building reflects a relaxed, urban 1960s lifestyle. Designed by lesser-known figures in the architecture community, Joe W. Passero and Vernon Welborn, the project was commissioned by Russell Mangum Company, Realtors and Developers. The complex featured one- and two-bedroom units priced between $13,000 and $18,500.

The 25-unit building spoke volumes to a style of modern living that factored in light and air, play and work. Outfitted with many grand items, the units included tiled kitchens with all the amenities, plastic snack bars, tiled baths, wall-to-wall carpeting, and custom drapes. The cool design aesthetic of the exterior puts forward a concrete patterned wall, a steel stairwell visible through panes of glass, and a geometric configuration of light-turquoise panels, glass, and concrete that march up the four-story building. A fantastic curvilinear concrete awning in the same shade protrudes over the front entrance. A wall of small subway tiles in brown and beige tones sneaks under the dynamic awning structure.

Even though the building is worn from lack of proper attention, its fabulous coat still shows off an architecture that is fresh and new.

1

2

3

Paul Edward Tay Office and Apartments

76
MAP 1, C5

LOCATION
3365 CREST DR.
DATE
1964
ARCHITECT
PAUL EDWARD TAY
ADJACENT
HUGH GIBBS & DONALD GIBBS
ARCHITECTS OFFICE BUILDING (74)
HOWARD CDM (96)
CAMBRIDGE OFFICE BUILDING (67)

1./ *Exterior view of triplex*

Located across from the San Diego Freeway onramp, the A-framed triplex that once housed Paul Edward Tay's architectural firm looks both incongruous and strangely appropriate. Perhaps this is due to the fact that Tay expertly reconciled the constant buzz of cars with his quest for a woodsy environment. The inherent limitations of noise and a sloping hillside lot would have driven most away. To complicate matters, Tay also had to conform to the R-zoning restrictions, which required the inclusion of residential quarters on the site. So he and his wife Ruth lived on the premises for a few years in one unit and occupied the other two units with their respective offices.

The triplex is situated on the lower part of the sloped lot, so that only the three separate peaked roofs are visible from the street. Steps drop off the driveway to the first-level approach of the units, whose cool and verdant gardens offer a respite from the frantic activities just yards away. Inside, the ceilings soar to 15 feet at the peak. Skylights and full glass walls flood the living areas with sunshine. The open floor plans of the interior spaces contribute to the sense of freedom and movement. The use of built-ins in the kitchens and living areas offers unobstructed views of adjoining rooms, and elements such as floated or cantilevered fireplaces foster a continuity of space. Exterior walls extend to four feet beyond the interiors, serving as windbreaks for the decks.

The landscaping, executed by Edward Lovell and maintained by Tay's mother, is integral to the plan. Eucalyptus trees rise above the roofs, sheltering the structure, and lush plantings create a sense of privacy and escape. The interior design with many levels also encourages plants to weave and grow throughout the spaces to create a unified whole with the outdoors.

Tay studied architecture at the University of Southern California and went on to design many residences in Long Beach and Lakewood during the 1950s and 1960s. In several instances, he broke from the box concept and experimented with hexagonal modules that he so admired in the work of Frank Lloyd Wright. As with the triplex, his process always involved an acute assessment of the site and the clients' needs.

1

Galaxy Tower

Standing as the tallest building on Ocean Boulevard in Bluff Park, the Galaxy Tower sits back on the scenic street and overlooks the city and surrounding elegant neighborhood. Developed by Lloyd Whaley, visionary of Park Estates, the Galaxy was unlike any other residential project in Long Beach. Hugh Gibbs & Donald Gibbs Architects designed the 20-story condominium complex and modeled it to promote high-rise urban living for an ever-growing population.

Set at an angle on the curvature of the shoreline, the Galaxy's cruciform plan produces four separate towers connected by a circular well that forms a garden and landscaped atrium court. A total of 80 dwelling units, 20 in each tower, rhythmically march up the building. Only four apartments occupy each floor, making the Galaxy a deluxe and intimate space for living. The units extend from the building's central core and incorporate three exposures, providing maximum views of the coastline. No unit shares a common wall.

Marketed as fine living at the time of its opening, the Galaxy featured the newest type of communication service with a security door intercom, a porte-cochere canopy off the building's entrance door, and two high-speed elevators for access to all levels including the subterranean garages. The striking metallic-blue color of the exterior is baked-on prefabricated glass-weld panels set into aluminum frames. This material, which does not require painting, was used to keep maintenance costs low and show the efficiency of city living.

During the early 1960s the city had rezoned the bluff area to encourage high-rise developments. The Galaxy was the only manifestation of this permissive zoning. Blocking the views, the Galaxy was an anomaly in this residential neighborhood. With the controversy that brewed over building at this height, the Ocean Boulevard thoroughfare returned to its original zoning to accommodate its much more docile low-rise luxury mansions and grand private properties. This act, along with the securing of historic district status in 1982, protected the fabric of the neighborhood from further tall developments.

77
MAP 1, E10
MAP 2, H4

LOCATION
2999 E. OCEAN BLVD.
DATE
1966
ARCHITECT
HUGH GIBBS & DONALD GIBBS
ARCHITECTS
ADJACENT
MARINA TOWER MODEL APARTMENT (68)
RAYMOND HOUSE (12)
LONG BEACH MUSEUM OF ART (9)

1./ Aerial view
2./ Exterior view across Bluff Park

1

2

Grace United Methodist Church

78
MAP 1, E10
MAP 2, G3

LOCATION
2325 E. 3RD ST.
DATE
1966
ARCHITECT
PALMER W. POWER
ADJACENT
ART THEATER (20)
ROSE TOWERS (36)
LONG BEACH MUSEUM OF ART (9)

1./ *Exterior view*
2./ *Hexagonal dome ceiling and skylight*
3./ *Colored-glass windows and pendant lighting*

Unusual in its circular shape, Grace United Methodist Church sits prominently at the intersection of 3rd Street and Junipero Avenue. The church has had a meaningful existence on this site. The first chapel was built in 1906, and in 1913 a large, wooden sanctuary was added to the structure. In 1964, both buildings burned to the ground in an arson fire.

Palmer W. Power rebuilt the church in 1966. Power, an extremely prolific Long Beach architect in the 1950s and 1960s, was responsible for the designs and alterations of many religious and public structures in the city. Breaking away from historic church design, Power took advantage of the curved site and presented a contemporary plan. A semicircular colonnade of high arches with minimal ornamentation encases the circular structure of the sanctuary and acts as an intermediate space. A large mosaic, consisting of 175,000 tesserae, individually cut from glass and rock, adorns the front. Inside the sanctuary, a shallow hexagonal dome and skylight top the two-story space. Filtering in natural light, the skylight and an array of 136 vertically oriented colored-glass windows create an intimate and spiritual space. Pendant lighting in a 1960s mode line the space and float under the flood of brilliant light.

International Tower

79
MAP 1, C10
MAP 2, D3

LOCATION
660 E. OCEAN BLVD.
DATE
1966
ARCHITECT
CARL B. TROEDSSON AND
CHARLES BOLDON
ADJACENT
VILLA RIVIERA (39)
ADELAIDE A. TICHENOR HOUSE (4)
COOPER ARMS (22)

1./ *Exterior view*

Situated across the street from the Villa Riviera, the International Tower provides a striking contrast to the city's more traditional architecture. In fact, another old vestige of the beachfront, the El Mirador Hotel, was cleared to make way for its erection. The shape of the 32-story circular structure drew a great deal of attention while under construction. A July 1964 article in the *Press-Telegram* predicted it would be "one of the most unusual structures ever erected here." More recently, it has been referred to by locals as the "beer can."

The International Tower claimed to be the tallest prestressed-concrete structure in the world. An intricate web of steel formed the 130-foot diameter foundation and, in total, more than 1,000 tons of reinforcing bars were used to strengthen the foundation mat, floor slabs, and inner- and outer-core walls. It was built by the slip-form method, in which wooden forms were airlifted to position and the concrete was poured. Operating 24 hours a day, the process allowed the tower to rise about one foot an hour and form completely in two weeks.

The initial plans called for commercial space on the bottom floors and 204 residential units composing 25 floors of eight apartments plus one floor containing four penthouses. The exterior consists of a glass-curtain wall, recessed to form continuous balconies, with unobstructed views in every direction. Shortly after the grand opening, owner Henry Sassoon considered converting the tower into an apartment hotel because of lack of tenants. He also proposed a revolving restaurant atop the building. Neither was realized. In the mid-1980s, the International Tower was sold and approved for condominium status.

1

Oil Drilling Islands

80
MAP 1, E11
MAP 2, E4

LOCATION
OFFSHORE
DATE
1966
ARCHITECT
LINESCH & REYNOLDS
ADJACENT
LIFEGUARD HEADQUARTERS,
CHERRY AVENUE (50)
LONG BEACH MUSEUM OF ART (9)
GALAXY TOWER (77)

1./ *View of White Island from Bluff Park*
2.–4./ *Images at sunset*

Four offshore oil-drilling islands were constructed from 1965 to 1966 to tap into one of the nation's largest oil reserves, the East Wilmington Field, lying under some 6,500 acres of Long Beach. Each man-made island has a rock perimeter containing approximately 160,000 tons of granite rock barged from Santa Catalina Island, and a dredged-sand-filled interior core. Three islands are 10 acres each and one island is 8.8 acres.

The San Francisco-based landscape architecture firm of Linesch & Reynolds was commissioned by Texaco, Humble, Union, Mobil, and Shell (THUMS) to beautify the islands. The challenge was described in a 1967 *TIME* magazine article as "how to preserve the innocent charm of the beach front and at the same time exploit what lies immediately below the city and its bay: an estimated billion barrels of crude oil." Though the islands altered the coastline, they were praised for their outstanding engineering achievements and "successful" compatibility between industry and aesthetics.

The execution of the site plan, which included trees, shrubs, camouflaged and soundproofed derricks, and sculptural forms, averaged more than $1 million per island. The appearance of the closest island, only 800 feet from the recreational beach, caused the most concern because it could be looked down upon from the bluff's high-rise apartments. In an effort to safeguard against unsightliness to the surrounding area's natural beauty, this island is the most extensively decorated.

The design is characterized by strong colors and artistic concrete forms. Each drilling tower is mounted on a track for easy mobility around the perimeter, moving with the full grown trees and shrubs as it advances around the island from one drilling site to another. The 180-foot drilling rigs are encased in colorful terra-cotta and steel shells and ringed with balconies to mirror the urban feel of condominiums along the coastline. Sculptural panels made of thin-shell gunite concrete screen views of industrial activity. The forms consist of various shapes—finlike, cylindrical, conoidal—and range up to 80 feet in height. They are anchored to a four-foot-thick concrete slab with aid of special cables to withstand hurricane force winds. Some of them provide a frame for waterfalls that plunge 45 feet to the ocean. Hundreds of fully grown palms and shrubs were barged to the islands and transplanted, with the tallest trees towering 60 feet in height. The island forms are particularly prominent at night when illuminated with multicolored lights.

The islands became known as the Astronaut Islands—Grissom, White, Chaffee, and Freeman—named after four astronauts who lost their lives in the nation's space program. Early in the islands' existence, it was reported that once oil operations cease (estimated by 2015), the city plans to convert them into offshore recreation centers, maybe even with an aerial tramway connecting the islands to the mainland.

1

2

3

4

Penn/Crowell House

81
MAP 1, H11

LOCATION
218 RIVO ALTO CANAL
DATE
1976
ARCHITECT
RAY KAPPE
ADJACENT
NAPLES CANAL HOUSE (88)
FRANK HOUSE, CASE STUDY #25 (73)
OPDAHL HOUSE (65)

1./ *Exterior of front with glass boxes*
2./ *Exterior detail*
3./ *Alley/garage entrance*

Limited by the footprint of a narrow 30-by-80-square-foot lot in the waterfront community of Naples, the Penn/Crowell House is a showcase of innovative design and energy efficiency. The residence, sited at a 90-degree angle, forms a point in the front, commanding unparalleled views of Alamitos Bay.

Though the house has three levels and a roof terrace, it qualifies as a two-story dwelling with a height of 40 feet. The vertically exaggerated, wood and glass tower is punctuated by specially designed solar projections. These geometric shapes lend to the structure's dynamic form and the interlocking planes yield five roofs (all flat), eight wooden decks, and two rooftop observation levels. The interior floor plan consists of a series of intersecting cubes. Though the rooms are intimate in scale, a sense of openness and flow exist between linked spaces. A prominent staircase weaves through the warm yet rough redwood surfaces of the interior, imparting a further sculptural dimension and sense of motion. Architect Ray Kappe employs the use of glass to make rooms seem more voluminous and produce a rich range of natural lighting. Despite the limitations of the lot, landscaping is a key element. Soaring eucalyptus trees reduce the contrast of house with its neighbors and frame the view to the water.

For every square foot of floor, there is 0.77 of glass. Nonetheless, the house maintains a comfortable temperature and is not air-conditioned. The sun warms the house quickly on clear or even slightly overcast days and heat is gradually lost at night through the glass. Kappe specified tinted glass to minimize glare and heat gain, with louvered blinds installed inside the glass for added control. Beneath the balconies off the third-story bedrooms, he hung glass boxes that shield the second-story windows from wind. The boxes are open at the bottom to prevent buildup of heat. Kappe placed three-story-tall shafts in the corners of the living room to provide air circulation throughout the house.

Kappe founded the Los Angeles architecture school SCI-Arc in 1972 and served as its director until 1985. He is known for his residential work in Rustic Canyon, Santa Monica, which combines nature with contemporary California modernism.

Long Beach City Hall and Public Library

LOCATION
333 W. OCEAN BLVD. AND 101 PACIFIC AVE.
DATE
1977
ARCHITECT
ALLIED ARCHITECTS (HUGH GIBBS
& DONALD GIBBS ARCHITECTS;
FRANK HOMOLKA AND ASSOCIATES;
KILLINGSWORTH, BRADY & ASSOCIATES;
AND KENNETH S. WING AND ASSOCIATES)
ADJACENT
LONG BEACH PUBLIC SAFETY BUILDING
AND LONG BEACH COUNTY BUILDING (70)
CALIFORNIA VETERANS MEMORIAL
STATE OFFICE BUILDING (86)
FIRST CONGREGATIONAL CHURCH (10)

1./ Bird's-eye view
2./ Clocktower
3./ Elevation rendering
4./ Aerial view of rooftop garden

The history of Long Beach's city halls involved rapid urban growth and changing architectural styles over the course of more than a century. The original two-story Greek Revival hall was located at Broadway and Pacific avenues. Occupied from 1899 to 1923, it resembled a large residence with a simple rectangular plan. By 1923, spatial requirements for the rapidly growing city departments necessitated the construction of a new facility. The architect, W. Horace Austin, described his seven-story composition as Renaissance Revival, but the towers at each corner of the rectangular plan so strongly resembled minarets that they gave the building a decidedly Moorish appearance. The disastrous 1933 earthquake toppled the city hall towers and caused the collapse of the red terra-cotta roof. As the hall's primary structure did not suffer major damage, city fathers decided to install new facades to the existing building. The architect, Cecil Schilling, provided a Streamline Moderne design. This glistening, white-painted concrete edifice was utilized until 1978. As early as the 1940s, it was evident that the existing hall was inadequate for city departmental needs and the subsequent scattering of departments caused administrative problems and public confusion as to where the various city services were located.

In 1974, a consortium of architects proposed a bold solution to the city hall problem: the Long Beach Civic Center. They planned to consolidate all of the city departments into a single tower, together with council chambers, conference rooms, briefing areas, administrative spaces, and a main computer facility. Furthermore, the proposed city hall tower would be the central component of a six-square-block redevelopment. The stated design intention for the complex was to create a town square and a center of community activity.

The completed civic center consists of several distinctive components, including a main public library bound and concealed by streetside sloping planted earth berms. Though the library entry is at the plaza level, a majority of the 135,000-square-foot facility, including a 286-seat auditorium, is located one story below ground. An extension of sloping earth berms and rooftop plazas continues west along Ocean Boulevard, interrupted only by several tunnel entries leading to an enclosed, broad, brick-paved plaza. The plaza is the setting for Long Beach City Hall, a 14-story tower that encompasses 280,000 square feet of space. The square tower plan is rotated 45 degrees to Ocean Boulevard. A vertical, exposed, rough, form-board finish enlivens all concrete surfaces. Spanning between the towers, bronze aluminum-curtain walls and glazing subtly delineate each floor. High public contact areas, such as the ones designated for city council chambers, the city treasurer, city clerk, and licensing and utilities agencies are directly accessed from the street-plaza level. The uppermost two floors contain offices for the mayor, city council members, and city manager. From these heights, appropriately, the entire city of Long Beach can be observed.

1

2

3

4

Museum of Art, City of Long Beach

83
MAP 1, B10
MAP 2, C3

LOCATION
UNREALIZED
DATE
1977
ARCHITECT
I. M. PEI & PARTNERS

1./ *View of scale model*
2./ *View of scale model depicting main semicircular entrance*

In 1977, the Long Beach Museum of Art planned to move from its 1912 Anderson House facilities on Bluff Park to the center of downtown at Ocean Boulevard and Pacific Avenue. The museum would have joined the Civic Center infrastructure making downtown a core of cultural and political activities. The Long Beach Museum of Art Foundation, in concert with the City of Long Beach, commissioned New York-based architect I. M. Pei to conceive this new museum space. Pei's roster of projects include renowned museums such as the East Building of the National Gallery of Art in Washington, D.C., and the pyramid structures at the Louvre's entrance in Paris.

For his museum project, called the "Arts Forum," Pei presented a plan for an 80,000-square-foot museum that would accommodate many artistic disciplines, including theater, dance, painting, and film. At a projected cost of $15.6 million, the museum was slated to be a world-class arts institution and center for the communication of ideas.

Pei's design proposed three distinctive masses for articulating the museum's spaces. An intersection of platonic forms included a rectangle with a protruding smaller square rotated at a 45-degree angle and an elevated semicircular wedge on pilotis that would have anchored the site. A series of symmetrically placed windows on the wedge were arranged in two rows allowing natural light to penetrate the facade. The forms were physically separated with a glass atrium that acted as a connective tissue tying the buildings into a cohesive statement. A body of water intermingled with the circular form while the landscape provided a gateway to the museum and shading for a serene courtyard. The plan incorporated a solar-energy system, which was considered advanced for a museum at this time.

Projected oil revenue slated for use in the public-improvement reserve fund and general-purpose fund was anticipated. With this money, the city proposed paying off the bond-debt service for both a new Long Beach City Hall and Public Library project and the museum. However, due to lower than expected oil monies, financing would have only lasted through 1981–82. Years later, a *Press-Telegram* article noted that the alternative was a tax increase, which obviously caused community reservations. In the end, the museum never materialized, but the museum and the City of Long Beach were forward-thinking in coupling a multidisciplinary artistic program with an architecturally significant building.

1

2

227

Spruce Goose Dome
(Hercules [H-4] Flying Boat Hangar)

84
MAP 1, C11

LOCATION
231 WINDSOR WAY
DATE
1982
ARCHITECT
DONALD L. RICHTER, TEMCOR
ADJACENT
AQUARIUM OF THE PACIFIC (91)
CALIFORNIA STATE UNIVERSITY,
CHANCELLOR'S HEADQUARTERS (92)
ARCO CENTER TOWERS (85)

1./ *Detail of dome*
2./ *View of dome*
3./ *Preparing nose of Spruce Goose*
   for transport

How do you house a 200-ton plane with eight piston engines and a 320-foot wingspan? This was the challenge Wrather Corporation faced in determining a proper place to display the Howard Hughes Hercules (H-4) Flying Boat, also known as the "Spruce Goose," which had been residing in a hangar across the Long Beach harbor since World War II. The solution came in the form of one of the world's largest aluminum domes, designed by Donald L. Richter of Temcor. Built alongside the Long Beach harbor and the Queen Mary, it was erected in a matter of months to the relatively inexpensive tune of $4 million.

Assuming the principles of a Buckminster Fuller geodesic dome—low cost and large span—the dome's 415-foot clear-span structure stands 130 feet high and covers 135,266 square feet of display floor in the round. The aluminum framing incorporates approximately 4,000 triangular modules. Seemingly identical, the modules actually vary slightly from bottom to top. The circular tier diminishes in circumference with height, dropping out modules until all that remains at the apex is a hexagon. Yet the structure was erected from the top down and raised gradually on a mast as ironworkers moved farther from the center. The mast was removed on completion and the dome essentially floats on the sand. No piles were driven, nor other deep foundation measures employed for the project. The transfer of the aircraft from the hangar to the dome involved a series of carefully orchestrated steps. The aircraft was picked up with a large Navy crane mounted on a barge and tugged across the harbor, nose first. To ensure a smooth transfer, the operation was planned for high tide so that the barge and landing were at the same elevation. On reaching its destination the plane was rolled onto the beach landing and into the dome tail-first. Once inside, the construction proceeded to final completion.

The Spruce Goose was the largest airplane in the world at the time of its construction. Designed in 1942 as the prototype for a transport seaplane envisioned for extensive use during World War II, it was not completed until 1947. It is a propeller-driven craft of wood construction. Equally compelling was its chief designer and builder Howard Hughes. A self-made billionaire and successful filmmaker, Hughes accomplished just about any task he set his mind to. Although his craft only flew once, in 1947, and then for a very short distance, the experimental seaplane garnered an important niche in the annals of U.S. aviation history.

The Spruce Goose was relocated to a new aircraft museum in McMinnville, Oregon, in 1993. The former hangar is now a reception area for the Carnival Cruise terminal.

1

2

3

Arco Center Towers

85
MAP 1, B10
MAP 2, B3

LOCATION
200–300 OCEANGATE
DATE
1983
ARCHITECT
LUCKMAN PARTNERSHIP INC.
ADJACENT
LONG BEACH PUBLIC SAFETY BUILDING
AND LONG BEACH COUNTY BUILDING (70)
LONG BEACH CITY HALL AND PUBLIC
LIBRARY (82)
CALIFORNIA STATE UNIVERSITY,
CHANCELLOR'S HEADQUARTERS (92)

1./ Exterior view of towers

Long Beach, a city of oil production, appealed to Arco Transportation Company as an ideal location for its new headquarters. Placed off the Long Beach Freeway at Shoreline Drive, the Arco Center Towers resemble giant doors and act as gates into the city. The angled monolithic structures dissect the center's plaza. Designed by Luckman Partnership Inc., a firm best known for its work of large-scale commercial and entertainment developments, the twin towers are indicative of late 1970s and early 1980s corporate modernism.

Placed on a plinth one level above the street, the 14-story project was an enormous complex at the time of its realization. Measuring 440,000 square feet in office space, the towers dominate the four-acre site. Taking into account the ultimate reflective quality when water meets glass, the architecture firm paid homage to the mirror effect and designed the glass towers to ensure privacy. Evocative of big architecture, the towers are sheathed entirely of large panels of black glass. The glazing system blocks a large percentage of the solar heat gain. A steel frame locks the panels into place giving the appearance of a stealthy machine ready for action. Facing off each other with unique faceted wall curvatures on the rear, the towers would fit together like snug puzzle pieces if touching. The strategic placement allows many offices to have windows on three sides.

A glass-atrium pavilion links the structures. Designed at a later date, this intermediate space closed the opening between the two towers to consolidate all points of access, cordoning off the area for security reasons.

1

California Veterans Memorial State Office Building

86
MAP 1, C9
MAP 2, C3

LOCATION
254 W. BROADWAY
DATE
1983
ARCHITECT
HUGH GIBBS & DONALD GIBBS
ARCHITECTS AND KENNETH S. WING SR.
AND KENNETH WING JR.
ADJACENT
FIRST CONGREGATIONAL CHURCH (10)
LONG BEACH CITY HALL
AND PUBLIC LIBRARY (82)
LONG BEACH PUBLIC SAFETY BUILDING
AND LONG BEACH COUNTY BUILDING (70)

1./ *Detail of exterior*
2./ *Exterior view*

The California Veterans Memorial State Office Building was established to consolidate state offices that were scattered throughout the city in leased buildings. The timing of its commission dovetailed with the state architect's heightened interest in creating examples of environmentally sensitive structures. The architects employ natural lighting as the main approach to energy conservation. Because the building was located in a temperate climate, they were able to use single panes of glass, allowing large amounts of indirect daylight to illuminate the work spaces. Complex shading keeps direct sun out and light sensors were installed to ensure unneeded lights are turned off.

Large frames with glass infill fan out around a central core. These three-dimensional forms create the internal spatial arrangements that further increase day lighting. The glass walls hang on heavy timber. Wood was selected as a renewable resource. At 156,000 square feet, this was almost the maximum size for a wood-frame structure based on the building code, which had a limit of four stories and 160,000 square feet. Steel frames seismically reinforce the building.

In contrast to the monumental architecture often used for civic structures, the design reflects a human scale. The interior space is comfortable and warm, and the infusion of sunlight promotes a more natural environment as well as saves energy.

The relation to the site is one of detachment except for its piers touching the ground, similar to a floating island. Anticipating foot traffic to and from city hall, the architectural team sited the building on a diagonal axis line. Two ramps lead to the complex's two first floors, which were planned to accommodate the state agencies with the highest volume of visitors. The ramps provide an energy-saving alternative to the elevator.

The state legislature declared the building surplus property in the mid 1990s and employees vacated the premises in 1998. The property was subsequently sold and now houses commercial office space.

1

2

University Art Museum, California State University, Long Beach

87
MAP 1, H8

LOCATION
UNREALIZED
DATE
1986
ARCHITECT
EISENMAN/ROBERTSON ARCHITECTS
AND HUGH GIBBS & DONALD GIBBS
ARCHITECTS

1./ Exploded axonmetric
2./ Perspective

Peter Eisenman, architect and educator, said, "At Long Beach, there is a cut between two figural masses. The cut is not a grid, but an unstable absence, a constantly dilating series of figures shearing, compressing, tensioning, undulating from its length like a vibrating or burning line, a series of after images." A fundamental aspect of Eisenman's architecture projects is analyzing and tracing the lay of the land. In his proposal for the University Art Museum, the architect did just that: He investigated the history of the museum site and mapped the surrounding topographies.

The design team for the University Art Museum presented a premier cultural institution for Long Beach and the third-largest museum in Los Angeles County. Programmatically, the 67,000-square-foot building incorporated the following designed spaces: a black-box theater, four galleries, storage space, a cafeteria, and an outdoor sculpture space. In addition, the plan introduced landscaped terraces, a courtyard, and botanical gardens with a two-acre pond. The 23-acre arboretum and ancillary spaces defined the museum and were revealed methodically, similar to discovering an archeological artifact.

Uncovering the Newport-Inglewood fault zone, Eisenman figuratively incised the site to expose layers of its history and geography. A series of maps with significant dates showed notations—non-scale specific—of the following (at right): green for original land divisions, blue for ranch houses, pink and red for the university's campus, and gold for eroded riverbeds and irrigation systems. The fault line between the two dislocated Atlantic and Pacific plates shows the patterns of civilization as looking toward the future. From this point, Eisenman superimposed map over map, revealing history and nonhierarchical conditions of how the culture organized itself.

Other building components proposed for the site included the relocation of the Greene & Greene-designed Adelaide A. Tichenor House, a commemorative old oil derrick, and a rebuilt version of the 1920s Rainbow Pier. By creating a fictitious narrative between old and new buildings, a unique museum proposal emerged.

The president of CSULB at the time was the project mentor. He resigned in 1987 and construction of the project ceased due to lack of funding and priority.

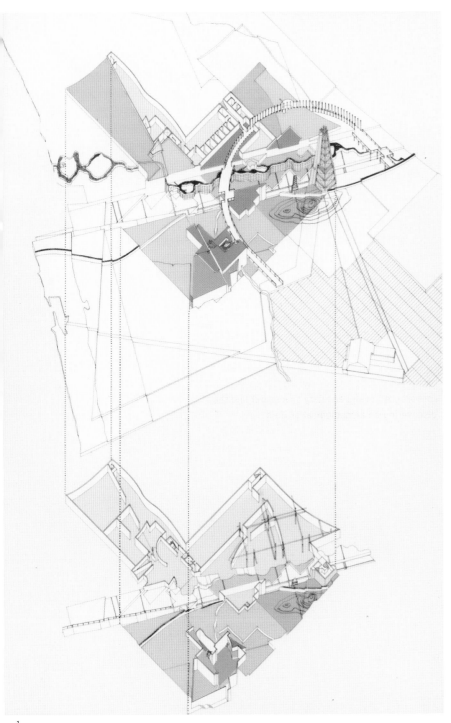

1

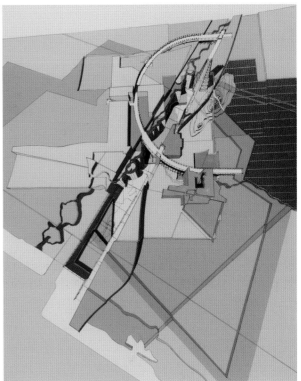

2

Naples Canal House

LOCATION
5610 NAPLES CANAL
DATE
1989
ARCHITECT
RON KAPPE
ADJACENT
PENN/CROWELL HOUSE (81)
FRANK HOUSE, CASE STUDY #25 (73)
OPDAHL HOUSE (65)

1./ *View across canal*
2./ *Side view*

The Naples Canal House takes full advantage of its south-facing position. Sited on the canal, this house is open to the exterior elements of water, neighboring houses, and strolling pedestrians, yet it maintains an intimate and private feel. Tucked into a confined lot, the 2,400-square-foot house still provides openness with a fluid floor plan. The house creates levity with transparent and opaque spaces and features two bedrooms and two bathrooms.

A unique house detail is the steel-hybrid frame that combines sheer walls on the back portion and an open steel structure on the front. The steel—painted with a high-grade polymer that protects it from saltwater effects—encases the entire house. The stringent building-height restriction of 25 feet challenged architect Ron Kappe to create a two-story volume with varying levels. Flowing over the garage, the double height space steps down from the kitchen into the dining-room area then toward the living room, which is closest to the canal. The kitchen is the most intimate space in the house while the living room is the most public. The private living spaces occupy the second floor and a large angled window protrudes from the front of the structure forming the master bedroom area.

Light is a key element in the design and is introduced with central skylights, a glass-block stairwell, and an atrium of glass block. Large windows, top and bottom, wrap around the south and north faces and extend to the side, framing ideal views of the water and canal. These big panes of glass facing the canal are north-oriented and do not get direct sun, which make the bedroom more comfortable (heat gain is through the south-facing glass and the skylights). To channel light into all spaces, Kappe uses a series of skylights placed rhythmically throughout the house. At night, the walls of glass act as a lantern for passing boats.

The architect planned a reflective pool for the front of the house to mirror the imagery of boats against the canals. But this design feature never materialized due to safety codes set by the city. The entrance still offers a daring elevation and a compelling deviation from the more traditional facades in the neighborhood.

1

2

Pyramid, California State University, Long Beach

One of the largest space-frame buildings in the United States, the 1994 Pyramid building houses the physical-education and athletic-events center for California State University, Long Beach. The first gymnasium, containing only 1,900 seats, was built in 1954 when the campus had an enrollment 5,000. In the 1970s, when the student population ballooned to more than 30,000, the university initiated discussions for the construction of this new facility. Its realization took nearly 20 years.

The four-sided, pyramid-shaped edifice includes entrances centered on each side of a perfectly square base. It is built over an 18-foot-deep, 70,000-square-foot excavation that contains a wooden playing surface, locker rooms, meeting rooms, lower seating levels, a truck-accessible staging area, and physical-education space. The Pyramid rises to a point 178 feet above ground. Sheathed in a cobalt-blue pleated steel roof that covers an area of 170,000 square feet, the structure is visible for miles.

The structural steel frame weighs less than half as much as conventional framing, which typically employs massive girders and foundations. It consists of a multiple-layer space grid assembled with individual tubular steel struts bolted at their ends to a plate node. More than 15,000 interconnecting steel tubes are laid out in subassemblies of small pyramids measuring six feet in height and 12 feet along the base.

Designed to hold as many as 7,000 spectators for 49er basketball and volleyball, the facility features a one-of-a-kind seating system mounted on moveable platforms. The four lower-level seating sections can be hydraulically raised to expose 39,000 square feet of beechwood flooring that accommodates three full-court and six half-court basketball areas and five volleyball courts.

This $22 million geometric abstraction is a striking visual departure from the rest of campus and among just a handful of true pyramid structures in the United States, which include the Pyramid Arena in Memphis and the Luxor Hotel and Casino in Las Vegas.

89
MAP 1, I8

LOCATION
1250 BELLFLOWER BLVD.
DATE
1994
ARCHITECT
HUGH GIBBS & DONALD GIBBS
ARCHITECTS
ADJACENT
CALIFORNIA STATE UNIVERSITY,
LONG BEACH (58)
VA LONG BEACH HEALTHCARE
SYSTEM (57)
FARMERS & MERCHANTS BANK,
LOS ALTOS BRANCH (94)

1./ Exterior view

1

Bikestation Long Beach

90
MAP 1, C10
MAP 2, C3

LOCATION
105 THE PROMENADE NORTH
DATE
1996
ARCHITECT
FERNANDO VAZQUEZ/STUDIO
AND CARLSON & COMPANY
ADJACENT
SECURITY PACIFIC NATIONAL BANK (25)
INSURANCE EXCHANGE BUILDING (24)
MASONIC TEMPLE (3)

1./ *View from Promenade*

Embracing progressive functionality, Bikestation* Long Beach is the first facility of its type in the United States. The city-owned unit was built to assist the Long Beach Metro Blue Line's commuter population and recreational cyclists. Taking ingenious concepts from European models of temporary pavilionlike structures, architect Fernando Vazquez designed the station using basic ideas of flexibility, mobility, low cost, and effortless access.

Evoking a bicycle's form of motion, Vazquez laid out a series of modular structures—triangle, circle, and arc—for the plan. Assembled on site, the forms and corrugated metal in yellow and red produce an elevation of colliding lines and shapes. Using these colors of sport, the building displays positive propaganda calling attention to the beneficial attributes of cycling. Engineering a trellis frame of white steel tubes for bike hanging, the architect, along with fabricator Peter Carlson, created an exposed cage that envelopes the station and lets it breath. The taut fit of the frame and bold colors of the station are in direct reference to form-fitting, colorful bike-riding gear, celebrating the activity and its benefits.

Bikestation offers amenities such as attended bicycle parking, 24-hour access to lockers, bike repair, rentals (both traditional and electric), restroom/changing room, accessory shop, snack shop, and even Internet access to transit and bike-commuting users.

Designated as a temporary facility to accommodate denser redevelopment, the Bikestation will move to a new site in 2004 or 2005. With this prerequisite, the architect looks to regenerate the structure in another iteration. Recycling the parts and using similar principles as the current station, a new customized Bikestation will emerge.

The first model spawned the development and creation of three additional Bikestations in Palo Alto, Berkeley, and Seattle with dozens of new facilities in the planning phases.

* *Bikestation is a protected trademark.*

1

Aquarium of the Pacific

91
MAP 1, B10
MAP 2, B4

LOCATION
100 AQUARIUM WAY
DATE
1998
ARCHITECT
HOK (HELLMUTH, OBATA
+ KASSABAUM INC.)
IN A JOINT VENTURE WITH
EHDD (ESHERICK, HOMSEY,
DODGE AND DAVIS)
ADJACENT
CALIFORNIA STATE UNIVERSITY,
CHANCELLOR'S HEADQUARTERS (92)
ARCO CENTER TOWERS (85)
SPRUCE GOOSE DOME (84)

1./ Exterior view
2./ Exterior view, evening

Adding to the revitalization of the late 1990s development of the Queensway Bay area and Shoreline Drive, the Aquarium of the Pacific sits as a welcome sign into the city. One of the largest aquariums in the United States at 156,735 square feet, it exclusively represents the Pacific Ocean, housing more than 12,000 ocean animals.

At first glance, the building resembles a wave formation rising and falling with the curve of the beach. Sheltered by a series of metal roof planes, the forms undulate in rhythm to this image of ocean swells. An extensive aluminum curtain wall punctuated with sea-green glass creates the entry and west wall. Other colors of blue and gray enhance the movement of the structure's shifting elevations.

Two buildings in one, the aquarium is divided into a lobby, shop, and restaurant on the dry side and preview tanks of sea life on the wet side. The interior and exterior areas flow in a unified plan. Once inside, visitors get an immediate sense of the magnitude of the space. The lobby houses large-scale objects such as a whale replica, and intimate spaces are created to encounter the underwater creatures. Aquatic exhibits from around the Pacific appear in natural settings along with several interactive displays.

Creatively challenged with the aquarium's specialized program, the architecture team of HOK, in collaboration with the Monterey Bay Aquarium architect EHDD and exhibit consultant Joseph A. Wetzel Associates Inc., developed an atypical structure and form. Special attention focused on minimizing danger to the fish life and building if an earthquake occurred. The aquarium's life-support systems and structure are sited on floating rafts. The rafts consist of numerous rock columns built 85 feet into the ground. Filled with gravel, the rock columns create soil stabilization and aid the support systems in case of a disaster.

The aquarium's design complements the city skyline and references the basic attributes of Long Beach's fine natural resources: sea, sun, and light.

1

2

California State University, Chancellor's Headquarters

92
MAP 1, B10
MAP 2, B4

LOCATION
401 GOLDEN SHORE DR.
DATE
1999
ARCHITECT
LPA, INC.
ADJACENT
ARCO CENTER TOWERS (85)
AQUARIUM OF THE PACIFIC (91)
GERALD DESMOND BRIDGE
REPLACEMENT (100)

1./ *Detail of building's curved vertical lip*
2./ *Exterior view*

The Chancellor's Headquarters is the administrative nerve-center for the largest university system in the country. Knowing the significance of a building such as this, LPA, Inc., a corporate architecture firm known for educational work, added sharpness to a relatively isolated group of eclectic neighbors: a protected marine biological reserve, a world-class port, and an RV park.

In 1971, state legislation granted authorization to lease tidelands in Long Beach to California State University (CSU). This parcel of land with an existing building became the headquarters facility for the next 25 years. In the early 1990s, the old structure needed a major renovation. But after a seven-year evaluation process and feasibility study, LPA, Inc., determined the building ceased to accommodate the ever-growing CSU's needs.

Realized in 1999 to house the chancellor's office for all 23 CSU campuses, the 165,000-square-foot building succeeds architecturally as well as programmatically. Flanked by two parking structures, the headquarters is oriented toward the water, exposing a solid face to the south. Roughly rectilinear except for a slight curved vertical lip, the form of the structure is sleek and stately. A steel moment frame with aluminum metal panels, light enough for landfill, creates a durable boxlike house for the evenly placed rows of green glass.

Fine materials—stone, aluminum, and concrete—delineate the exterior cladding and interior flooring and walls. Solnhofen, a light-colored stone quarried from a mine in Germany, flows in and out. The building's six floors feature almost identical plans and house 500-plus staff. All offices occupy the central spine therefore opening up the building to multiple views from the outer corridor. Functions include offices for the chancellor and administrative support for all operating departments, as well as offices for auditors; the legal, finance, and informational technology departments; and various international and summer-arts programs.

From the building's inception, landscape played a dominant role in the design. The architecture firm integrated a grove of trees into the new vision. Various types—redwood, coral, eucalyptus, live oak, and palm—symmetrically decorate the site. Different-colored gravel representing the three primary topographies of California—desert, redwood trees, and fertile central valley farmland—creates organic patterns that can only be seen from above. Several art installations were commissioned, including one at the entrance and one en route from the front parking lot. The entrance piece presents a timeline of significant historical themes juxtaposed with CSU's growth from 1850 to the present. The other one features 23 lights and spells out CSU in Morse code when activated.

International Elementary School

Charged with the complex task of creating a public school in the midst of a downtown urban environment, the collaborative efforts of Morphosis and Thomas Blurock Architects produced a unique solution that maximizes play area, addresses security concerns, and responds to the surrounding neighborhoods. The design of the International Elementary School challenges traditional notions, presenting a radical departure from typical single-story suburban school structures that are situated on more expansive sites.

Constrained by a two-and-a-half-acre former parking lot, the 34-classroom school consists of two buildings. A one-story concrete structure houses K-2 classrooms, secured staff parking, and the majority of the school's administrative and extracurricular rooms. A three-story, steel-framed building contains classrooms for grades 3–5. The architects addressed the issue of open space by configuring a playfield on the roof of the concrete structure, offering the children an enclave that never loses contact with the ground or the sky. This vertical layering reduced the site requirement by 50 percent. Thus the majority of the program is subterranean. The classroom space occupies the periphery of the site, maximizing natural lighting and supporting the courtyard above.

To protect children, a perimeter fence encloses the playfield on three of the four sides. Yet this boundary is transformed into a three-dimensional, sculptural unit, what Morphosis principal Thom Mayne refers to as "the skin without the body," eschewing a forceful, divisional image reminiscent of a prison yard. Vibrant hues of blue and brick define the massing and also help to soften the image.

Despite the varying pragmatic constraints—budget, size, configuration—of school design, the International Elementary School manages to achieve a rare balance between the institutional nature of the building and the more personal, intimate activities of the interior.

Santa Monica-based Morphosis has completed other successful educational facilities in Southern California, as well as numerous international projects. The firm is responsible for changing the perception of architecture in the public realm, transforming mundane programs into engaging and inspirational spatial environments.

93
MAP 1, C9
MAP 2, C2

LOCATION
700 LOCUST AVE.
DATE
1999
ARCHITECT
MORPHOSIS AND THOMAS BLUROCK ARCHITECTS
ADJACENT
YORK RITE MASONIC TEMPLE (31)
KRESS BUILDING (19)
WALKER'S DEPARTMENT STORE (40)

1./ Side view
2./ Window detail
3./ Interior courtyard

1

2

3

Farmers & Merchants Bank, Los Altos Branch

94
MAP 1, H7

LOCATION
2302 BELLFLOWER BLVD.
DATE
2003
ARCHITECT
FERNALD DESIGN GROUP
ADJACENT
PYRAMID, CALIFORNIA STATE
UNIVERSITY, LONG BEACH (89)
CALIFORNIA STATE UNIVERSITY,
LONG BEACH (58)
MATLOCK HOUSE (61)

1./ *Front view*
2./ *Front view with landscaping*
3./ *Side view*

The new F&M Bank displays roadside architecture in a contemporary and direct way. The first building to be inaugurated into the family-owned bank in 30 years, the Los Altos branch straddles the conservative nature of bank operations and the modern requirements of today's paperless banking system.

In 1960, F&M Bank purchased the lot and building—the former 1950s Queen's City Ford car dealership—and turned it into a financial banking center. The bank is set amidst a 1950s middle-suburbia neighborhood of ranch houses, shopping-plaza developments, and large expansive streets for automobile access. Knowing the bank's need for modernization, F&M Bank commissioned Fernald Design Group to renovate the existing structure. After analyzing the site's options, the architects determined that a completely new structure built from the ground up would be the best solution.

The bank's architecture comprises two major building elements. One is the public side that visibly opens to the street with double-height volume and glazing. The openness through windows creates an interior space that welcomes comfortable access. The other segment of the bank building is the solid part that offers no window penetrations or open views. This dense wall element purposefully reinforces the bank's primary operation, which is to securely protect its holdings.

The architects placed an emphasis on revealing the true function of the materials: metal, stone, and glass. The curved-metal roof panels pass through the main space elevation and transition into a perforated-metal ceiling system, continuing the architecture element in and out of the building. Chocolate sandstone wraps the solid wall and allows the glass to insert itself, shifting into the public domain.

Showing the building's connective steel tissue, the architects provide an understanding of how the parts cohere. This structural element, called a side plate, is a seismic system that was developed after the 1993 Northridge earthquake. Most buildings hide this apparatus, but in the case of the bank, it is prominently featured showing the function as it is: a structural support. Another visible part of the building's innards is the large bank vault located in the main space. It has a 24-inch concrete box with heavy rebar and fortifies the image of a secure and stable facility.

"Rooted in tradition, wired for the future" is the bank's dictum. This is reinforced with the Los Altos branch as well as other F&M banks appearing on the scene, including branches in Belmont Shore and Huntington Beach.

1

2

3

Livable Places Competition

What does it take to regenerate a major boulevard in a city? Can a decayed area be turned into an environment that promotes alternative housing with an emphasis on contemporary design? Intervening in urban redevelopments is the forward approach of Livable Places, an organization that strives to promote a more livable and sustainable Los Angeles region. The nonprofit housing developer assumes an inevitability of growth and injects affordable housing and social equity in all of its projects. By concentrating on a particular area in need of redevelopment, Livable Places avoids spotty interventions and focuses on density.

Funded by the National Endowment for the Arts, Livable Places launched the Innovations in Community Design and Housing Competition in 2003. The competition brief sought to explore prototypical solutions for the reuse of low-density, commercial strip-style corridors. A 10-acre site thick with low-income housing and in proximity of a transit station served as the competition canvas. Requirements included 50 units of sustainable mixed-use housing and a plan for the surrounding area. Of the 90 submissions received, the Livable Places jury of architects, landscape architects, urban designers, and civic leaders selected McCormick, Smith & Others in collaboration with Lloyd Russell to realize their project.

The winning scheme put forth two different cost models for living. One included common courtyards and located parking on the rooftops of condominiums, and the other focused on fully independent properties on separate parcels. "The prototypes proposed minimal infrastructure costs, such as below-grade parking structures, elevators, and corridor systems, allowing larger proportions of the given budget to be devoted to the architecture of the units themselves," expressed principal Ted Smith of McCormick, Smith & Others.

Another scheme was designed by Touraine + Richmond Architects and entitled "Houses on Top." Using Archizoom's 1971 *No-Stop City*—the position of architecture as an open structure—as a thematic underpinning, this firm challenged density through diversity. By developing a mix of uses—housing, school, social, and business—to suit the transit-oriented neighborhood, they produced a plan that answers the realities of the urban context. A third finalist, Behnisch, Behnisch & Partners with Blackbird Architects, proposed an urban alternative to gridlock and smog with green arteries of townhouses.

The competition recharged the possibility of co-mingling design and affordability in housing. The next phase for Livable Places is to realize the project of McCormick, Smith & Others. The organization owns a small portion of the site and is in the process of acquiring the entire parcel for this development.

95
MAP 1, C7

LOCATION
LONG BEACH BLVD.
AND PACIFIC COAST HIGHWAY
DATE
2003
ARCHITECT
MCCORMICK, SMITH & OTHERS IN
COLLABORATION WITH LLOYD RUSSELL;
BRIAN HEALY ARCHITECTS; BEHNISCH,
BEHNISCH & PARTNERS WITH
BLACKBIRD ARCHITECTS; CENTRAL
OFFICE OF ARCHITECTURE; AND
TOURAINE + RICHMOND ARCHITECTS
ADJACENT
OLIVE COURT (98)
ATLANTIC AVENUE WORKFORCE
HOUSING DEVELOPMENT (97)
LONG BEACH POLYTECHNIC
HIGH SCHOOL (48)

1./ *Perspective rendering*
   McCormick, Smith & Others
2./ *Bird's-eye view of model,*
   Touraine + Richmond Architects
3./ *Perspective rendering of street,*
   Touraine + Richmond Architects

1

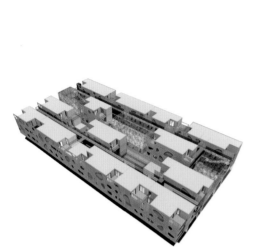

2

3

Howard CDM

96
MAP 1, C4

LOCATION
3777 BIXBY AVE.
DATE
2004
ARCHITECT
SCHWEITZER BIM
ADJACENT
CAMBRIDGE OFFICE BUILDING (67)
KILLINGSWORTH, BRADY & SMITH
OFFICE BUILDING (63)
BIXBY RANCH HOUSE (1)

1./ *View across Long Beach*
   Boulevard
2./ *Rear of building and annex*
   space

Sensing the rapid transformation of Bixby Knolls from a sleepy, nondescript suburban strip to a rejuve-nated urban center, the development partnership 3777 + Partners LP seized the opportunity in 2002 to acquire a group of buildings on a three-acre parcel at the junction of Long Beach Boulevard and Bixby Avenue.

Purchasing three 1950s- and 1960s-era office complexes with little character, the developer started by revamping the first major eyesore: 3777 Bixby Avenue. Built in 1959 for Western Land Company, the building had a series of owners and tenants, including IBM and the engineering firm Earth Tech. The latter company occupied the structure from 1977 to 1989 and transformed it from three stories into five stories with a roof-top tennis court. In doing this awkward addition, the architectural character was lost. For 13 years the building stood vacant and residents in the bucolic area tried unsuccessfully to condemn the off-putting structure. Without occupants, it had its share of vandalism, including stripping of all wiring, doorjambs, copper utilities, and fixtures, until almost all that was left was its shell.

Using the building's existing foundation and structure, Josh Schweitzer of the architecture firm Schweitzer BIM reconstructed the core, subtracting what was left of its tattered innards and building upon the bones. Maximizing its site, the 44,000-square-foot office building fills the lot.

Reducing a Mondrian painting to patterns, the architect accentuated the building's horizontal and vertical structural apparatus. Wanting to inject the curtain wall with life, Schweitzer decided to make it a visual—instead of an invisible—structural system. The result reveals the skeleton of the building, underscored by the color palette. Breaking up the flat surface into various smaller geometric planes, a game of solids and voids plays into the facade. In another turn of innovation, the building utilizes an energy-efficient system by installing photovoltaic cells around the top to harness electricity.

Howard CDM occupies the two-story, 8,000-square-foot annex space and leases the additional office area to commercial clients.

1

2

Atlantic Avenue Workforce Housing Development

The Atlantic Avenue Workforce Housing Development presents a comprehensive approach to urban planning, one not forged in isolation but with great consideration to the surrounding environment. The project proposal, planned for implementation in 2005, extends beyond the standard housing solution by incorporating suggestions and actions for enhancing the physical character of the community. Related components include infrastructure improvements such as repairing broken curbs, restoring sidewalk planter strips, introducing new street trees, and repaving roadways; improving existing civic institutions with facade and landscape upgrades; and recommending policy changes such as advocating against street widening and reducing existing parking requirements. Integral to this plan is the creation of a pedestrian-friendly environment that encourages the use and interaction of proximal amenities, including residential neighborhoods, retail stores, civic institutions, and transit stops.

The residential-development plan utilizes courtyard housing and quadplexes, with a mix of two-, three-, and four-bedroom units evenly dispersed throughout. A minimum of two architectural styles is sought to avoid monotony, and varying cornices and roof slopes are encouraged over monolithic building facades. Materials such as cementitious fiberboard or metal siding provide an alternative to plaster cladding, and the use of deep, saturated colors articulate massing. Windows and doors will be recessed at least three-and-a-half inches from the face of the exterior finish to prevent wall surfaces from appearing tediously flat.

Landscaping is an essential component of the plan, which integrates drought-resistant plants, enclosed private spaces, pathways of permanent materials, and at least one fountain in each main courtyard. Even the parking lots—with tree and bush plantings and accommodations for recreational activities such as basketball—are designed as usable and attractive places.

Architects Elizabeth Moule and Stefanos Polyzoides are committed to the idea of coherence in design. They believe that the only way to treat the visual chaos and formlessness present in many of today's cities and suburbs is to adopt a role that supports both newness and continuity. As a result, their projects develop as an integral part of a larger order.

97
MAP 1, C7

LOCATION
WEST SIDE OF ATLANTIC BETWEEN
20TH AND HILL STREETS
DATE
2005
ARCHITECT
MOULE & POLYZOIDES ARCHITECTS
AND URBANISTS
ADJACENT
OLIVE COURT (98)
LIVABLE PLACES COMPETITION (95)
LONG BEACH POLYTECHNIC HIGH
SCHOOL (48)

1./ *Rendering of site plan*
2./ *Bird's-eye rendering*
3./ *Section of street users*

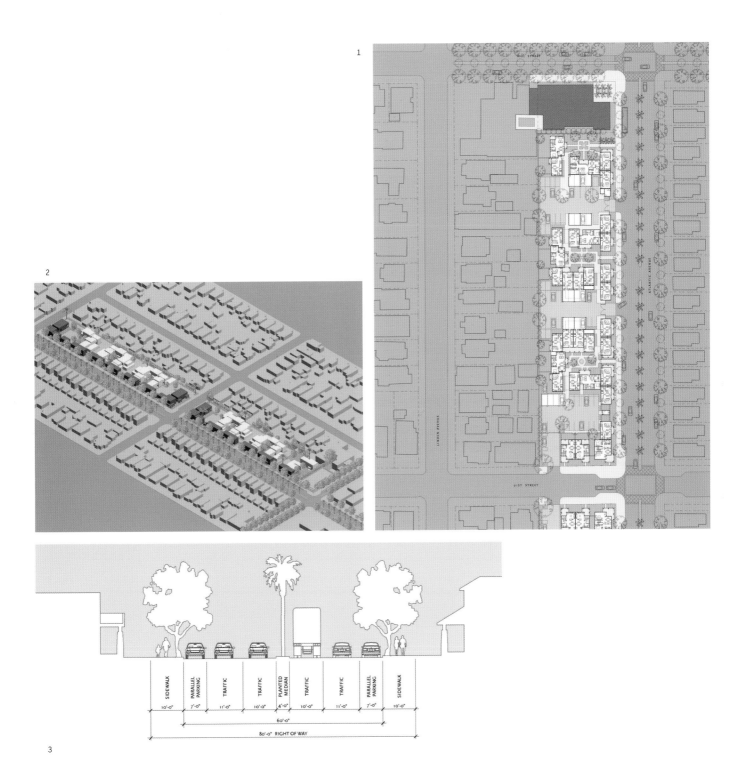

Olive Court

98
MAP 1, C7

LOCATION
1856–1890 LONG BEACH BLVD.
DATE
2005
ARCHITECT
STUDIO E ARCHITECTS AND NESTOR
+ GAFFNEY ARCHITECTURE LLP
ADJACENT
ATLANTIC AVENUE WORKFORCE
HOUSING DEVELOPMENT (97)
LIVABLE PLACES COMPETITION (95)
LONG BEACH POLYTECHNIC HIGH
SCHOOL (48)

1./ Bird's-eye view of scale model
2./ Detail of scale model
3./ Elevation rendering

Responding to the Los Angeles region's severe housing crisis, nonprofit housing developer Livable Places dedicates its efforts to promoting affordable housing in existing urban areas. Rather than contributing to the sprawling and rapid habitation of outlying areas where excessive development destroys open space, generates more traffic, and harms the environment, the organization aims to establish models for smart growth infill development where it can help revitalize the community. Central Long Beach provides an ideal location to carry out this vision due to its ample transit connections, neighborhood stores, and nearby civic, cultural, and recreational amenities.

Currently underway is Olive Court, a medium-density development consisting of 58 new for-sale condominium homes in central Long Beach. Designed by Studio E Architects, the project aims to enhance an underutilized and blighted commercial strip on Long Beach Boulevard by replacing it with a residential community that possesses a financial stake in the neighborhood.

In order to alleviate the contrast between the small scale of the development and the fast pace of the adjacent boulevard, the buildings will be situated around a protected, semipublic courtyard in the tradition of the region's bungalow courts. Residences along Long Beach Boulevard will be arranged in two- to four-story buildings with smaller gated courtyards feeding onto the sidewalk.

Olive Court will offer a range of townhouses and flats between 800 and 1,400 square feet in one-, two-, three-, and four-bedroom configurations. Many will be affordable to low- and moderate-income families earning between $35,000 to $60,000 a year. The homes will be constructed using environmentally friendly materials and will feature energy-efficient design and appliances to reduce utility costs. Committed to reducing automobile dependency, Livable Places selected a site one block north of the Metro Blue Line light rail station at Pacific Coast Highway.

Construction is anticipated to begin in 2004 with units ready for occupancy in mid-2005.

1

2

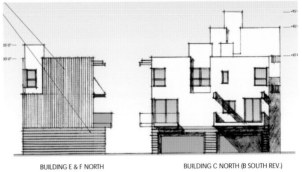

BUILDING E & F NORTH   BUILDING C NORTH (B SOUTH REV.)   3

MacArthur Park Neighborhood Library

The MacArthur Park Neighborhood Library represents an inspired new library building, the first in Long Beach since 1977. The library, a recipient of the California Reading and Literacy Improvement and Public Library Construction and Renovation Bond Act 2000, surpassed approximately 60 other applicants to be one of 12 selected for funding. The conceptual team involved Manuel Oncina Architects (MOA) of La Jolla, California, a firm that is familiar with the challenges of contemporary library facilities with projects in Cardiff, Encinitas, and San Ysidro.

Located in an ethnically diverse neighborhood, the current Mark Twain Library structure is outmoded in square footage, amenities, and technological capacity, making it difficult to serve the burgeoning local community of 70,000. The present collection reflects Long Beach's Cambodian population—the largest outside of Cambodia—with an extensive collection of Khmer literature, setting a precedent for the new building to cater to multilingual users. Furthering the cultural convergence, the proposed library design suggests a variety of functions, connecting the structure to its environment and inviting a symbiotic relationship between the park and surrounding inhabitants.

MOA will scale the 16,155-square-foot, one-story structure to the acre site and introduce an abstract frame of a sweeping roof structure and a series of horizontal window bands. These elements will reinforce openness to the north and grounding to the site. The strong, saturated colors and exuberant forms of the exterior will translate into interior volumes. The community room will be located underneath the peaked roof, while large and small vaulted spaces will house the collection and meeting rooms. More than just a well-designed building, the library will provide a community locus for the exchange of many cultural voices.

As part of the new Leadership in Energy and Environmental Design rating system implemented by the City of Long Beach, the design envelopes a series of green principles. The structure is situated on a north-south axis with the majority of the glass fronting the north side. Large overhangs and louvers will protect the glass on the south, east, and west sides. Proposed photovoltaic cells and a low-velocity displacement ventilation system speak to sustainable architecture. With its wireless connections, the MacArthur Park Neighborhood Library should set the standard for future energy-conscious municipal projects.

99
MAP 1, D8

LOCATION
1401 E. ANAHEIM ST.
DATE
2006
ARCHITECT
MANUEL ONCINA ARCHITECTS INC.
ADJACENT
LONG BEACH POLYTECHNIC
HIGH SCHOOL (48)
HANCOCK MOTORS (34)
ATLANTIC AVENUE WORKFORCE
HOUSING DEVELOPMENT (97)

1./ *Parking lot elevation rendering*
2./ *Alley elevation rendering*
3./ *Anaheim Street elevation rendering*

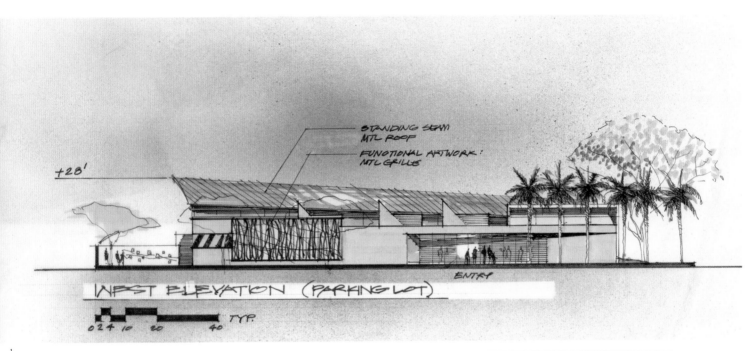

STANDING SEAM
MTL ROOF

FUNCTIONAL ARTWORK:
MTL GRILLE

+28'

WEST ELEVATION (PARKING LOT)

0 2 4 10   20   40   TYP.

ENTRY

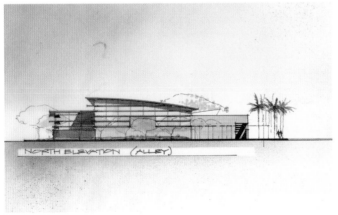

NORTH ELEVATION (ALLEY)

2

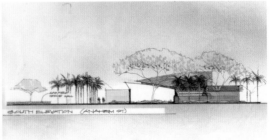

SOUTH ELEVATION (ANAHEIM ST)

3

1

Gerald Desmond Bridge Replacement

As unique architectural and structural undertakings, bridges carry a huge responsibility of overcoming the forces to which they are subjected. In an 1883 *Harper's Weekly* article, writer Montgomery Schuyler articulates this assertion: "The work which is likely to be our most durable monument, and to convey some knowledge of us to the most remote posterity, is a work of bare utility; not a shrine, not a fortress, not a palace, but a bridge." Of all the waterborne containers that pass through U.S. ports each year, 15 percent use the Long Beach Freeway and 10 percent traverse the Gerald Desmond Bridge. Infrastructural needs at the world's third-busiest port require structural provisions for this tremendous commerce. The current 560-foot-span Gerald Desmond Bridge, named after Long Beach civic leader and former city attorney Gerald Desmond, was erected in 1968 to aid in the passage between Long Beach and Terminal Island. Designed by the company Moffatt & Nichol Engineers, the bridge resembles an erector set and funnels an estimated 40,000 vehicle crossings each day. This number is expected to double by 2020.

With the increasing volume of activity and traffic, the modernization of the bridge requires both raising and widening. The port authorities will demolish the overburdened, dated structure to make way for an engineering wonder with architectural tenacity designed by Poul Ove Jensen, a partner from the Copenhagen, Denmark, firm of Dissing and Weitling, in collaboration with the joint venture team Parsons/HNTB Corporation. The group submitted several architectural designs; among the ideas included were a slanted *H* (the roadway rests on the horizontal span between the *H*), single mast (cables stretch from two single towers), and delta frame (inverted pyramids sit atop two shorter single-mast towers). The selected design, slanted *H*, consists of a single tower at each pylon with shear links. Its specific elements include a total span of 2,000 feet, three traffic lanes in each direction, and a 200-foot-plus vertical clearance for ship passage.

An objective for all new bridges is to provide a balanced finesse between art and science, and the Gerald Desmond Bridge Replacement achieves this equilibrium. The design shows off the cable-stayed bridge—the first in California—that incorporates load-bearing cables, which radiate from concrete towers in a fanlike pattern to the road deck. Lighting created by Brandston Partnership Inc., known for its work on the Statue of Liberty, will illuminate the roads.

In an effort not to cease port operations, the bridge will rise next to the existing Gerald Desmond Bridge and, when completed, the old structure will be removed. This bridge is the first component to be realized under the I-710 Corridor/Gerald Desmond Bridge Gateway Program that proposes a comprehensive, strategic approach to addressing the congestion and safety issues in the corridor between the ports of Long Beach and Los Angeles and State Route 60.

100
MAP 1, A10

LOCATION
SPANS THE BACK CHANNEL OF THE
PORT OF LONG BEACH
DATE
2010
ARCHITECT
PARSONS/HNTB CORPORATION AND
POUL OVE JENSEN OF DISSING AND
WEITLING, JOINT VENTURE TEAM
ADJACENT
CALIFORNIA STATE UNIVERSITY,
CHANCELLOR'S HEADQUARTERS (92)
ARCO CENTER TOWERS (85)
AQUARIUM OF THE PACIFIC (91)

1./ *Computer rendering of proposed design*

1

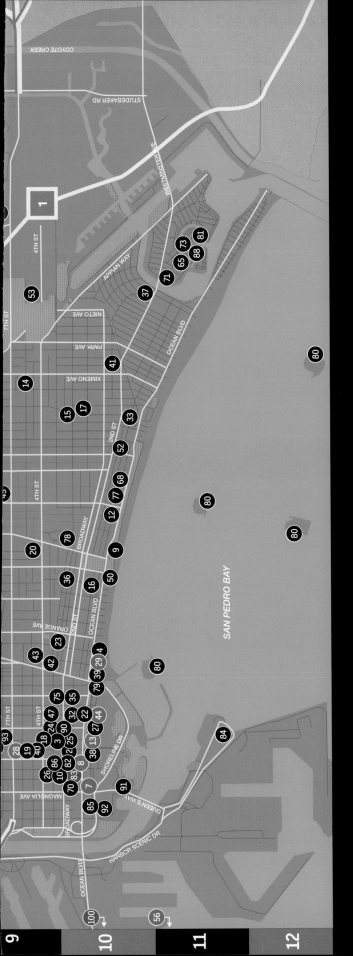

MAP 1

LEGEND

○ INTACT

● DEMOLISHED

● UNREALIZED/PROJECTED

▬ INTERSTATE

▬ HIGHWAY

▬ MAJOR STREETS

▬ SECONDARY STREETS

▬ PARKS

1. Bixby Ranch House
2. First National Bank
3. Masonic Temple
4. Adelaide A. Tichenor House
5. Bembridge House
6. Physical Testing and Chemical Laboratory (Southern Pacific Depot)
7. Hotel Virginia
8. Carnegie Public Library
9. Long Beach Museum of Art
10. First Congregational Church
11. Harnett House
12. Raymond House
13. Markwell Building/Jergins Trust Building and Jergins Subway
14. Seashell House
15. Belmont Heights United Methodist Church
16. Better Home Electrical
17. Captain Ponto House
18. Farmers & Merchants Bank and Tower
19. Kress Building
20. Art Theater
21. Community Hospital of Long Beach
22. Cooper Arms
23. Ebell Club and Theater
24. Insurance Exchange Building (Middaughs' Boys' Shop)
25. Security Pacific National Bank (Security Trust and Savings Bank)
26. The Willmore
27. The Breakers Hotel
28. YWCA
29. Pacific Coast Club
30. Pray/Dawson House
31. York Rite Masonic Temple
32. Broadlind Hotel
33. Casa Grande Apartment Building (La Casa Grande)
34. Hancock Motors
35. Lafayette Complex
36. Rose Towers (El Cordova Apartments)
37. Engine Company No. 8
38. Ocean Center Building
39. Villa Riviera
40. Walker's Department Store
41. Gaytonia
42. Long Beach Skating Palace
43. The Koffee Pot Cafe
44. Municipal Auditorium
45. The Skinny House (Newton P. Rummond House)
46. Henry Clock House
47. U.S. Post Office and Federal Building
48. Long Beach Polytechnic High School
49. Cheney/Delaney House
50. Lifeguard Headquarters, Cherry Avenue
51. Tichenor Orthopedic Clinic for Children
52. Apartment Building on 1st
53. Kimpson/Nixon House
54. Craig/McLeod House
55. Long Beach Airport
56. Roosevelt Naval Base, Terminal Island
57. VA Long Beach Healthcare System (Navy Hospital)
58. California State University, Long Beach
59. Alexander House
60. George's Fifties Diner
61. Matlock House
62. Moore/Hafley Twin Houses
63. Killingsworth, Brady & Smith Office Building
64. Java Lanes Bowling Alley
65. Opdahl House
66. Ruth Bach Neighborhood Library
67. Cambridge Office Building
68. Marina Tower Model Apartment
69. Long Beach Elks Lodge No. 888
70. Long Beach Public Safety Building and Long Beach County Building
71. Portofino (Toledo Tower)
72. Duffield Lincoln-Mercury Agency
73. Frank House, Case Study #25
74. Hugh Gibbs & Donald Gibbs Architects Office Building
75. Linden Tower
76. Paul Edward Tay Office and Apartments
77. Galaxy Tower
78. Grace United Methodist Church
79. International Tower
80. Oil Drilling Islands
81. Penn/Crowell House
82. Long Beach City Hall and Public Library
83. Museum of Art, City of Long Beach
84. Spruce Goose Dome (Hercules [H-4] Flying Boat Hanger)
85. Arco Center Towers
86. California Veterans Memorial State Office Building
87. University Art Museum, California State University, Long Beach
88. Naples Canal House
89. Pyramid, California State University, Long Beach
90. Bikestation Long Beach
91. Aquarium of the Pacific
92. California State University, Chancellor's Headquarters
93. International Elementary School
94. Farmers & Merchants Bank, Los Altos Branch
95. Livable Places Competition
96. Howard CDM
97. Atlantic Avenue Workforce Housing Development
98. Olive Court
99. MacArthur Park Neighborhood Library
100. Gerald Desmond Bridge Replacement

MAP 2   LEGEND   ◯ INTACT   ▬ INTERSTATE
         ◉ DEMOLISHED   ▬ MAJOR STREETS

F G H I J

10TH STREET

WALNUT AVE
CHERRY AVE
JUNIPERO AVE
TEMPLE AVE
OBISPO AVE
REDONDO AVE

④⑤

4TH STREET

②⓪

3RD STREET

③⑥

⑦⑧

2ND STREET

BROADWAY

3RD STREET

①⑤

VISTA STREET

①⑦

1ST STREET

①⑥

OCEAN BLVD

⑤⓪ ⑨

LINDERO AVE
MOLINO AVE
ORIZABA AVE
PALOMA AVE

①② ⑦⑦ ⑥⑧

1ST STREET

MIRA MAR AVE
TERMINO AVE

2ND STREET

⑤②

③③

2. First National Bank
3. Masonic Temple
4. Adelaide A. Tichenor House
5. Bembridge House
7. Hotel Virginia
8. Carnegie Public Library
9. Long Beach Museum of Art
10. First Congregational Church
12. Raymond House
13. Markwell Building/Jergins Trust
    Building and Jergins Subway
15. Belmont Heights United Methodist
    Church
16. Better Home Electrical

17. Captain Ponto House
18. Farmers & Merchants Bank
    and Tower
19. Kress Building
20. Art Theater
22. Cooper Arms
23. Ebell Club and Theater
24. Insurance Exchange Building
    (Middoughs' Boys' Shop)
25. Security Pacific National Bank
    (Security Trust and Savings Bank)
26. The Willmore
27. The Breakers Hotel
28. YWCA

29. Pacific Coast Club
31. York Rite Masonic Temple
32. Broadlind Hotel
33. Casa Grande Apartment Building
    (La Casa Grande)
35. Lafayette Complex
36. Rose Towers (El Cordova
    Apartments)
38. Ocean Center Building
39. Villa Riviera
40. Walker's Department Store
42. Long Beach Skating Palace
43. The Koffee Pot Cafe
44. Municipal Auditorium

45. The Skinny House (Newton P.
    Rummond House)
47. U.S. Post Office and Federal
    Building
50. Lifeguard Headquarters, Cherry
    Avenue
52. Apartment Building on 1st
68. Marina Tower Model Apartment
70. Long Beach Public Safety Building
    and Long Beach County Building
75. Linden Tower
77. Galaxy Tower
78. Grace United Methodist Church
79. International Tower

80. Oil Drilling Islands
82. Long Beach City Hall and Public
    Library
83. Museum of Art, City of Long Beach
85. Arco Center Towers
86. California Veterans Memorial State
    Office Building
90. Bikestation Long Beach
91. Aquarium of the Pacific
92. California State University,
    Chancellor's Headquarters
93. International Elementary School

PROJECT SOURCES

Public files provided by the Office of Historic Preservation, Department of Planning and Building, City of Long Beach, served as a primary source of research for the majority of the pre-1960s buildings cited in the project entries. Files from the National Register of Historic Places also were utilized in compiling the text. Additional resources are noted below.

Bixby Ranch House
- Berner, ed., "Sketches from Way Back," *Los Fierros*, Vol. 2, July 1965.
- Bixby to Rancho Los Cerritos, pre-1965, La Linda Drive file, Rancho Los Cerritos.
- *Long Beach Daily Press*, "Very Beautiful Home," March 12, 1904, 6.

First National Bank
- Brown, "Restoration Planned for Landmark," May 16, 1983, 1.
- Case, "Clocks on Bank Building," September 7, 1947, B4.
- Clements, letter to the editor, May 23, 1983.
- *Long Beach Press*, "Twelve Story Structure," September 19, 1923, 17.

Adelaide A. Tichenor House
- Bosley, *Greene & Greene*, 67–69.
- Case, *History of Long Beach*, 568.
- Edward R. Bosley (director, Gamble House), interview by Cara Mullio, March 2003.
- *House Beautiful*, "New Life," February 1956, 88–95.
- Makinson, *Greene & Greene*, 99.

Bembridge House
- Long Beach Heritage, *Bembridge House*, 2004, 4.
- Lehrer, "Bembridge House in Long Beach," 2002.
- Masterson, "The Long Beach Story," November 1977, 4–8.

Hotel Virginia
- Bassett, "Hotel Virginia Locks Front Door," October 2, 1932, 3.
- Berner, *A Step Back in Time*, 43.
- *Daily Telegram*, "Victory of Big Hotel," September 8, 1905, 1.
- *Daily Telegram,* "Woman Designs Hotel Gardens," February 13, 1908, 1.
- *Daily Telegram*, "World's Finest Seaside Hostelries," October 31, 1913, 4.
- *Evening Tribune*, "Hotel Bixby," September 30, 1905, 1.
- Hotel Virginia Shopping Guide Co., *Hotel Virginia: Guide and Shopping List.*

Carnegie Public Library
- Brown, "Public Library Here," April 1922, 13.
- Case, *Long Beach Community*, 87.
- *Daily Telegram*, "Carnegie Library Will be Built," July 10, 1908, 1.
- *Daily Telegram*, "Carnegie Public Library," September 5, 1908, 1.
- *Daily Telegram*, "Formal Dedication of City Library," June 15, 1909, 1.
- *Long Beach Press*, "Opening of Library Auspicious," June 15, 1909, 1.

Long Beach Museum of Art
- Long Beach Museum of Art, "A Brief History," 2003.
- Joseph Coriaty (partner, Frederick Fisher and Partners Architects), interview by Cara Mullio and Jennifer M. Volland, June 2003.

First Congregational Church
- Pryor, "Landmark," 50.

Harnett House
- Polly and George Johnson (owners, Harnett House), interview by Cara Mullio and Jennifer M. Volland, March 2004.

Raymond House
- Hines, *Irving Gill*, 207–209.

Markwell Building/Jergins Trust Building and Jergins Subway
- Aschieris, "The Jergins Subway," July 29, 1979, 1.
- Berner, "My Experiences," 60–62.
- Case, "Did You Know," March 15, 1932, 1.
- Hillburg, "Preservers Dig In for Old Subway," January 6, 1992, B1.
- Long Beach Coalition, "The Jergins Trust 1979–87," November 1987.
- Lungren, "Arcade Offered Splendid Shopping," February 1981, 3.
- Rees, "Jergins Building Must Go," November 24, 1987, 1.

Belmont Heights United Methodist Church
- Barrett, "From the Pastor's Desk," October 22, 1972.
- Belmont Heights Methodist Church, *Dedication*, June 15–22, 1923.
- *Press-Telegram*, "Belmont Methodist Drive," August 10, 1947, 1.

Better Home Electrical
- *Long Beach Press*, "Electrical Home on First Street," February 23, 1923, 12.
- *Long Beach Press*, "Electricity Aids Advancement," February 21, 1923, 22.
- *Long Beach Press*, "Harold E. Ketchum," February 21, 1923, 24.
- *Long Beach Press*, "Labor-Saving Is Exhibit Theme," February 21, 1923, 23.
- *Long Beach Press*, "Model Electrical Home," February 21, 1923, 21.
- *Long Beach Sunday Press*, "Electrical Home Now Reality," February 18, 1923, E3.

Captain Ponto House
- *Daily Telegram*, Miner R. Smith advertisement, April 30, 1922, D7.
- Florence Smith Ballinger (daughter of Miner R. Smith), interview by Peter Devereaux, April 1985.
- *Long Beach Press*, Miner R. Smith advertisement, January 20, 1923, 13.

Farmers & Merchants Bank & Tower
- *Long Beach Press*, "New Structure is Monument Built by Conservative Policy," April 16, 1923, 118.

Kress Building
- Thomas, *America's 5 & 10 Cent Stores.*

Art Theater
- Hillburg, "Last Small Theater Reeling," December 18, 1992, A10.
- Howard Linn (owner, Art Theater), interview by Jennifer M. Volland, March 2004.

Community Hospital of Long Beach
- Allen, "Renovation Saves Hospital Landmark," February 16, 1979, 175.
- Dilday-Davis, *Doctors, Dreamers & Doers.*

Cooper Arms
- Bentley-Smith, "Cooper Arms," August 14, 2000, 1.
- "Cooper Arms," 1922.

Insurance Exchange Building (Middoughs' Boys' Shop)
- Morrell, "City Well Supplied," January 1, 1939, 3.
- Morrell, "First Court Here," February 10, 1938, 1.
- *Press-Telegram*, "Middough Edifice," August 17, 1930, A12.

Security Pacific National Bank (Security Trust and Savings Bank)
- *Long Beach Press*, "Security Bank to Build," September 19, 1923, 17.

YWCA
- Boutelle, *Julia Morgan, Architect*, 97–100.
- Kusel, "'Y' Denies Building Condemned," March 2, 1976, B1.
- *Long Beach Press*, "Corner of Sixth and Pacific," October 11, 1922, 1.
- Murrell, "Daughter of Pool Victim," February 29, 1976, A3.
- Murrell, "YWCA Shuts Building," March 10, 1976, B1.
- Pack, "An Edifice Wrecked," June 25, 1978, LS1.
- Pack, "New Contractors to Take Crack," August 17, 1978, A17.
- Pack, "YW Building Defies Demolition," June 25, 1978, LS1.
- *Press-Telegram*, "YWCA Building Gets Face-Lift," October 1, 1958, B1.

Pacific Coast Club
- Bemis, "PCC 'Barons' Will Celebrate," October 21, 1951, A34.
- Inaugural Volume, *Pacific Coast Club*, 30.
- *Long Beach Press*, "Club Building Plan Nearly Complete," September 9, 1923, 1.
- Otto, "The Pacific Coast Club," October 18, 1987, 7.
- Zappe, "Pacific Coast Club Plan Ok'd," April 4, 1987, 1.

Pray/Dawson House
- Stewart, "Urban Problems," February 1, 1983, A1.

York Rite Masonic Temple
- Case, *History of Long Beach*, 286.
- Frye, "Local Developer to Renovate," February 27–March 12, 2001, 2.
- Helin, "New, Urban Remodel," January 28, 2002, 1.
- Joseph Coriaty (partner, Frederick Fisher and Partners Architects), interview by Cara Mullio, March 2004.

Casa Grande Apartment Building (La Casa Grande)
- *Press-Telegram*, "Now Open for Inspection," August 26, 1928, 11.

Hancock Motors
- Doherty, "Not Just an Old Wreck," January 27, 1991, J1.
- *Great Cars*, "Mass Produced Pioneer," 991.
- Ivers, "Evolution of Modern Architecture," 266.
- Rosenbaum, "Hancock Motors: Adaptive Use," Spring 1994.

Lafayette Complex
- Hillburg, "Lafayette Owners Work to Restore," June 2, 1992, B1.
- Ivers, "Cecil Schilling, Long Beach Architect," 171–204.
- Lafayette Association of Homeowners Inc., "History of Lafayette," http://www.thelafayettelb.org/history.html.
- *Press-Telegram*, "Hotel Lafayette Will Open," October 27, 1929, A6.
- *Press-Telegram*, "Hotel Modernization Program Progresses," October 21, 1960, B9.

Rose Towers (El Cordova Apartments)
- Polyzoides et al., *Courtyard Housing in Los Angeles.*

Villa Riviera
- Hillburg, "Preserving Memories," July 7, 1996, A1.
- *Los Angeles Times*, "Skyscraper Rises Rapidly," September 23, 1928, V1.
- Michael W. Traub (senior member, Villa Riviera Architectural Committee), interview by Cara Mullio and Jennifer M. Volland, February 2004.

- Pool, "Villa Riviera's Gothic Walls," June 12, 2003, B2.
- *Press-Telegram*, "Villa Riviera Put Foremost," February 10, 1938, 3.

Walker's Department Store
- Lindborg Development, *History of The Walker Building*, 2002.
- *Long Beach Press*, "Marti Company Plans Modern Building," January 20, 1924, 1.
- *Press-Telegram*, "Hugh Marti Firm to Open," November 3, 1925, 2.
- *Press-Telegram*, "New Marti Store," October 28, 1928, A1.

Gaytonia
- Musselman, "Gaytonia Overlooks the Shore," October 11, 1990, 23.

Long Beach Skating Palace
- Cox, "Foundation Helping Village Renaissance," March 12, 2001, A13.

Municipal Auditorium
- Hinkey, *Federal Art in Long Beach*, 7–16.
- *Independent Press-Telegram Southland Magazine*, "Southland's Hall of Famous Names," March 3, 1957, 3.
- *Long Beach Convention News*, "Wrecker's Ball Rolling," February 1975, 1.
- Long Beach Municipal Officials et al., "Forward Steps," 1933.
- McKay, "Thousands See City Mosaic," January 30, 1938, 5.
- Piper, "A Mosaic Tile Mural," August 1938, 495.
- *Press-Telegram*, "Municipal Auditorium Monument of Progress," December 31, 1930, B1.
- Southern California State Office and Art Gallery, "Federal Art Project Works Progress Administration," January 1938.
- Stevens, "Colorful Adventures of Recreation," June 11, 2000, 1.
- Williams, "Long Beach Municipal Auditorium," March 3, 1957, 3.

The Skinny House (Newton P. Rummond House)
- Christensen, "Skinny House," May 31, 1980, H1.
- Gill, "Skinny House," Summer 1989, 14.
- Kelly, "Built on Dare," June 28, 1980, HL5.
- Oliver, "A Mere Slip of a Home," August 15, 1999, K1.
- Purcell, "America's Thinnest House," January 2, 1949, 7.
- Shannon, "Three-Story L.B. House," May 12, 1955, 2.
- Swanson, "Freak Home but Comfortable," February 10, 1932, A12.

Henry Clock House
- Matthews, *Kirtland Cutter*, 358–360.

U.S. Post Office and Federal Building
- Burmester, "Five Thousand Attend Post Office Opening," September 2, 1934, A14.
- Long Beach Post Office Customer Service, *Long Beach Post Office*, 2003.
- *Press-Telegram*, "New Post Office to Open," August 19, 1934, 1.
- *Press-Telegram*, "Notables Talk at Post Office," December 7, 1935, 1.
- *Sun*, "Our New Federal Building," June 6, 1931, 1.

Long Beach Polytechnic High School
- Hinkey, *Federal Art in Long Beach*, 29–32.
- Ivers, *Hugh Davies: Architect and Innovator*, 2002.
- *Press-Telegram*, "Architect's Suggestions for Poly High," October 1, 1933, 1.
- *Press-Telegram*, "Mural is Dedicated," June 5, 1939, A8.
- *Press-Telegram*, "Poly High School Structure," February 3, 1921, 1.
- *Press-Telegram*, "School Theater Ready," June 16, 1935, 1.

Lifeguard Headquarters, Cherry Avenue
- Miller and Gould, "Men in the Waters," http://www.ci.long-beach.ca.us/fire/.
- *Press-Telegram*, "City replacing lifeguard towers," November 17, 1981, 3.
- Russell, "L.B.'s Lifeguard Legacy," December 7, 1994, C1.

Tichenor Orthopedic Clinic for Children
- *Press-Telegram*, "Reception at Hospital Tomorrow," January 28, 1938, 1.
- *Press-Telegram*, "Tichenor Clinic," January 2, 1936, 7.

Kimpson/Nixon House
- *Arts & Architecture*, "Long Beach Single Family House," 34.
- Gebhard and Von Breton, *Los Angeles in the Thirties*, 111–114.
- Gladys Nixon (owner, Kimpson/Nixon House), interview by Cara Mullio and Jennifer M. Volland, May 2003.
- McCoy, *The Second Generation*, 151.
- Wegener, *Raphael Soriano*, 171.

Craig/McLeod House
- Newland, *Johnson, Kaufmann, Coate*, 43.
- Steve McLeod and Kelly Sutherlin McLeod (owners, Craig/McLeod House), interview by Cara Mullio and Jennifer M. Volland, March 2004.

Roosevelt Naval Base, Terminal Island
- *Architectural Record*, "Roosevelt Naval Base, Terminal Island", May 1944, 58–70.
- Crawford, "Architectural Properties on the Naval Station," January 1992, 1–6.
- Foster, "Roadblock Removed in COSCO Deal," June 1, 1998, 1.
- Hillburg, "Waves of Protest," March 16, 1997, A1.
- Sterngold, "West Coast Naval Base," September 16, 1996, A8.
- Weikel, "Navy Recommends Razing," May 27, 1998, B3.
- William Manley Consulting, *Historical and Architectural Assessment, Naval Station Long Beach*, June 24, 1994, 6.

VA Long Beach Healthcare System (Navy Hospital)
- Anthony, "V.A. Hospital Project," April 13, 1965, B3.
- Estella Murray (public affairs officer, VA Long Beach Healthcare), interview by Cara Mullio and Jennifer M. Volland, April 2004.
- *Independent Press-Telegram*, "VA Okays Hospital Plan," August 27, 1955, B3.
- *Press-Telegram*, "Naval Opens Hospital at Long Beach," December 15, 1942, B1.

California State University, Long Beach
- Coar, "Long Beach Beautiful," April 23, 1972, B10.
- Gloady, "This Eden was Planned," 11–12.
- Killingsworth, "History of the Sculpture Symposium," April 1967.
- *Los Angeles Times*, "College Union Rising," September 14, 1969, J1.
- Wilcox, "LBSC Plan Approved," January 13, 1963, A1.

Alexander House
- Campbell-Lange, *John Lautner*, 14.
- Escher, *John Lautner, Architect*, 72–75.
- Grace Alexander (owner, Alexander House), interview by Cara Mullio and Jennifer M. Volland, June 2003.

George's Fifties Diner
- Hess, *Googie: Fifties Coffee Shop*.
- Rice, "Bixby Knolls Diner Receives Historic Landmark Nomination," September 29, 2003, 4.
- Wallace, "Coffee Shops Modern," April 1, 1993, B1.

Matlock House
- Hines, *Richard Neutra*, 268.
- Margie Masterson (owner, Matlock House), interview by Cara Mullio and Jennifer M. Volland, November 2003.

Moore/Hafley Twin Houses
- Hines, *Richard Neutra*, 268.
- Janice Atzen (owner, Moore House), interviews by Cara Mullio and Jennifer M. Volland, October 2003 and March 2004.

Killingsworth, Brady & Smith Office Building
- McCoy, "What I Believe...," February 3, 1957, 46–49.

Java Lanes Bowling Alley
- Douglas, "Survivor: Java Lanes," September 9, 2002, 8.
- Russell, "Long-Gone Era," June 2, 1997, B3.

Opdahl House
- George, "Tribute to Fine Architecture," May 1, 1960, 12.
- *House & Garden*, "New Living in Old Neighborhoods," 132–135.
- *Independent Press-Telegram*, "Unique Long Beach Home," September 20, 1959, A17.
- Mulcahy, "Principle of Simple Design," February 14, 1960, VI1.
- Niece, *Art: An Approach*, 26–27.
- *Sunset*, "On a 30-Foot Lot...," October 1959, 80–81.

Ruth Bach Neighborhood Library
- Halferty, "Pride of Long Beach, December 1, 1957, 3,036.

Cambridge Office Building
- *Harvard Business School Bulletin*, "Art is Our Partner," February 1961, 16.
- *Independent Press-Telegram*, "Long Beach Architects Win," December 20, 1961, 1.
- *Los Angeles Times*, "Southland Architects Win," January 14, 1962, J1.
- Mulcahy, "Honor Award Given by AIA," October 16, 1960, J1.

Marina Tower Model Apartment
- *Arts & Architecture*, "Cooperative Apartments," 26.
- *Independent Press-Telegram*, "Big Interest Shown," September 6, 1959, B5.
- *Independent Press-Telegram*, "Marina Tower Plans Revised," August 30, 1959, R1.
- *Independent Press-Telegram*, Marina Tower advertisement, October 5, 1958, R3.
- Moore Realty, *Marina Tower*, 1958.

Long Beach Elks Lodge No. 888
- Long Beach Elks Lodge No. 888, *Dedication Brochure*, September 15–25, 1960.

Long Beach Public Safety Building and Long Beach County Building
- Maddock, "New County Building," December 21, 1960, A1.
- Weeks, "Police to Move," January 31, 1960, B2.

Portofino (Toledo Tower)
- Donald Gibbs (principal, Hugh Gibbs & Donald Architects, FAIA), interviews by Cara Mullio and Jennifer M. Volland, October 2003 and January 2004.

Duffield Lincoln-Mercury Agency
- *Independent Press-Telegram*, "Local Building Judged," September 3, 1967.

Frank House, Case Study #25
- *Arts & Architecture*, "Case Study House No. 25," 16–17.

Hugh Gibbs & Donald Gibbs Architects Office Building
- Currie, "Firm has family touch in design," December 12, 1988, C1.
- Donald Gibbs (principal, Hugh Gibbs & Donald Architects, FAIA), interviews by Cara Mullio and Jennifer M. Volland, October 2003 and January 2004.

Linden Tower
- *Press-Telegram*, "Open House Today," May 17, 1964, R7.

Paul Edward Tay Office and Apartments
- Krec, "A-Framed Beauty," February 8, 1970, 14–15.

- Paul Edward Tay (architect, Paul Edward Tay Architects), interview by Jennifer M. Volland, December 2003.

Galaxy Tower
- Chilcote, "17-Story Own-Your-Own," April 15, 1962, R1.
- Donald Gibbs (principal, Hugh Gibbs & Donald Architects, FAIA), interviews by Cara Mullio and Jennifer M. Volland, October 2003 and January 2004.
- The Galaxy, Galaxy Information Bulletin, circa 1970.
- *Press-Telegram*, "Raze 2 Sea Front Houses," March 3, 1963, 1.

International Tower
- Brown, "International Towers Sold," June 5, 1986, 1.
- Howland, "Planning Board Approves Condo Permit," July 17, 1981, B4.
- *Press-Telegram*, "Beach Tower Converting," April 14, 1966, B1.
- *Press-Telegram*, "Circular Foundation for Skyscraper," June 7, 1964, R1.
- *Press-Telegram*, "Clear Site for Construction.," January 19, 1964, R1.
- *Press-Telegram*, "Firm Foundation," August 2, 1964, R1.
- *Press-Telegram*, "It's the Height," July 5, 1964, R1.

Oil Drilling Islands
- Baldwin, "Landscaping on Closest Oil Island," March 14, 1967, B4.
- Baldwin, "Oil Island Glamour Plans," May 19, 1966, A1.
- Baldwin, "Oil Islands Near Completion," July 14, 1968, 5.
- Carlton, "Drilling Islands to be Beautified," February 20, 1966, A8.
- City of Long Beach Department of Oil Properties, "Long Beach's Oil Islands."
- Gore, "Beauty Belies Oil-Producing Purpose," April 8–9, 1978, X1.
- *Independent Press-Telegram*, "Beauty Treatment Set," January 9, 1966, A3.
- *Independent Press-Telegram*, "Oil Islands to Resume," August 8, 1974, B7.
- Schaff, "Oil Islands Lose Derricks, Facades," August 3, 1992, 1.
- *TIME*, "Decorating the Derricks," September 15, 1967, 49.

Penn/Crowell House
- Ron and Susan Crowell (owners, Penn/Crowell House), interview by Cara Mullio and Jennifer M. Volland, December 2003.
- Webb, *Themes and Variations*, 54–58.

Long Beach City Hall and Public Library
- *Aqueduct*, "Long Beach," Fall 1975, 5.
- Brackenbury, "New City Hall Designed," July 4, 1976, 47.
- City of Long Beach, *Your New City Hall*, 1976.
- Sherman, "City Hall Finish Postponed," August 30, 1976, 1.

Museum of Art, City of Long Beach
- Brackenbury, "Art Museum OK in Doubt," March 12, 1976, B1.
- Brackenbury, "Art Museum Price $15.6 Million," June 28, 1976, B1.
- Emery, "A Place of Life," August 31, 1975, L/S1.
- Gallegos and Korber, "Design for $15 Million Edifice," June 26, 1986, A1.
- Gallegos, "Museum of Art Got Left Behind," June 26, 1988, 1.
- Museum of Art, "Long Beach Museum of Art Progress," Fall 1974.
- Sutton, "Public Opposition," February 20, 1977, 1.

Spruce Goose Dome
- *Construction Contracting*, "415-ft. Dome, Only $4 Million," 28–29.
- Grobaty, "The Spruce Goose," May 13, 1983, 1.

Arco Center Towers
- Howland, "Arco Center to Sparkle," February 3, 1981, B2.
- *Press-Telegram*, "Tower is Topped Out," May 4, 1982, B1.
- Ross, "Last Hurdle Cleared," August 4, 1981, 1.
- Zappe, "Arco Center Suits 'A Team' Star," October, 3, 1983, 1.

California Veterans Memorial State Office Building
- Cox, "Idea for Lofts and Parking," January 3, 2002, A13.
- Donald Gibbs (principal, Hugh Gibbs & Donald Architects, FAIA), interviews by Cara Mullio and Jennifer M. Volland, October 2003 and January 2004.
- Houser, "New State Office Building," April 16, 1983, C1.
- Howland, "End is Near for State Building," September 22, 1981, B2.
- *Press-Telegram*, "State Office Building," April 25, 1997, C2.

University Art Museum, California State University, Long Beach
- Fillip, "Architecture for Art's Sake," May/June 1987, 23.
- *GA Document*, "University Art Museum," April 18, 1987.
- Payne, "Design for the University Art Museum," 357.

Naples Canal House
- Ron Kappe (architect, Kappe + Du), interview by Cara Mullio, March 2004.

Pyramid, California State University, Long Beach
- Crowe, "No Pyramid Scheme," August 19, 1994, C1.
- DeGanyar et al., "Space-Frame Pyramid," November 1994, 69.
- *Press-Telegram*, "Pyramid in the Right Place," June 1, 1992, B4.
- Saltzgaver, "Dreams Come True," October 31–November 3, 1994, 1–2.
- Woolard, "LBSU Arena on Schedule," February 6, 1994, D1.

Bikestation Long Beach
- Fernando Vazquez (architect, Fernando Vazquez/Studio), interview by Cara Mullio, February 2004.
- Georgia Case (project director, Bikestation Long Beach), interviews by Cara Mullio, February and March 2004.
- *Metro Quarterly*, "Chain Reaction," Spring/Summer 2003.
- Nero, "Clean Rides Drive, Scoot," April 20, 2002, 2.
- Olson, "In Freewayland Without a Car," March 28, 1999, 28.
- Snyder, "Ancillary Facilities," January 1998.
- Streeter and Wride, "Commuter's Headache Cure," January 29, 2002, B1.
- Webb, "Free Wheelin'," September 1998, 14.

Aquarium of the Pacific
- Aquarium of the Pacific, Chuck Davis (senior partner, Esherick, Homsey, Dodge and Davis), http://www.aquariumofpacific.org/vistor_info/aqua_arch.html.

California State University, Chancellor's Headquarters
- Lori J. Erdman (executive project manager, Chancellor's Headquarters), interview by Cara Mullio, March 2004.

International Elementary School
- Futagawa, *GA Document Extra*, 124–129.
- Mayne et al., *Morphosis: Buildings and Projects*, Appendix 11:26–27.

Farmers & Merchants, Los Altos Branch
- Pedro Blanco (architect, Fernald Design Group), interview by Cara Mullio, March 2004.

Livable Places Competition
- Angela Brooks (president, Livable Places), interview by Cara Mullio, February 2004.
- Coupland, "Livable L.A.," March 2003, 1.
- Milionis, "Winner Announced," September 9, 2003, 1.
- Olivier Touraine and Debbie Richmond (architects, Touraine + Richmond), interview by Cara Mullio, February 2004.

Howard CDM
- Martin Howard (developer, Howard CDM), interview by Cara Mullio and Jennifer M. Volland, January 2004.

Atlantic Avenue Workforce Housing Development
- Moule & Polyzoides Architects and Urbanists, *Housing Development Master Plan*, 2003.

Olive Court
- Studio E Architects, *Olive Court Project Concept Document*, 2003.

Gerald Desmond Bridge Replacement
- Gateway Cities Council of Governments, *I-710 Corridor/Gerald Desmond Bridge Gateway*, 2003.
- Higginbotham, "A Bridge Too Small," May 4, 2001, A1.
- Johnson, "Towers May be a First," December 16, 2003, A2.
- Schuyler, "Bridge as a Monument," May 1883, 1.

BIBLIOGRAPHY

Books

- Banham, Reyner. *Los Angeles: The Architecture of Four Ecologies.* New York: Penguin Books, 1971.
- Berner, Loretta. *A Step Back in Time.* Long Beach: Historical Society of Long Beach, 1990.
- ———, ed. *Earthquake '33: A Photographic History.* Long Beach: Historical Society of Long Beach, 1981.
- ———. *Shades of the Past.* Long Beach: Historical Society of Long Beach, 1995.
- ———. *Sketches from Way Back.* Long Beach: Los Cerritos Ranch House Museum, 1965.
- Bidwell, John. *A Journey to California with Observations about the Country, Climate and the Route to this Country.* San Francisco: John Henry Nash Printer, 1937.
- Border, Iain, ed. *The Unknown City.* Cambridge: MIT Press, 2001.
- Bosley, Edward R. *Greene & Greene.* London: Phaidon Press Ltd., 2000.
- Boutelle, Sara Holmes. *Julia Morgan, Architect.* New York: Cross River Press Ltd., 1988.
- Boyer, M. Christine. *The City of Collective Memory: Its Historical Imagery and Architectural Entertainments.* Cambridge: MIT Press, 1996.
- Briegel, Kaye. *Bixby Land Company 1896–1996: A Centennial History.* Long Beach: Bixby Land Co., 1996.
- Burnett, Claudine. *Haunted Long Beach.* Long Beach: Historical Society of Long Beach, 1996.
- ———. *Strange Sea Tales Along the Southern California Coast.* Long Beach: Historical Society of Long Beach, 2000.
- Calvino, Italo. *Invisible Cities.* New York: Harcourt Brace & Company, 1974.
- Campbell-Lange, Barbara-Ann. *John Lautner.* Köln, Germany: Taschen, 1999.
- Case, Walter H. *History of Long Beach.* Long Beach: Press-Telegram Publishing Company, 1935.
- ———. *History of Long Beach and Vicinity.* Vol. 1. Chicago: The S.J. Clarke Publishing Company, 1927.
- ———. *Long Beach Community Book.* Long Beach: Arthur H. Cawston, 1948.
- Conrads, Ulrich. *Programs and Manifestoes on 20th Century Architecture.* Cambridge: MIT Press, 2002.
- Crump, Spencer. *Ride the Big Red Cars: How Trolleys Helped Build Southern California.* Los Angeles: Crest Publications, November 1962.
- Cuff, Dana. *The Provisional City: Los Angeles Stories of Architecture and Urbanism.* Cambridge: MIT Press, 2000.
- Curtis, William J.R. *Modern Architecture Since 1900.* London: Phaidon Press Limited, 1982.
- Davis, Mike. *City of Quartz.* New York: First Vintage Books Edition, 1992.
- ———. *Ecology of Fear.* New York: Metropolitan Books/Henry Holt and Company, 1998.
- DeAtley, Richard. *Long Beach: The Golden Shore, A History of the City and the Port,* Houston: Pioneer Publications Inc., 1988.
- Dilday-Davis, Pamela. *Doctors, Dreamers & Doers, A History of Long Beach Community Medical Center.* Long Beach: Community Publications, 1999.
- Epley, Malcom. *Highlights & Anecdotes: Long Beach's 75 Years.* Long Beach: Long Beach Diamond Jubilee Inc., 1963.
- Escher, Frank. *John Lautner, Architect.* New York: Princeton Architectural Press, 1998.

- Ferriss, Hugh. *The Metropolis of To-morrow.* New York: Princeton Architectural Press, 1986.
- Gebhard, David and Harriette von Breton. *Los Angeles in the Thirties: 1931–1941.* Santa Monica: Hennesesey & Ingalls Inc., 1989.
- Gebhard, David and Robert Winter. *Los Angeles: An Architectural Guide.* Salt Lake City: Gibbs Smith, Publisher, 1994.
- Gratz, Roberta Branders. *The Living City.* New York: John Wiley & Sons Inc., 1989.
- GUST, ed. *The Urban Condition: Space, Community, and Self in the Contemporary Metropolis.* Rotterdam, The Netherlands: 010 Publishers, 1999.
- Hall, Peter and Colin Ward. *Sociable Cities: The Legacy of Ebenezer Howard.* New York: John Wiley & Sons, 1998.
- Hannaford, Donald R. and Revel Edwards. *Spanish Colonial or Adobe Architecture of California.* New York: Architectural Book Publishing Company Inc., 1931.
- Harris, Cyril M., ed. *Illustrated Dictionary of Historic Architecture.* New York: Dover Publications Inc., 1977.
- Hayden, Dolores. *The Power of Place: Urban Landscapes of Public History.* Cambridge: MIT Press, 1995.
- Hess, Alan. *Googie: Fifties Coffee Shop Architecture.* San Francisco: Chronicle Books LLC, 1986.
- Hillburg, Bill. *Long Beach: The City and Its People.* Carlsbad, CA: Heritage Media Corporation, 2000.
- Hines, Thomas S., *Irving Gill and the Architecture of Reform.* New York: The Monacelli Press Inc., 2000.
- ———. *Richard Neutra and the Search for Modern Architecture.* Berkeley and Los Angeles: University of California Press, 1994.
- Hinkey, Douglas M. *Federal Art in Long Beach: A Heritage Rediscovered.* Long Beach: Hippodrome Gallery, 1991.
- Howard, Ebenezer. *Tomorrow: A Peaceful Path to Real Reform.* London: Swan Sonnenschein, 1898. Republished as *Garden Cities of Tomorrow,* Swan Sonnenschein: London, 1902.
- Ivers, Louise. *Hugh Davies: Architect and Innovator.* Dominguez Hills, CA: University Art Gallery, California State University, 2002.
- Jacobs, Jane. *The Death and Life of Great American Cities.* New York: Vintage Books, 1961.
- Kirker, Harold. *California's Architectural Frontier.* San Marino, CA.: The Huntington Library, 1960.
- Koolhaas, Rem. *Delirious New York.* New York: Monacelli Press, 1994.
- Krythe, Maymie. *Port Admiral: Phineas Banning 1830–1885.* San Francisco: California Historical Society, 1957.
- Lefebvre, Henri. *The Production of Public Space.* Translated by Donald Nicholson-Smith. Oxford, England, and Cambridge, MA: Basil Blackwell, 1991.
- Lewis, Oscar. *Here Lived the Californians.* New York: Rinehart & Company Inc., 1957.
- Lynch, Kevin. *The Image of the City.* Cambridge: MIT Press, 1960.
- Makinson, Randell L. *Greene & Greene: Architecture as a Fine Art.* Salt Lake City: Peregrine Smith Books, 1977.
- Matthews, Henry C. *Kirtland Cutter: Architect in the Land of Promise.* Seattle: University of Washington Press, 1999.
- Mayne, Thom, Tony Robins, and Anthony Vidler. *Morphosis: Buildings and Projects 1993–1997.* New York: Rizzoli International Publications Inc., 1999.
- McCawley, William. *The First Angelinos: The Gabrielino Indians of Los Angeles.* Banning, CA: Malki Museum Press/Ballena Press, 1996.
- McCoy, Esther. *Case Study Houses 1945–1962.* 2nd ed. Los Angeles: Hennessey & Ingalls Inc., 1977.

- ———. *The Second Generation.* Salt Lake City: Peregrine Smith Books, 1984.
- McGroarty, John Steven, ed. *History of Los Angeles County.* Vol. 3. Chicago: The American Historical Society Inc., 1923.
- Meyer, Larry L. and Patricia L. Kalayjian. *Long Beach: Fortune's Harbor.* Tulsa, OK: Continental Heritage Press Inc., 1983.
- Mumford, Lewis. *The City in History: Its Origins, Its Transformations, and Its Prospects.* New York: Harcourt, Brace & World Inc., 1961.
- Newland, Joseph N., ed. *Johnson, Kaufmann, Coate: Partners in the California Style.* Santa Barbara: Capra Press, 1992.
- Olmsted Brothers and Bartholomew and Associates. *Parks, Playgrounds and Beaches for the Los Angeles Region.* Report submitted to the Citizens' Committee on Parks, Playgrounds, and Beaches, Los Angeles, 1930. In *Eden by Design: The 1930 Olmsted-Bartholomew Plan for the Los Angeles Region,* by Greg Hise and William Deverell. Berkeley and Los Angeles: University of California Press, 2000.
- *Pacific Coast Club,* Inaugural Vol. Long Beach: Pacific Coast Club, 1926.
- Payne, Alina. "Design for the University Art Museum, California State University Long Beach, California." In *Architecture and Its Image, Four Centuries of Architectural Representation, Works from the Collection of the Canadian Centre for Architecture,* edited by Eva Blau and Edward Kaufman. Cambridge: MIT Press, 1989.
- Poe, Stanley. *Naples: Its History in Words and Pictures 1784–1987.* Long Beach: The Naples Improvement Association, 1987.
- Polyzoides, Stefanos, Roger Sherwood, and James Tice. *Courtyard Housing in Los Angeles.* New York: Princeton Architectural Press, 1992.
- Queenan, Charles F. *Long Beach and Los Angeles: A Tale of Two Ports.* Northridge, CA: Windsor Publications Inc., 1986.
- *Ranchos of the Sunset: The Story of Long Beach.* Long Beach: Security Trust & Savings Bank, 1925.
- Relph, Edward. *The Modern Urban Landscape.* Baltimore: The Johns Hopkins University Press, 1987.
- Robinson, Irene. *Ranchos Become Cities.* Pasadena, CA: San Pasqual Press, 1939.
- Rolle, Andrew. *Los Angeles: From Pueblo to City of the Future.* San Francisco: Boyd & Fraser Publishing Company, 1981.
- Rowe, Peter G. *Modernity and Housing.* Cambridge: MIT Press, 1993.
- Salzer, George. *Rancho Los Alamitos.* Ramona, CA: Acoma Books, 1975.
- Sinclair, Upton. *Oil!* Berkeley and Los Angeles: University of California Press, 1997.
- Smith, Elizabeth A. T., ed. *Blueprints for Modern Living: History and Legacy of the Case Study Houses.* Cambridge: The MIT Press, 1989.
- Smith, Sarah Bixby. *Adobe Days.* Lincoln and London: University of Nebraska Press, 1987.
- Soleri, Paolo. *Archeology: The City in the Image of Man.* Cambridge: MIT Press, 1969.
- ———. "Citizens of the Cosmos." Conversation with Jeffrey Cook in *The Urban Ideal: Conversations with Paolo Soleri,* edited by John Strohmeier. Berkeley: Berkeley Hills Books, 2001.
- Starr, Kevin. *Endangered Dreams: The Great Depression in California.* New York and Oxford: Oxford University Press, 1996.

- Thomas, Bernice L. *America's 5 & 10 Cent Stores : The Kress Legacy*. New Jersey: John Wiley & Sons and the National Building Museum, 1997.
- Venturi, Robert. *Complexity and Contradiction in Architecture*. New York: Museum of Modern Art, 1966.
- Waldie, D.J. *Holy Land: A Suburban Memoir*. New York: W.W. Norton & Company, 1996.
- Waters, Maxine. "Unheard." In *Twilight: Los Angeles, 1992*, by Anna Deavere Smith. New York: First Anchor Books Edition, 1994.
- Webb, Michael. *Themes and Variations: House Design by Ray Kappe*. Mulgrave, Australia: The Images Publishing Group, 1998.
- Wegener, Wolfgang. *Raphael Soriano*. New York: Phaidon, 2002.
- Whyte, William H. *The Social Life of Small Urban Places*. Washington: Conservation Foundation, 1980.

Articles

- Allen, Rex Whitaker. "Renovation Saves Hospital Landmark." *Hospitals, J.A.H.A., Design and Construction*, February 16, 1979, 175.
- Anthony, Vern. "V.A. Hospital Project in Gear at L.B." *Independent*, April 13, 1965, B3.
- *Aqueduct*. "Long Beach," Fall 1975, 5.
- *Architectural Record*. "Roosevelt Naval Base, Terminal Island," May 1944, 58–70.
- *Arts & Architecture*. "Case Study House No. 25," January 1962, 16–17.
- ———. "Cooperative Apartments by Killingsworth, Brady and Smith," February 1959, 26.
- ———. "Long Beach Single Family House for D. Kimpson, R. Soriano, Architect. Views and Floor Plans." April 1941, 34.
- Aschieris, Rick. "The Jergins Subway." *Independent Press-Telegram*, July 29, 1979, 1.
- Baldwin, Jack O. "Most Landscaping on Closest Oil Island." *Press-Telegram*, March 14, 1967, B4.
- ———. "Oil Island Glamour Plans Bared," *Independent*, May 10, 1966, A1.
- ———. "Unique Oil Islands Near Completion—Artistry in Camouflage." *Independent Press-Telegram*, July 14, 1968, 5.
- Bassett, Hugh. "Hotel Virginia Locks Front Door: Noted Hostelry Closed." *Press-Telegram*, October 2, 1932, 3.
- Bemis, Sterling. "PCC 'Barons' Will Celebrate." *Independent*, October 21, 1951, A34.
- Brackenbury, Don. "Art Museum OK in Doubt." *Press-Telegram*, March 12, 1976, B1.
- ———. "Art Museum Price $15.6 million." *Press-Telegram*, June 28, 1976, B1.
- ———. "New City Hall Designed as Symbol of L.B." *Independent Press-Telegram*, Bicentennial Survey 1976, July 4, 1976, 47.
- Brown, Scott. "International Towers Sold, to be Converted to Condos." *Press-Telegram*, June 5, 1986, 1.
- ———. "Restoration Planned for Landmark." *Press-Telegram*, May 16, 1983, 1.
- Brown, Zaidee. "Public Library Here Loans 523,946 Books in Single Year." *Daily Telegram, Industrial and Development Number*, April 1922, 13.
- Burmester, H.F. "Five Thousand Attend Post Office Opening." *Press-Telegram*, September 2, 1934, A14.
- Carlton, Mary Ellis. "Drilling Islands to be Beautified." *Press-Telegram*, February 20, 1966, A8.
- Case, Walter H. "Clocks on Bank Building See City Grow 100-fold." *Press-Telegram*, September 7, 1947, B4.
- ———. "Did You Know That — ?," *Long Beach Sun*, March 15, 1932, 1.

- Chilcote, Ken. "17-Story Own-Your-Own to be Added to Skyline." *Press-Telegram*, April 15, 1962, R1.
- Christensen, Joyce. "Skinny House." *Press-Telegram*, May 31, 1980, H1.
- Coar, Roger. "Long Beach Beautiful." *Independent Press-Telegram*, April 23, 1972, B10.
- *Construction Contracting*. "415-ft. Dome, Only $4 Million." March/April 1982, 28–29.
- Coupland, Ken. "Livable L.A." *Metropolis*, March 2003, 1.
- Cox, John W. "Foundation Helping Village Renaissance." *Press-Telegram*, March 12, 2001, A13.
- ———. "New Idea for Lofts and Parking." *Press-Telegram*, January 3, 2002, A13.
- Crowe, Jerry. "No Pyramid Scheme." *Los Angeles Times*, August 19, 1994, C1.
- Currie, Don. "Firm Has Family Touch in Design." *Press-Telegram*, December 12, 1988, C1.
- *Daily Telegram*. "Carnegie Library will be Built by W. Crowell." July 10, 1908, 1.
- ———. "The Craig Ship Plant: Our First Big Industry Now Employing 240 Men and Needing More Skilled Labor." April 4, 1910, 3.
- ———. "Formal Dedication of City Library." June 15, 1909, 1.
- ———. "Hotel Virginia One of World's Finest Seaside Hostelries." October 31, 1913, 3.
- ———. "Laying Corner Stone of Carnegie Public Library." September 5, 1908, 1.
- ———. "Long Beach Is Home of Widely Known Film Producing Company: $300,000 Investment Made— Employees Number 250—Many Famous." November 18, 1915, 11.
- ———. "Woman Designs Hotel Gardens." February 13, 1908, 1.
- ———. "Wow! What a Time! Whole Town and its Relatives Out to Celebrate Victory of Big Hotel." September 8, 1905, 1.
- *Daily Telegram, Industrial and Development Number*. "No 'Closed Season' Here For Motor Car" April 1922, 17.
- ———. "Religious Life A Civic Factor." April 1922, 13.
- *Daily Telegram, Industrial and Tourist Edition*. "Our Building Activity: All Lines of Construction Represented—Home-Building a Big Feature in City's Growth." November 1917, 23.
- Davis, Chuck. "End of the Cyclone." *Independent Press-Telegram, Southland Magazine*. July 21, 1968, 5.
- DeGanyar, Tejav J., Michael D. Griffin, and Michael R. Patterson. "Space-Frame Pyramid." *Civil Engineering*, November 1994, 69.
- Doherty, Shawn. "Not Just an Old Wreck: Hupmobile Agency Was Once Showplace." *Los Angeles Times*, January 27, 1991, J1.
- Douglas, Theo. "Survivor: Java Lanes Still has a Few Strikes Left," *Press-Telegram*, September 9, 2002, 8.
- *Downtown Gazette*. "Cooper Arms." August 14, 2000, 1.
- Drake, Colonel Charles Rivers. "Life Just Long, Sweet Song and I Would Live it Again, Says Colonel." *Press-Telegram*, February 12, 1925, 3.
- Emery, Elise. "New Museum: 'A Place of Life." *Press-Telegram*, Sunday, August 31, 1975, L/S1.
- *Evening Tribune*, "Hotel Bixby as Seen from the Bay." September 30, 1905, 1.
- Fillip, Janice. "Architecture for Art's Sake." *Architecture California*, May/June 1987, 23.
- Foster, Sarah. "Roadblock Removed in COSCO Deal: Navy Ok's City's Plan for Long Beach Naval Station." *World Net Daily*, June 1, 1998, 1.
- Frye, Cindy. "Local Developer to Renovate Historic York Rite Masonic Temple into Contemporary Living Environment." *Long Beach Business Journal*, February 27–March 12, 2001, 2.

- Futagawa, Yoshio. *GA Document Extra 09 Morphosis*. A.D.A. Edita Tokyo, 1997, 124–129.
- *GA Document*, "University Art Museum California State University, Long Beach, California," April 18, 1987.
- Gallegos, Karen A. "Museum of Art Got Left Behind the Long Beach Cultural Surge." *Press-Telegram*, June 26, 1988, 1.
- Gallegos, Karen A. and Dorothy Korber. "Grand Design for $15 Million Edifice Went Pfft." *Press-Telegram*, June 26, 1986, A1.
- George, Stella. "Tribute to Fine Architecture." *Independent Press-Telegram, Southland Magazine*, May 1, 1960, 12.
- Gill, Larry. "The Skinny House." *Interchange*, Summer 1989, 14.
- Gore, Robert J. "Islands' Beauty Belies Oil-Producing Purpose." *Los Angeles Times, Southeast Weekend Edition*, April 8–9, 1978, X1.
- Griswold, Earl. "Last Crop Being Planted on Los Altos Farm Land." *Press-Telegram*, April 25, 1957, P20.
- Grobaty, Tim. "The Spruce Goose." *Press-Telegram, Souvenir Edition Weekend*. May 13, 1983, 1.
- Halferty, Guy. "Pride of Long Beach." *Library Journal*. December 1, 1957, 3,036.
- Helin, Kurt. "Masonic Temple to Get New, Urban Remodel." *Downtown Gazette*, January 28, 2002, 1.
- Higginbotham, Keith. "A Bridge too Small." *Press-Telegram*, May 4, 2001, A1.
- Hillburg, Bill. "Lafayette Owners Work to Restore Their Complex." *Press-Telegram*, June 2, 1992, B1.
- ———. "Last Small Theater Reeling." *Press-Telegram*, December 18, 1992, A10.
- ———. "Preservers Dig in for Old Subway." *Press-Telegram*, January 6, 1992, B1.
- ———. "Preserving Memories: At Villa Riviera, It's Just a Matter of Pride." *Press-Telegram*, July 7, 1996, 1.
- ———. "Waves of Protest." *Press-Telegram*, March 16, 1997, A1.
- *House & Garden*. "New Living in Old Neighborhoods." October 1958, 132–135.
- *House Beautiful*. "A New Life for a Grand Old Ruin." February 1956, 88–95.
- Houser, Bob. "New State Office Building Dedicated." *Press-Telegram*, April 16, 1983, C1.
- Howland, Richard. "Arco Center to Sparkle." *Press-Telegram*, February 3, 1981, B2.
- ———. "End is Near for State Building." *Press-Telegram*, September 22, 1981, B2.
- ———. "Planning Board Approves Condo Permit for International Tower." *Press-Telegram*, July 17, 1981, B4.
- *Independent*. "Hotel Modernization Program Progresses." October 21, 1960, B9.
- ———. "Long Beach Architects Win World Fame and Honors." Dec. 20, 1961, 1.
- ———. "Long-Range Freeway Plan Bright." July 23, 1959, C5.
- ———. "Oil Islands to Resume Waterfalls and Lighting." August 8, 1974, B7.
- ———. "VA Okays Hospital Plan." August 27, 1955, B3.
- *Independent Press-Telegram*. "Beauty Treatment Set for L.B. Oil Islands." January 9, 1966, A3.
- ———. "Big Interest Shown in Marina Tower." September 6, 1959, B5.
- ———. "Local Building Judged Grand Prix Winners." September 3, 1967.
- ———. "Marina Tower Plans Revised to Offer Smaller Residences." August 30, 1959, R1.
- ———. "Unique Long Beach Home Wins Architectural Design Award." September 20, 1959, A17.

- Ivers, Louise H. "Cecil Schilling, Long Beach Architect." *Southern California Quarterly*, Vol. 79, Summer 1997, 171–204.
- ———. "The Evolution of Modern Architecture in Long Beach." *Southern California Quarterly*, Vol. 68, Fall 1986, 266.
- Ivy, Carol. "Long Beach's Developing Controversy." *Independent Press-Telegram*. October 28, 1973, L/S1.
- Jergler, Don. "Planning Pine Avenue." *Press-Telegram*, January 23, 2004, A17.
- Johnson, Eric. "Span's Towers May be a First." *Press-Telegram*, December 16, 2003, A2.
- Kelley, Daryl. "New Lease on Life: Rehabilitation Rekindles Hope at Housing Project, but Critics Say It Isn't Enough." *Los Angeles Times*, January 3, 1988, IX1.
- Kelly, Erin. "Built on Dare, It's Only 10 Feet Wide." *Los Angeles Times*, June 28, 1980, HL5.
- Koolhaas, Rem. "Toward the Contemporary City." *Design Book Review 17*, Winter 1989, 15–16.
- Krec, Ellen. "A-Framed Beauty on a Problem Site." *Independent Press-Telegram, Southland Magazine*, February 8. 1970, 14–15.
- Kusel, Denise. " 'Y' denies building condemned." *Independent*, March 2, 1976, B1.
- LaRiviere, Anne. "Skinny House Not for Everyone." *Los Angeles Times*, Jan. 29, 1983, 1.
- Light, Bill. "Shore Wars." *LA Weekly*, May 21–27, 1999, www.laweekly.com/ink/99/26/news-light.php.
- *Long Beach Convention News*. "Wrecker's Ball Rolling on New Convention Center." February 1975, 1.
- *Long Beach Daily Paper*. "A Very Beautiful Home: Brief Description of the Improvements Made by Geo. H. Bixby In His Residence." March 21, 1904, 6.
- *Long Beach Press*, "Club Building Plan Nearly Complete." September 9, 1923, 1.
- ———. "Corner of Sixth and Pacific for New Structure." October 11, 1922, 1.
- ———. "Electrical Home on First Street Formally Opened." February 23, 1923, 12.
- ———. "Electricity Aids Advancement of Woman of Today." February 21, 1923, 22.
- ———. "Harold E. Ketchum, Builder, Designed Electric Home." February 21, 1923, 24.
- ———. "Hugh A. Marti Company Plans Modern Building." January 20, 1924, 1.
- ———. "Knoll Northeast of City Would Make A Beautiful Site For Municipal Park: Charles Mulford Robinson Expresses Views on What He Terms a Golden Opportunity to Aid in Making Long Beach a City Beautiful." December 14, 1908, 1.
- ———. "Labor-Saving is Exhibit Theme at Electrical Home." February 21, 1923, 23.
- ———. "Model Electrical Home." February 21, 1923, 21.
- ———. "Opening of Library Auspicious Affair." June 15, 1909, 1.
- ———. "Security Bank to Build Million Dollar Home at First and Pine; Twelve Story Structure is Designed." September 19, 1923, 17.
- ———. "Setting Nation's Style in Homes: from Swiss Chalet and Bungalow to Aeroplane and Spanish Type Long Beach has led country in changing fashions in homes." November 5, 1922, 6.
- *Long Beach Sunday Press*. "Electrical Home Now Reality." February 18, 1923, E3.
- "Long Beach: Where Oil and Water Do Mix!" *Harbor Highlights Magazine*, 7.
- *Los Angeles Times*. "College Union rising Without Benefit of Public Tax Funds." September 14, 1969, J1.

- ———. "Skyscraper Rises Rapidly: Completion of Long Beach Apartment Project Set for Thanksgiving Day." September 23, 1928, V1.
- ———. "Southland Architects Win 1st Prize in International Design Exhibition." January 14, 1962, J1.
- Lungren, Nancy. "Arcade Offered Splendid Shopping Underground." *Long Beach Heritage*, Vol. 2, No. 1, February 1981, 3.
- Maddock, Don. "Warren Calls New County Building 'Symbol of Law.' " *Independent Press-Telegram*, December 21, 1960, A1.
- Masterson, Iola. "The Long Beach Story." *Long Beach Review*, November 1977, 4–8.
- McCoy, Esther. "What I Believe ..." *Los Angeles Times Magazine*, February 3, 1957, 46–49.
- McKay, Robert. "Thousands See City Mosaic Dedication." *Press-Telegram*, January 30, 1938, 5.
- *Metro Quarterly*. "Chain Reaction." Spring/Summer 2003.
- Milionis, Allison. "Winner Announced for NEA Community Design and Housing Competition." *Architecture Record*, September 9, 2003, 1.
- Miller, Richard and Noel Gould. "Men in the Waters: The History of the Long Beach Lifeguard Service." City of Long Beach, http://www.ci.long-beach.ca.us/fire/.
- Morrell, Harry. "City Well Supplied with Court Service." *Press-Telegram*, January 1, 1939, 3.
- ———. "First Court Here in Lean-to Under Trees." *Press-Telegram*, February 10, 1938, 1.
- Mulcahy, Frank. "Honor Award Given by AIA." *Los Angeles Times*. October 16, 1960, J1.
- ———. "Principle of Simple Design Basic to Sound Architecture." *Los Angeles Times*. February 14, 1960, VI1.
- Murray, Walt. "LBSU Reflects—and Affects—Life-style of L.B. Area." *Independent Press-Telegram*, September 24, 1972, A1.
- Murrell, Al. "Daughter of Pool Victim Persuaded Parents to Go." *Independent*, February 29, 1976, A3.
- ———. "YWCA Shuts Building, Plans to Move." *Press-Telegram*. March 10, 1976, B1.
- Musselman, Sheila. "Gaytonia Overlooks the Shore From the Heights." *Grunion Gazette*, October 11, 1990, 23.
- Nero, Mark Edward. "Clean Rides Drive, Scoot. Environment: Bikestation Long Beach Adds Rental Plan for Emission-free Vehicles." *Press-Telegram*, April 20, 2002, 2.
- Oliver, Marilyn Tower. "A Mere Slip of a Home." *Los Angeles Times*, K1.
- Olson, Martha Stevenson. "In Freewayland Without a Car." *New York Times*, March 28, 1999, 28.
- Omohundro, Thad. "Carmelitos Project is Under Way." *Long Beach Press-Telegram*, August 27, 1939, A5.
- Otto, Doug W. "The Pacific Coast Club: A Past—and a Future?" *Press Telegram*, October 18, 1987, 1.
- Pack, Susan. "An Edifice Wrecked." *Press-Telegram*, June 25, 1978, L/S1.
- ———. "New Contractors to Take Crack at Stubborn YWCA Building." *Independent*, August 17, 1978, A17.
- ———. "YW Building Defies Demolition." *Press-Telegram*, June 25, 1978, L/S1.
- Piper, Natt. "A Mosaic Tile Mural." *Pencil Points*, August 1938, 495.
- Pool, Bob. "Villa Riviera's Gothic Walls Have Tales to Tell." *Los Angeles Times*, June 12, 2003, B2.
- *Press-Telegram*, "A pyramid in the right place," June 1, 1992, B4.
- ———. "Architect's Suggestions for Poly High School," October 1 1933, 1.
- ———. "Beach Tower Converting to an Apartment Hotel," April 14 1966, B1.

- ———. "Belmont Methodist Drive to Complete Plant Opens." August 10, 1947, 1.
- ———. "Cerritos Circle to Open in L.B. Country Club District." June 7, 1964, R4.
- ———. "Circular Foundation for Skyscraper." June 7, 1964, R1.
- ———. "City Replacing Lifeguard Towers." *Press-Telegram*, November 17, 1981, 3.
- ———. "Clear Site for Construction of 31-Story Circular Tower in L.B." January 19, 1964, R1.
- ———. "Firm Foundation for This Round Tower." August 2, 1964, R1.
- ———. "Hotel Lafayette Will Open Doors Monday; Festivities Planned." October 27, 1929, A6.
- ———. "Hotel Virginia Locks Front Door; Noted Hostelry Closed." October 2, 1932, 3.
- ———. "Hugh Marti Firm to Open Enlarged Store Tomorrow." November 3, 1925, 2.
- ———. "It's the Height—of Something or Other." July 5, 1964, R1.
- ———. "La Casa Grande is Now Open for Inspection." August 26, 1928, 11.
- ———. "Middough Edifice Now One of Most Modern in City." August 17, 1930, A12.
- ———. "Municipal Auditorium Monument of Progress." December 31, 1930, B1.
- ———. "Mural is dedicated at Poly High School." June 5, 1939, A8.
- ———. "Naval Opens Hospital at Long Beach." December 15, 1942, B1.
- ———. "New Marti Store to Cost $750,000 Will Be Erected." October 28, 1928, A1.
- ———. "New Post Office to Open Next Saturday." August 19, 1934, 1.
- ———. "Notables Talk at Post Office Dedication," December 7, 1935, 1.
- ———. "Open House Today." May 17, 1964, R7.
- ———. "Poly High School Structure Erected at Cost of $200,000." February 3, 1921, 1.
- ———. "Raze 2 Sea Front Houses for High-Rise." March 3, 1963, 1.
- ———. "Reception at Hospital Tomorrow: Tichenor Clinic Plans to Receive Many Visitors at Opening Event," January 28, 1938, 1.
- ———. "School Theater Ready for Use." June 16, 1935, 1.
- ———. "State Office Building in Long Beach to be Closed." April 25, 1997, C2.
- ———. "Tichenor Clinic Aims at Having Own Structure, Many Organizations Help to Make Life Brighter for Crippled Children." January 2, 1936, 7.
- ———. "Tower is Topped Out." May 4, 1982, B1.
- ———. "Villa Riviera Put Foremost Among Apartments Here." February 10, 1938, 3.
- ———. "YWCA Buildings Gets Face-Lift." October 1 1958, B1.
- *Press-Telegram, Southland Magazine*, "Long Beach Municipal Auditorium 25 Years Old; Southland's Hall of Famous Names." March 3, 1957, 3.
- Purcell, Everett. "America's Thinnest House." *Press-Telegram*, January 2 1949, 7.
- Rees, Julie. "Jergins Building Must Go." *Press-Telegram*, November 24, 1987, 1.
- Rice, Jenny Lee. "Bixby Knolls Diner Receives Historic Landmark Nomination." *Downtown Gazette*, September 29, 2003, 4.
- Ross, Andrew. "Last Hurdle Cleared by Arco Towers." *Independent*, August 4, 1981, 1.
- Russell, Kelle. "L.B.'s Lifeguard Legacy." *Press-Telegram*, December 7, 1994, C1.
- ———. "Long-gone Era Seen in a Bowling Alley Sign." *Press-Telegram*, June 2, 1997, B3.

- Saltzgaver, Harry. "Dreams Come True As Pyramid Reaches To Sky." *Gazette Newspapers Special Section*, October 31–November 3, 1994, 1.
- Schaff, Bob. "Skyline Changing as Oil Islands Lose Derricks, Facades," *Downtown Gazette*, August 3, 1992, 1.
- Schuyler, Montgomery. "The Bridge as a Monument." *Harper's Weekly*, May 1883, 1.
- Shannon, Herb. "Three-story L.B. House on 10-foot Lot for Sale." *Press-Telegram*, May 12 1955, 2.
- Sherman, Kris. "City Hall Finish Postponed Again." *Independent Press-Telegram*, August 30, 1976, 1.
- Sitton, Tom. "It's A Question of Interpretation: The Dilemma of Rancho Los Cerritos." *Terra* 30, No. 1, Fall 1991, 24–29.
- Sterngold, James. "West Coast Naval Base Belatedly Stirs Passions." *New York Times*, September 16, 1996, A8.
- Stevens, Joe. "Colorful Adventures of 'Recreation': The Mosaic Mural Has a History of Controversy that Continues as it Becomes Part of the Long Beach Plaza Redevelopment." *Press-Telegram*, June 11, 2000, 1.
- Stewart, Jill. "Urban Problems." *Press-Telegram*, February 1, 1983, A1.
- Streeter, Kurt and Nancy Wride. "Bike Station is a Commuter's Headache Cure." *Los Angeles Times*, January 29, 2002, B1.
- *Sun.* "Here's Our New Federal Building." June 6, 1931, 1.
- *Sunset.* "On a 30-foot Lot... the Luxury of Space Indoors and Out." October 1959, 80–81.
- Sutton, Charles. "Public Opposition May Have Sunk L.B. Museum Plan." *Independent Press-Telegram*, February 20, 1977, 1.
- Swanson, Ed. "Freak Home but Comfortable." *Press-Telegram*, February 10, 1932, A12.
- *TIME.* "Decorating the Derricks." September 15, 1967, 49.
- Wallace, Amy. "Coffee Shops Modern." *Los Angeles Times*, April 1, 1993, B1.
- Webb, Michael. "Free Wheelin'," *Westways*, September 1998, 14.
- Weeks, George. "Police to Move in on New Quarters." *Independent Press-Telegram*, January 31, 1960, B2.
- Weikel, Dan. "Navy Recommends Razing of Former Base's Historic Buildings." *Los Angeles Times*, May 27, 1998, B3.
- Wilcox, Robert. "LBSC Plan Approved: $60 Million Campus for 20,000 Students." *Independent Press-Telegram*, January 13, 1963, A1.
- Williams, Vera. "Southland's Hall of Famous Names." *Press-Telegram*, March 3, 1957. 3.
- Woolard, John. "Pyramid Progress: LBSU Arena on Schedule Despite $3.7 Million Shortfall." *Press-Telegram*, February 6, 1994, D1.
- Zappe, John. "Pacific Coast Club Plan Ok'd." *Press-Telegram*, April 4, 1987, 1.
- ———. "Arco Center Suits 'A Team' Star to a T." *Press-Telegram*, October, 3, 1983, 1.

Other

- Adams, Thomas R. "City Planning." *Community Bulletin Vol. 4, No. 8*, Long Beach Chamber of Commerce, 1920, 1.
- Armstrong, Mike. "Long Beach: Livable Places Profile." Report for the Southern California Association of Governments, June 1998.
- Barrett, Truman A. "From the Pastor's Desk." *Voice of Belmont Heights United Methodist Church*. Newsletter, October 22, 1972.
- Belmont Heights Methodist Church. *Dedication.* Pamphlet, June 15–22, 1923.
- Bixby, David. Letter to Rancho Los Cerritos, pre-1965.

- Cerritos Park advertisement. *Press-Telegram*, October 31, 1937, A13.
- City of Long Beach. "Green Building Policy for Municipal Buildings." *Green Building Policy for New Municipal Building Projects*, 2.1, 2004.
- ———. "Your New City Hall... Main Library Directory." Fact sheet for facilities, 1976.
- City of Long Beach Department of Oil Properties. *Long Beach's Oil Islands.* Circa 1970s.
- Clements, Karen. Letter to the editor. *Press-Telegram*, May 23, 1983.
- Cooper Arms. *Cooper Arms.* Brochure, 1922.
- Crawford, Kathleen. *Architecture, Historic and Architectural Properties on the Naval Station.* Report for State of California, Resources Subcommission, Department of Parks and Recreation, Office of Historic Preservation, January 1992, 1–6.
- Davis, Chuck, senior partner, EHDD. Interview on Aquarium of the Pacific website, http://www.aquariu-mofpacific.org/vistor_info/aqua_arch.html.
- Fogg, Neeta and Paul Harrington. "Growth and Change in the California and Long Beach/Los Angeles Labor Markets." Report for Conference of Mayors, Workforce Development Summit, Long Beach, CA, May 3, 2001.
- The Galaxy. *Galaxy Information Bulletin.* Circa 1970s.
- Gateway Cities Council of Governments. *The I-710 Corridor/Gerald Desmond Bridge Gateway Program Booklet.* 2003.
- Gilbert Arnold Sanchez Architects. *Historic Structure Report: Rancho Los Cerritos.* Report for City of Long Beach, 1987.
- Gloady, Rick. "This Eden was Planned." California State University, Long Beach, 2000, 11–12.
- Harnik, Peter. *The Excellent City Park System.* Report, published by Trust for Public Land, San Francisco, 2003, 38.
- *Harvard Business School Bulletin.* "Art is Our Partner." February 1961, 16.
- Hotel Virginia Shopping Guide Co. *Hotel Virginia: Guide and Shopping List.*
- Killingsworth, Edward. "History of the Sculpture Symposium." Lecture, meeting of student counselors at California State College at Long Beach, April 1967.
- L. S. Whaley Company Development. University City Business Center marketing brochure. Circa 1950.
- Lafayette Association of Home Owners. "History of Lafayette." http://www.thelafayettelb.og/history.html.
- Lehrer, Ruthann. "The Bembridge House in Long Beach." *Historical Society of Long Beach Newsletter*, 2002.
- Lindborg Development. *History of The Walker Building.* Brochure, 2002.
- Long Beach Coalition. *The Jergins Trust 1979-87.* Presentation to Redevelopment Agency, Long Beach, CA, November 23, 1987.
- Long Beach Elks Lodge No. 888. *Dedication Brochure.* September 15–25, 1960.
- Long Beach Heritage. *Bembridge House.* Brochure, 2004.
- Long Beach Municipal Officials, Chamber of Commerce Executive, and Others. "Forward Steps." Report, 1933.
- Long Beach Museum of Art. *A Brief History of the Long Beach Museum of Art's Historic Home.* Brochure, 2003.
- ———. "Long Beach Museum of Art Progress." Newsletter, Fall 1974.
- Long Beach Post Office. *Long Beach Post Office.* Pamphlet, 2003.
- Long Beach Strategic Plan Task Force, *Long Beach 2010 Strategic Plan*, January 2001.
- Long Beach Transit. "Long Beach: A New Wave in Transit." Http://www.lbtransit.com/history6.html.

- Lumley, Kathleen Chandler. "Redevelopment—More than Tearing Down Old Buildings and Putting up New Ones." California State University, Long Beach Network, Vol. 34 No. 12, April 2, 1982, 2.
- Marie Jones Consulting. *Art Exchange Feasibility Study.* City of Long Beach Redevelopment Agency, January 7, 2004.
- Marina Tower advertisement. *Independent Press-Telegram*, October 5, 1958, R3.
- Members of Los Altos Association. *Protective Restrictions for Tract 15545 Park Estates.* September 14, 1953.
- Miner R. Smith advertisements. *Long Beach Press*, 1923.
- Moore Realty. *The Marina Tower.* Brochure, 1958.
- Moule & Polyzoides Architects and Urbanists. *Atlantic Avenue Workforce Housing Development Master Plan*, 2003.
- Naples advertisement. *Long Beach Daily Telegram*, July 21, 1905, 3.
- Poelzig, Hans. "Das Deutsche Kunstgewerbe (Third German Exhibition of Applied Art) 1906." In *Lesebuch für Baumeister.* Berlin: Karl H. Henssel Verlag, 1947.
- Pryor, Luanne. "Landmark." *The Pilgrim.* Long Beach: The First Congregational Church of Long Beach, 1979. Reprinted from *Long Beach Review*, October 1978, Vol. II, No. II, 50.
- Robinson, Charles Mulford. Abstract from "Suggestions for Municipal Improvement in Long Beach California," City of Long Beach, January 1909.
- Roosevelt, Franklin Delano. Address at Oglethorpe University, Atlanta, GA, May 22, 1932.
- Rosenbaum, Debra. "Hancock Motors: Adaptive Use of an Historic Auto Showroom to run a Community Cultural Art Center." Paper for UCLA course AUP 277, Historic Preservation, Spring 1994.
- Snyder, Ryan. "Ancillary Facilities." Report for the Federal Highway Administration, January 1998.
- Southern California State Office and Art Gallery. *Federal Art Project Works Progress Administration.* News release, 1938.
- Studio E Architects. *Olive Court Project Concept Document.* 2003.
- William Manley Consulting. *Historical and Architectural Assessment, Naval Station Long Beach.* Report for Lowell Martin, Southwest Division, Naval Facilities Engineering Command, June 24, 1994, 6.
- Willmore City advertisement. *Los Angeles Times*, April 8, 1883, 1.

ACKNOWLEDGEMENTS

We wish to thank our publisher Hennessey + Ingalls for recognizing Long Beach as a city in need of a publication on its architecture. In particular, we are indebted to owner Mark Hennessey and editor Robert Barrett for believing in *Long Beach Architecture: The Unexpected Metropolis* from inception to realization.

We extend tremendous gratitude to the Long Beach Navy Memorial Heritage Association (LBNMHA) for its generous support of our project. This organization's funding made the book feasible. We also wish to thank Farmers & Merchants Bank and Kenneth Walker for their kind contribution.

Our profound gratitude goes to key individuals who participated intimately in the production of the book: Michael Worthington for capturing the essence of Long Beach and creating a graphic structure with the highest quality design and detail; Gabrielle Gayagoy for her precise editing and organizational skills; Soo Kim for making Long Beach a visual reality with her photography; and Michael Forbes for his expertise in capturing tall and difficult buildings.

D. J. Waldie and Thom Mayne eloquently situated the book within a historical and contemporary context, and we thank them for their insightful observations.

We are beholden to the readers, writers, and historians who contributed invaluable information, facts, and memories to this publication. These individuals include Ruthann Lehrer, former Preservation Officer, City of Long Beach, for being our most unwavering supporter and trusted consultant, and allowing us unfettered access to the city's files; Sheilah Nelson for her dedicated assistance and lovely spirit; Ron Lindgren for his articulate writing style; Long Beach Public Library Department Librarian Claudine Burnett and her staff for continuously tracking down information with smiles; Ken Larkey for not only contributing the bulk of historical photographs but also for imparting his expertise on the city's chronology; and Peter Devereaux for his recollection of key moments in Long Beach's history and the many contacts he provided us. The editorial comments and critiques from the following individuals resulted in immeasurable improvements to the text: Ellen Calomiris, Karen Clements, Lester Denevan, Tim Grobaty, Barbara Lamprecht, Sarah Schrank, and Mary Sullivan.

There are also many individuals we would like to thank for opening doors in our exploratory investigations and hard-core research process: Bob Andrews, Helene Ansel, Julie Bartolotto, Kathy Berry, Michael Bogner, Michael Bohn, Ted Bosley, Claire Bowin, Sue Cannon, Georgia Case, Sue Castillo, George Choma, Tom Ciosek, Anita Colangelo, Joseph Coriaty, Scotty Dixon, Lori J. Erdman, Frederick Fisher, Ed Frank, Ron and Nancy Frank, Donald Gibbs, John Glasgow, Charlotte Goforth, Juan Gomez-Novy, Sharon Hayes, Thomas Hines, Martin Howard, Steven Iverson, Clifton S. Jones, Veena Kedia, Edward and Laura Killingsworth, Geraldine Knatz, Gary Lamb, Marilyn Leckman, Ryan Lehman, Bill Lindborg, Howard Linn, Long Beach Design Forum, Alan Lowenthal, Marmol Radziner and Associates, Judy McKee, Tony Merchell, Tiffany Minor, Estella Murray, Hal Nelson, Doug Otto, Henry Pardo, Alan Pullman, Jean Bixby Smith, Jennifer Stevens, Paul Tay, Michael Traub, Fernando Vazquez, and Robert Zur Schmiede.

Special thank-you to the homeowners who graciously welcomed us and answered our many inquires: Grace Alexander, Janice Atzen, Susan and Ronald Crowell, Thomas Hoehn and Kevin Poi, Polly and George Johnson, Margie and John Masterson, Kelly Sutherlin McLeod and Steve McLeod, Gladys Nixon, Wally Simmons, Gerry Smith and Duane Rose, Andreas Stevens, and Karen and Ronald Van Wert.

We offer our sincerest appreciation to the institutions and individuals who lent images, without which the pages would not have come alive: Bixby Land Co., Henry Cabala, Canadian Center for Architecture, City of Long Beach, Galaxy Tower, Historical Society of Long Beach, I.M. Pei & Partners, Bobby June, Ron Kappe, KSLW and Associates Architects, Leland Lee, Livable Places, Long Beach Heritage Museum, Long Beach Public Library, Manuel Oncina Architects Inc., Moule & Polyzoides Architects and Urbanists, Port of Long Beach, *Press-Telegram*, Rancho Los Cerritos, Marvin Rand, Larry Rich, Julius Shulman, Tim Street-Porter, Studio One Eleven at Perkowitz + Ruth Architects, Paul Turang, and Wayne Thom Associates.

We would like to acknowledge Meina Co, Daniel Hernandez, Tracy Hopcus, Megan McGinley, and Kim Rogers for their assistance with design and photography.

A steady stream of encouragement from the Mullio, Moser, Volland, and Wheeler clans, fueled this project. In particular, we extend a heartfelt thanks to Adam Wheeler and Lance Volland for their love, support, acceptance, and ability to share.

INDEX

PHOTO CREDITS:

Courtesy Bixby Land Co.: 35(3)

Henry Cabala: 10; 47(1); 48(2); 56; 181(1); 239; 243(2); 245(1,2); 247(1,2,3)

Courtesy Canadian Centre for Architecture, Montreal: 235 (1,2)

Courtesy City of Long Beach: 16; 71(2)

Fred Daly: 233(2)

Courtesy Lester Denevan: 26; 33(1); 57(1)

William B. Dewey, Port of Long Beach: 45(4); 173(1,2,3)

Michael Forbes: 97; 99(1); 105; 107; 115(1); 123(1); 131(1); 137; 139; 141; 155(2); 161(1,2); 169; 211(1); 219; 253(1,2)

Ron Frank and Frank Bros. Archives: 37(9)

Courtesy Charlotte Goforth: 75(2)

Courtesy Historical Society of Long Beach: 30; 34(2); 125(1); 127(3); 189(1); 229(3)

Hugh Gibbs & Donald Gibbs Architects F.A.I.A. Archives: 177(1); 233(2)

I. M. Pei & Partners: 227(1,2)

Bill Inch, *Press-Telegram*: 43(1)

Bobby June: 14–15; 51(1)

Killingsworth, Stricker, Lindgren and Wilson Archives: 35(5); 197(2,3); 225(3)

Soo Kim: 63(1); 67(1); 71(1); 73(1); 81(1,2,4); 83; 85; 89; 91(2); 93(1,3); 95; 101(1,2,4,5); 103(1); 121; 125(2); 127(1,2); 129(1,2); 133; 135(2); 141; 143(2,3); 145(1); 147(1,2,3); 151; 153; 157(1); 159; 163; 165(1,2); 167(2,3); 171(1,2); 179(1); 181(2); 189(2); 193(2); 197(1); 209(2); 211(2); 217(1,2,3); 221(1,2,3,4); 223(1,2,3); 229(1,2); 231; 237(1,2); 249(1,2,3)

Courtesy Ken Larkey, Long Beach Heritage Museum: front cover; 4–5; 6–7; 8; 19(4); 23(1); 24(2); 25(3); 26; 28(3); 60–61; 75(1); 77(1,2); 81(3); 87(1,2); 101(3); 109; 113; 123(2,3); 131(2,3); 145(2); 157(2,3); back cover

Leland Lee: 36(7); 213

Courtesy Livable Places: 251(1,2,3); 257(1,2,3)

Courtesy Long Beach Public Library: 12–13; 19(3); 20(5,6); 27(1); 28(4); 29(5); 35(4); 39(1); 40(2,3,4); 44(3); 52(3); 54(9); 65; 69(1); 73(2); 79(1,2); 93(2); 103(2); 111; 115(2); 117(1,2); 119; 149(1,2)

Manuel Oncina Architects Inc.: 259(1,2,3)

Elaine Marks: 42; 215(1)

Steve McLeod: 169(1,2)

Moule & Polyzoides Architects and Urbanists: 53(7); 255(1,2,3)

Courtesy Port of Long Beach: 38; 50; 261

Courtesy *Press-Telegram*: 21(7); 22; 25(4); 28(2); 31(1); 58(2); 67(2,3); 69(2); 91(1); 99(2); 135(1,3); 155(1); 143(1)

Courtesy Rancho Los Cerritos Historic Site, Long Beach CA: 17(1); 18(2); 63(2)

Marvin Rand: 1; 187(1,2,3); 191; 195; 243(1)

Larry Rich, City of Long Beach: 44(2)

Cristina Salvador, *Press-Telegram*: 48(4)

Julius Shulman: 2–3; 32; 36(6); 37(8); 167(1); 175(1); 177(2,3); 183(1,2); 185(1,2); 193(1,3); 199; 201(1,2); 203; 205; 207; 209(1); 215(2); 225(2)

Tim Street-Porter: 241

Studio One Eleven at Perkowitz + Ruth Architects: 55(10,11)

Paul Turang: 79(3)

Courtesy VA Long Beach Healthcare System: 175(2,3)

Jennifer M. Volland: 48(3); 49(5); 53(5); 54(8)

Lance Volland: 49(6)

Wayne Thom Associates: 46; 225(1,4); 233(1)

Adam Wheeler: 52(2,4); 53(6); 55(12); 58(3); 179(2,3); 211(3)

Andy Witherspoon, *Press-Telegram*: 45(5)

BACKGROUND IMAGES:

Page 1: Marina Tower scale model, 1958.

Pages 2–3: Portofino (Toledo Tower), 1961.

Pages 4–5: Aerial view of city and landfill, 1976.

Pages 6–7: Long Beach skyline, 1931.

Pages 12–13: Aerial view of Rainbow Pier and Long Beach harbor, c. 1950.

Pages 14–15: Downtown skyline, 2003.

Pages 60–61: Aerial view of downtown and Cyclone Racer, c. 1940.